Too Naked for the Nazis

Too Naked for the Nazis

Alan Stafford

The untold story
of sand dancing legends
Wilson, Keppel and Betty

fantom
publishing

First published in 2015 by Fantom Films
fantomfilms.co.uk

A catalogue record for this book is available from the British Library.

Hardback edition ISBN: 978-1-78196-149-0

Typeset by Phil Reynolds Media Services, Leamington Spa
Printed and bound by CPI Group (UK) Ltd, Croydon, CR0 4YY

For Andrea

and Betty Knox

in that order

Contents

Prologue: *Betty, Keppel and Wilson*   1
Foreword   3

1   A Bad Day for German Catching   5
2   The University of Experience   8
3   Wizard of the Wooden Shoe   13
4   Hobo Flappers to be Spanked   19
5   Picking 'Em Up and Laying 'Em Down   31
6   The Average Life of a Chorus Girl   37
7   Oodles of Sex Appeal   44
8   The Sultan of Zanzibar   59
9   The Gandhi Bit   62
10 Expressions That Would Make a Mummy Laugh   75
11 Bad for the Nazi Youth's Morals   85
12 Not Keen on Dancing   92
13 Give Me Two Weeks   108
14 It's the Kind of World I Want   118
15 Zowie   133
16 My Tomsky   145
17 Hey, Have You Heard?   156
18 We Will Teach You Democracy!   172
19 Hook, Line and Sinker   182
20 Married in Two Weeks   190
21 The Title is a Secret   195
22 Our Friends are Back   210
23 A Distant Tinkle   229
24 All the Old Paintings on the Tombs   235

Acknowledgements   242
Bibliography   245
Index   247

Contents

Prologue:
Betty, Keppel and Wilson

THE SCENE IS A PSYCHIATRIST'S CONSULTING ROOM. A petite woman with black beaded headdress, gold sequined top, bare waist and black shorts pours her heart out. She's every bit as important as the other two, so why are *their* surnames on all the posters while hers isn't?

She sits between two men in fezzes and short sleeveless mustard-coloured tunics. They have identical false droopy moustaches. Their arms are crossed. Their legs are crossed. A plentiful assortment of hairy male appendages is on display. The woman hasn't finished. Why is she just a first name, tacked on at the end? An afterthought. Why not in alphabetical order, with *her* name at the front?

The therapist discreetly enquires how things are at home. Betty blushes and giggles, while Wilson and Keppel arch their black grease-paint eyebrows and nod approvingly. Clearly no complaints in that department. There is a pause. A long awkward pause. Plenty of time to fill, but no one can think of anything else to say. Finally, in desperation, the trio leaps to its collective feet.

All three stand in profile, assuming an Egyptian pose – one hand (palm up) in front and the other (palm down) behind. As the pseudo-ethnic music strikes up, they begin to shuffle forward …

This sketch, from TV comedy series *Psychobitches*, first aired in November 2014. Samantha Spiro portrayed Betty Knox, double-act Seb Cardinal and Dustin Demri-Burns were Wilson and Keppel, and Rebecca Front was the resident therapist.

In less than two minutes this one sketch perfectly encapsulates public opinion of the trio. The bizarrely memorable combination of names. The sand dance that seems to be the sum total of their variety act. And the deep suspicion that a two-man-one-woman combo must surely have

1

got up to some rum shenanigans in the privacy of their theatrical digs.

Of course, the pedants amongst you would spot that Betty should have spoken with a Kansas accent. That the sand dance was a twosome, not a threesome. And that Wilson and Keppel would never – positively never! – have shuffled through the sand wearing *fezzes*.

Who cares? It's a great sketch. And the writers and producers clearly believed a significant proportion of their audience of contemporary comedy fans would be familiar with the names and dance moves of Wilson, Keppel and Betty. These days many of their routines are on YouTube. Anyone who happens across the sand dance can instantly share it with their Twitter followers and Facebook friends. Wilson, Keppel and Betty were constantly rediscovered throughout their career – and the process continues to this day.

Psychobitches got it spot on by suggesting Betty Knox was the creative centrepiece of the act. She's also the photographic centrepiece of a group of female war correspondents outside a Normandy hospital tent in 1944. From exotic dancer to war reporter. It was that total change of career that made me want to learn more about Betty. And what I discovered was a woman who, throughout her life, was courageous, rebellious, resilient and – above all – a right good laugh. Wilson and Keppel were a talented dance act. But Wilson, Keppel and Betty were a vaudeville sensation.

Nothing has been handed to me on a plate. There are no scrapbooks, unpublished biographies, or collected Wilson, Keppel and Betty archives to draw upon. Their lives have been reconstructed with the help of researchers, enthusiasts, newspaper collections and museums from throughout Britain, America, Australasia and Europe. Plus the personal recollections of a handful of people who were there.

These are the non-stop adventures of a trio for whom home was a succession of rooms in a succession of towns in a succession of countries. Australian circus, American vaudeville, British variety and Continental cabaret – they played them all. And Betty's adventures took her further still – to the battlefields of Normandy and the law courts of Nuremberg.

It's a fascinating tale, most of it never told before.

And at its very heart is a truly remarkable woman named Betty.

Alan Stafford, 2015

Foreword

ON MONDAY 5ᵀᴴ NOVEMBER 1945, the Royal Variety Performance, which had been suspended for the duration of the war, made its triumphal return. The Royal Box was occupied by King George VI and Queen Elizabeth, together with their teenage daughters Princess Elizabeth and Princess Margaret, who were experiencing a theatrical variety show for the very first time. On the bill that night were the comedy dancers Wilson, Keppel and Betty, who would perform an identical routine two years later to the same Royal party, with the addition of Princess Elizabeth's future husband, Lieutenant Philip Mountbatten.

In early 2015, I wrote to Buckingham Palace about Wilson, Keppel and Betty's Royal Variety appearances. Susan Hussey, Lady-in-Waiting to the Queen, replied:

> The Queen thought it was kind of you to write and ask if she remembers seeing their performances, and I can tell you that Her Majesty does indeed remember them well, and with great enjoyment.

I also asked a number of celebrities for their opinions or memories of Wilson, Keppel and Betty – starting with Samantha Spiro, who portrayed Betty Knox in the sketch show *Psychobitches*:

> An image comes to mind of a kind of dance entertainment that has had a huge and wide ranging influence. I can't help but giggle!

Matt Lucas, comedy actor of *Little Britain* fame:

> I've seen footage on TV over the years and always found them fascinating. This distinctive pair, replacing their 'Betty' as often as Spinal Tap replaced their drummer, were hugely successful in their heyday, and I'd love to know more about their life and work.

Glenda Jackson, who recently retired after a long career as Labour MP and (in a former life) once sand danced between Morecambe and Wise:

> My parents took me to a show at the Liverpool Empire when I was, almost, a teenager and they were on the bill. As was Anne Shelton and top-of-the-bill was Johnnie Ray, he who cried. I think Anne Shelton was the act my parents wanted to see, but I do remember Wilson, Keppel & Betty.

Playwright Peter Nichols, whose works include *A Day in the Death of Joe Egg* and *Privates on Parade*:

> Memories of 70 years ago are hazy but I'm sure I saw them, probably at Bristol Hippodrome. I remember one move where one dancer got in a contortion with the other so that he finished by seeming to be holding his balls. I think of them whenever pseudo-oriental music's played, such as Ketèlbey's 'In a Persian Market'.

Presenter and columnist Victoria Coren Mitchell, daughter of Alan Coren, satirist and erstwhile editor of *Punch*:

> I do remember my father mentioning the name of that act on the radio and it often helping him get a laugh, but I was too small and uninformed to know why!

And finally, although their theatrical billing for much of their career was 'Cleopatra's Nightmare', Dame Judi Dench told me of an occasion when the trio gave the Egyptian Queen nothing but sweet dreams:

> When I came to play Cleopatra for Peter Hall at the National Theatre in 1987, Peter was very clear that he wanted to see a live snake in Cleopatra's hand in the final scene. Being extremely nervous of worms, and slightly nervous of snakes, my husband (the late Michael Williams) suggested a way of getting over the fear by naming all the snakes. We had three (two understudies) and from that moment they were known as Wilson, Keppel and Betty. I overcame my fear and became very fond of them.
>
> As for the real Wilson, Keppel and Betty, I remember seeing them on film and thought they were wonderful.

1
A Bad Day for German Catching

(Paris 1944)

'… the oddest party I have ever been to …' (Betty Knox, 1944)

ON 8TH SEPTEMBER 1944, the *London Evening Standard* carried a report from one of its journalists currently based in France. Many articles were simply credited to an anonymous *Evening Standard Correspondent*. But this particular byline read: *From* BETTY KNOX, *Evening Standard War Reporter*.

Over the past year, Betty's name had become familiar to the paper's readership. Her style of writing was markedly different from that of many of her male colleagues. There was a folksy American warmth to it. Despite moving to England a dozen years ago, she was still a Kansas girl at heart. Her war reports were packed full of adventure, even humour. Most importantly they were about the people she met – British, American, French, German. She brought the war to life through the men, women and children who were caught up in it. At this moment she was in Paris – and Allied troops had victory within their grasp. If readers back home in London were scanning their papers in search of an uplifting thrilling escapade, Betty was not about to disappoint them:

> I've just returned from a three-day hunting trip with the French Forces of the Interior.
>
> In three shiny black staff cars and one truck, 30 young men in misfit

uniforms, carrying any weapons they could dig up, went German stalking. They all wore the silver skull and crossbones ensignia of the Corps France, one of the oldest resistance movements in France, now incorporated into the F.F.I.

I rode in the leading car with 'Captain Pierre', who is 22 years old, and for four years has been liaison officer between various resistance organisations.

Local resistance members informed us that there were Germans in a chateau this side of the river Oise.

Female correspondents were expected to provide a woman's perspective on the war – visiting hospitals and reporting how families were coping with food shortages. They were not supposed to hitch a ride with the French Resistance and go Nazi hunting! Betty was risking both her life and her career.

And did she give a damn? Not in the slightest:

We climbed out of the cars, and the 30 young men surrounded the chateau. There were no Germans; the servants said they had left a few hours before in an effort to escape over the river in row boats.

So Betty and the men got back in their cars and headed for a forest where Germans had been spotted:

We crawled through the forest at about five miles an hour. The lieutenant beside me levelled his German automatic pistol out of his window. In the truck that followed about half the squad had machine-guns, with about one burst of ammunition.

Everyone was very quiet. Nothing happened. If there were Germans in the forest they refused to be drawn out.

After conferences, mainly laments about the scarcity of left-over Germans and awed exclamations about the 'formidable' Americans, who went too fast to keep up with, the discouraged company decided it was a bad day for German catching.

In the town ahead was a large convoy of American troops, liberated that afternoon from a German internment camp. Food was scarce but, nevertheless, the locals decided to throw a party:

Music was provided by Joe Kannui, an aged Hawaiian guitarist, who had been playing in Paris night clubs since the last war.

Children went to sleep on benches around the recreation hall while mothers and daughters danced with the Americans, the F.F.I. and each other.

When we left for Paris at 5 a.m. with the disconsolate F.F.I. who hoped there would still be some Germans left to clean up, the oddest party I have ever been to was still going on.

They may not have nabbed any Germans, but they danced and partied the night away. And Betty could high-kick with the best of them. Dancing had been her life. She'd built a whole career out of it. She'd danced all over America, Britain and Europe. She'd even danced for the Nazis.

Dressed as Cleopatra, with bare midriff and bare legs, she'd clicked her finger-cymbals in a dance of seduction. Swaying sensually, in an attempt to drive her two minions, Jack Wilson and Joe Keppel, mad with desire. Nazi officials were gobsmacked – furious at this blatant display of naked flesh.

And what was the cause of such outrage? Betty Knox's womanly curves?

No. It was Wilson and Keppel's spindly legs.

2

The University of Experience

(Kansas 1906–1918)

'The main thing is, it saves five per cent.' (Charles Peden, 1912)

BETTY KNOX IS OFTEN PORTRAYED as the black sheep of the family. As one relative recalled, with a sniff of disapproval, 'Oh, she became some sort of dancer, or entertainer, or something.' If she had ever broached the subject of a possible career in vaudeville, her words would have been met with frowns, general tut-tutting and, if she persisted, a stern telling-off. The stage was not a place for nice young girls. The only sensible option was to do what she was told and forget all about it.

But Betty didn't want to forget all about it. Or do what she was told. She wasn't even that keen on being sensible. So she ran away from home. Twice. At least.

Why did she run away? What was she running away from? Unsalted buffalo meat, a length of ribbon and a sack of potatoes. Three items that shaped her childhood. They may not provide a full explanation of Betty's troubled teenage years, but they tell us quite a lot.

Unsalted Buffalo Meat ...

Betty was born Alice Elizabeth Peden (to rhyme with 'maiden') on 10th May 1906 in Salina (to rhyme with 'china'), Kansas, USA. She had an older brother, George, born in 1901. And in 1911, her younger brother Charles Peden Junior arrived. Her mother, Lizzie Peden, was daughter of Thomas Anderson, one of the first pioneer settlers to have made Salina his home.

Salina is home to Kim Novak's character in the 1958 Hitchcock classic *Vertigo*. In 1980, *Mad* magazine's *Up the Academy* (an ill-fated attempt to emulate *National Lampoon's Animal House*) was filmed entirely in and around Salina's St John's Military School.

Salina is now a thriving city located in one of the world's largest wheat producing areas, with a population close to 50,000. In 1861, when Thomas Anderson's wagon rolled into town, the population was just 30. With $12.50 in his pocket, he worked in a brick yard for $10 a month, surviving on unsalted buffalo meat and corn meal. One family member, who met him in her youth, described him as 'a pleasant but crusty old Scot'. Like many of Salina's early settlers, Scotland was the country of Thomas Anderson's birth. Fenwick, to be precise. In case you had any doubt that Alice Peden's grandpa was a self-made man (whose recollections of early hardships only remained clear through constant repetition) the *Standard History of Kansas and Kansans*, written in the quaint old language of the American tourist, makes it abundantly plain:

> ... he had attended the Scotch schools, but his real education came from the university of experience.

Thomas went on to become a successful farmer, was a sergeant in the Fifteenth Kansas Militia, fighting the (understandably) hostile Native American Indians, and then entered politics. In 1901 by far the most important issue for voters was the enforcement of the prohibition law, banning the consumption of alcohol. Most of the larger cities voted against prohibition. In Salina, however, Thomas Anderson – the temperance candidate for mayor – was elected by an overwhelming majority.

Doubtless young Alice Peden got a plentiful supply of career advice from this no-nonsense self-taught teetotal Presbyterian Scot, whether she wanted it or not. And if the great man was too busy to dispense his wisdom first-hand, she could always rely on one of his four sons and eleven daughters to pass it on. Indeed, not only did he help make Salina the place that it was – he also had a darned good try at populating it.

9

A Length of Ribbon …

Alice's father was Charles Edward Peden from West Virginia, described in his obituary as a dry goods merchant – 'dry goods' being ready-to-wear clothes, material and accessories. In Charles' early career he had been a travelling salesman, a clerk in a department store, and later he was the proprietor of the Peden Grocery; but in 1912, when Alice was six, he owned a dry goods store at 134 North Santa Fe Avenue, specialising in 'notions' (fabric, thread, ribbons and general sewing supplies – the equivalent of the British haberdasher's). And that was the year he announced to the world – or rather to trade magazine *Dry Goods Reporter* – his revolutionary new invention:

> The idea of this machine is to save the retailer his loss on ribbons through careless measuring, good nature and deliberate action on the part of salespeople in ribbon departments.

'Good nature' – the curse of the retail industry! Most shop assistants selling ribbon would first carefully measure the length, and then deliberately cut up to an inch more. That way the customer knew they'd got what they asked for, and didn't feel short-changed by the assistant. And, after all, it's only an extra inch of ribbon. But this was just not good enough for Charles. Those extra inches add up. So, first, the ribbon had to be placed into a specially constructed box:

> Then raise the spring and put the ribbon under and draw it through until you get the desired length … Then there is a rod one-fourth inch high across the board to slightly raise the ribbon so as to get a pair of shears underneath and one has always to cut it off at this place.

Whether or not Charles was inundated with orders for his sophisticated measuring apparatus, we don't know. Neither do we have any idea how patrons of his Salina store felt about being subjected to this elaborate ribbon rigmarole, specifically designed to ensure they got not one sixteenth of an inch more fabric than they paid for. It is said that, as a teenager, Alice used to serve in her father's shop. If ever she thought, 'To hell with this!' grabbed a ruler and made a hasty snip, she could expect a lengthy lecture on economics. For, in her father's own words:

> The main thing is, it saves five per cent on ribbon sales and perhaps more, for no merchant knows how much he loses, but it is enough.

A Sack of Potatoes ...

A month before Alice's 12th birthday, something terrible happened. All the more terrible because it's unthinkable that such a combination of events could occur today. Through present-day eyes it would be viewed as gross negligence. But, on 2nd April 1918, it was just a very unfortunate accident. *The Salina Daily Union* carried a report the following day:

> Charles Peden, Jr, six-year-old son of Mr and Mrs Charles E. Peden, 411 West Walnut street, has little chance of life today as the result of internal injuries sustained shortly after five o'clock last night when he was struck by a rear wheel of an automobile trailer.
>
> 'Only a fighting chance,' was the phrasing of one attending physician this afternoon in speaking of the boy's condition.

It happened at the junction of Fifth and Iron Avenues, virtually in front of the grocery store that Charles Peden Senior now owned. A customer named R. S. Carson had just purchased a sack of potatoes from the store and was driving them away in a farmyard motor trailer, which also contained a load of heavy cement. Charles Junior and his friend Clifford Thompson were riding in front. The boys weren't seated – they were standing on the running board, being held by Clifford's father, Jud Thompson, an employee of the Peden grocery. Suddenly young Clifford jumped and ran off. Then, before Jud realised what he was doing, Charles also broke loose and jumped to the pavement. He landed on his hands and feet and was instantly struck by the trailer. Almost 24 hours later, Alice's young brother was dead. The *Salina Journal* interviewed Mr Thompson:

> 'The wheel of the trailer did not run over Charles,' Jud Thompson said today. 'It was attached to the motor by a rope, instead of the usual coupling, and when it struck the boy the car rolled back a trifle, so that the wheel did not pass over his body. If it had, he would have been instantly killed, because of the heavy load carried.'

It's hard to see what point Jud Thompson was making, unless he was trying to justify the use of a rope to attach the trailer as some sort of safety measure. His words don't come over as particularly com-passionate, and it would have been small comfort to Charles' parents to know that he had a lingering painful death. But Alice was living in a different time. The whole matter-of-fact tone of the newspaper article seems to suggest that this kind of thing just happens from time to time. The headline is simply: *BOY'S JUMP COSTS LIFE*. A story in the next column, about police disrupting the funeral of a pet cat, carries the headline: *WASN'T THIS VERY CRUEL*.

Whatever Alice Peden's home life was like before the accident, right now her home was not a happy place. Away from home, with friends, maybe it was easier to put this family tragedy to the back of her mind. With friends, Alice could be a different person. And, with friends, Alice could – and would – run away.

3
Wizard of the Wooden Shoe

(Australia 1917–1920)

'I am not fit for any work now.' (Joe Keppel, 1918)

FIVE MONTHS EARLIER – in the Royal Australian Navy Sick Quarters, Garden Island, Sydney – the staff surgeon was writing his report on a stoker who had been invalided out. The letter was dated 11th November 1917:

> His weight has decreased from 148 pounds to 128 pounds within a few months. He complains of indigestion and pains after eating food. He has only three natural teeth in the upper jaw and nine in the lower jaw ... He becomes breathless after slight exertion, and is subject to attacks of giddiness. He is not a heavy smoker, and is, so he states, temperate in the use of alcohol ... His nervous system is excitable, possibly due to his high blood pressure and rapid pulse ... The Board of Medical Survey at Sydney 8th October 1917 considered that he was unfit for Naval Service either ashore or afloat.

John Joseph Keppel, an Irishman born in Cork, had been a stoker in the Royal Australian Navy since January 1915, spending his war service on three ships: the *Cerberus*, the *Encounter* and the *Tingira*. Having been discharged on 1st November 1917 with heart trouble, he pursued his claim for a war pension. The following letter was written, in Joe Keppel's own immaculate copperplate handwriting, on 14th December 1917:

Regarding this pension matter I have just received your note 13th inst & beg to inform you that I have been up country for the benefit of my health & did not receive it until now.

His journey up country was far from being a rest cure, according to the *Melbourne Argus* of 3rd December:

At the People's Concerts at the Temperance Hall on Saturday, successful first appearances were made by the Chi Lie's (conjurors), Hal Scott (baritone) and Joe Keppel (dancer).

The next month, January 1918, the Navy Office received further statements as to Joe's medical condition; the first from Jane Smith, with whom he was staying at the time:

He is suffering from malaria and heart trouble contracted I believe whilst on active service in the tropics ... He gets trembling attacks. He has no appetite and cannot sleep. These attacks come on frequently. He is very thin.

And this, from Joe Keppel himself:

I am not fit for any work now. My health is not improving. I am a single man.

Five days after these statements were written, the *Melbourne Argus* advertised another appearance:

PEOPLE'S CONCERTS. Temperance Hall. – Tonight, special engagement Harry Noye and Joe Keppel, simultaneous dancers.

It seems incredible that Joe Keppel was beginning to establish himself as a professional dancer at a time when his physical condition was so poor. However, fresh air and exercise may have been just what the doctor ordered; considerably less stressful than being a stoker on a warship.

When Joe Keppel joined the navy, he was described as: 5 feet 4¾ inches, black hair, brown eyes, sallow complexion, with a scar on his left forearm. Anyone who has seen film of Wilson and Keppel in action might easily assume the men were long and lanky. For two dancers of such short stature, this is some indication of how remarkably skinny they were. Whether or not Joe Keppel was careful about his diet before his illness, we do know that he later became quite fanatical about everything he ate and drank.

Some double acts last a lifetime, some don't. Noye and Keppel lasted no more than a few months, then Joe was back to being a solo act. As the war ended and peace resumed he made various appearances at Adelaide and Brisbane. By November 1919 he was a fully fledged vaudeville act at the Olympia Theatre, Rockhampton, Queensland:

> JOSEPH KEPPEL (The Wizard of the Wooden Shoe) who will introduce the Scottische Clog Dance, Waltz Clog, and the American Buck Dance.

Clog dancing has nothing to do with the all-wooden Dutch clog. The clogs used for this type of dancing are leather shoes with wooden soles. Lancashire is one area particularly associated with clog dancing, where clogs were the traditional footwear of the workers. It was not unlike tap dancing, except that the rhythmic sound created was far more important than the visual aspect. In fact, the aim was often to make it look as if the upper body was hardly moving at all. A vaudeville variation of the clog dance was the pedestal dance, in which the performer stood on a replica marble pedestal, their whole body motionless except for their frantically busy feet. Some pedestal dancers would cover their body in white make-up to complete the statue effect.

Early settlers from England, Ireland, Scotland and Wales are credited with spreading this form of dancing throughout the world. Gradually each culture added refinements of their own, which is reflected in Joe Keppel's international programme. The Scottische Clog Dance is a Scottish-style folk dance, popular all over Europe. The Waltz Clog is a dance in triple time (1-and-2-and-3) as opposed to the more usual 2 or 4 beats in a bar. The American Buck Dance is said to derive from traditional Cherokee tribal dancing, with more stomping and less shuffling.

Joe 'won rounds of applause for his clever dancing' and gave his last performance at Rockhampton on 1st December 1919. The following day, Colleano's Circus rolled into town, and this is where Joe went next.

Colleano (to rhyme with Beano) is the perfect circus name – it has a wonderfully exotic ring to it. And that's why the Sullivan family invented it. There were ten Colleano children in all, and various of them had appeared as solo acts or groups in other circuses around Australia before the Colleano family circus was formed in 1915.

Whether the audience was aware of the strong family presence – or indeed the frantic swapping between roles – is uncertain, as the bill boasted a vast variety of international performers. Look, there's Senorita Sanchez (Winnie Colleano) on trapeze! And Miss Katherine, the somersaulting horsewoman (Kate Colleano). And Zeneto, up there on the high wire (Con Colleano). And over there is the Hawaiian Orchestra, with its slightly out-of-breath trombonist (Con Colleano again, together with any members of the family who aren't hurriedly getting changed for the next act).

Con Colleano was arguably the supernova of this stellar family. His prowess on the tightrope earned him the epithet 'The Wizard of the Wire'. (Yet another wizard. Australia must have been overrun with them!) His speciality, which took years to perfect, was the forward somersault on the high wire, and he was the first performer to achieve it. The backward somersault is comparatively less dangerous as, once you're heading down again, you can see the wire coming towards you. The forward somersault doesn't have that advantage and, for the latter half of the manoeuvre, your only option is to look heavenwards and pray that no one's taken away the tightrope. During his career he picked up some fairly horrific injuries, but survived in good enough shape to enjoy a well-earned retirement.

Bonar Colleano, the eldest brother of the family, in addition to playing cornet in the band, combined clowning with precision balancing – doing a drunk act on the slackwire. He and wife Rubye were parents of the movie star Bonar Colleano Junior, who will reappear in this story much later. A 1970 edition of British theatrical newspaper *The Stage* provides us with Rubye's eyewitness account of a historic meeting:

> I met Joe Keppel when I was on the road in Australia with a family show at the age of 14. He used to roll out his dancing mat in 'The Colleano's Circus Ring' ... Jack [Wilson] came over on a boat from England, met Joe Keppel and they did a double act.

If you want your clog dancing to be heard in the middle of a circus ring, it makes sense to bring your own dancing mat (or sounding board) to amplify the clickety-clack of your feet. In those days its main purpose was to provide a clean dancing surface in the midst of a sawdust-strewn arena. A decade or so later they were to employ an almost identical piece

16

of equipment to achieve precisely the opposite.

It was only after the First World War that Colleano's Circus started to look beyond the immediate family for acts. By 1920 they had combined their resources to form 'Colleano and Sole Brothers' Huge Circus and Menagerie'. The circus now boasted '55 performers, 19 horses and ponies, and 8 cages of wild animals'. In February they advertised vacancies for several musicians, including a clarinettist. The clarinet was Jack Wilson's instrument, so it's highly likely he joined the circus at this time and met Joe.

Joe Keppel, as previously mentioned, came from Ireland. He was born John Joseph Keppel in Mary Street, Cork, on 5th May 1894. He had three older brothers and two sisters. As a young lad he's believed to have worked as an auxiliary fire fighter in Cork. He then joined the 5th (Royal Irish) Lancers; but it's said that he hated the marching and so decided to try the Royal Navy instead. At the age of 18 he enlisted for the customary twelve years. However, after only a month, he fell ill. He spent the next four months in Plymouth hospital before being discharged from the navy as unfit. Two years later (and half a world away) he joined the Royal Australian Navy where he fared much better, serving for almost three years before being invalided out. (One former neighbour reckoned that almost every resident of Mary Street subsequently emigrated – so there was nothing particularly extraordinary about Joe's decision to go to Australia.)

Jack was born John William Wilson on 30th January 1894 in Warrington, Lancashire. Though Jack and Joe were born the same year, they seldom told the press their true ages. *The Performer* magazine of 1933 adds six years to Jack's age and says Joe Keppel is two years his junior, whereas the *Birmingham Evening Argus* of 1958 has it the other way round, claiming Jack is the younger by two years.

Jack Wilson was one of five children, with two sisters (one older than him) and two younger brothers. His father worked as a tanner, converting animal skins into leather. After his father died, Jack's mother moved to nearby Liverpool and ran a boarding house. By the age of 17, Jack (along with his brothers and sisters) still lived in the family home, where he and younger brother Thomas continued the family tradition of working in the tannery trade.

And that may have been Jack's life, were it not for the adventure, travel and extreme peril offered by the outbreak of the First World War. He is said to have joined the Navy transport service and participated in the Gallipoli Landings in Turkey. After surviving the war, a trip to Australia to try his chances might not have seemed that daunting a task. He was an adept amateur musician and came from an area of Britain famed for its rich clog dancing tradition – though who could have imagined that these skills alone would earn him a good living? Surprisingly, he appears to have had little contact with his family for the rest of his life.

However, once Jack and Joe got together, the two clog dancers obviously 'clicked' in a way that Joe and Harry Noye hadn't. And, for a second time, Joe Keppel went from single act to double act – this time under the Colleano big top. But the opportunities and financial rewards weren't easy to come by and (in June 1920) Joe wrote again to the Navy Office:

> I should be very grateful if you could facilitate the forwarding of my war gratuity as I have an opportunity of leaving for USA on steam ship (*Niagara*) at the end of this month where I hope to secure a good engagement as things are not too good at present here.

A month or so later Joe Keppel and Jack Wilson took that massive career gamble (though possibly they didn't have that much to lose) and boarded the RMS *Niagara* bound for Canada. They had to fill out a Passenger's Declaration form in their own hand, and each claimed to have fifty dollars in their possession. And, in answer to one particular question, they were in total agreement:

> Intended occupation … Vaudeville Artist.

4

Hobo Flappers to be Spanked

(Kansas 1922–1925)

'That's just what they need and what they will likely get.' (Lizzie Peden, 1922)

Some scores of blood relatives of the Peden girl who still reside in and near Salina, Kas., think of the year 1923 as the date of the big 'scandal' in the family. That was the year Betty Peden, at the age of 14, threw off respectability, flouted tradition, thumbed her nose at Salina and showed up at the stage door of the Globe theatre in Kansas City.

Her grandpa, old Tom Anderson, who crossed the plains with a Bible in one hand and a bull whip in the other to become mayor of Salina and then a member of the state Legislature, knew the inevitable reward for such conduct. Salina realized the worst when Betty Peden bluffed her way into the chorus of a 'tab' show at the Globe and shook her skinny legs before the stares of its audiences.

MARCEL WALLENSTEIN, LONDON CORRESPONDENT of *The Kansas City Star*, wrote this in March 1944, after interviewing Betty Knox in the Savoy grill. So it's reasonable to suppose that the Globe theatre story came from Betty herself. (Incidentally, a 'tab' show is a compact mini-musical, intended to slot into a bill of vaudeville acts or between movie showings.) In 1923, Betty would have been 16 rather than 14. But most press articles that give Betty an age suggest she was born around 1909 (probably because that's what Betty told them) rather than 1906. The article concludes with a short paragraph added by a local reporter:

Betty Peden is remembered in Salina as an exceptionally pretty girl who possessed far more than usual charm, took part in amateur theatricals and finally ran away, dressed in overalls and posing as a boy … Her father was employed in various Salina mercantile establishments and eventually opened a small store of his own in which his daughter worked for a time … It is the recollection of old-timers in Salina who 'knew her when' that she was Alice Peden when she lived here.

In May 1922, Alice Peden (the young Betty Knox) had turned 16. Her elder brother George had first worked as a clerk in the family business, then later toured with the Frisco Exposition, selling tickets to one of the fairground sideshows – the Monkey Autodrome. This was a demolition derby (or banger racing) event, where the object was not so much to win the race but to smash up the other drivers' cars. But there was a twist – all the drivers were monkeys. At the time it was considered hilarious entertainment. Nowadays it would be a lethal cocktail of health, safety and animal welfare issues. But, for George, it was just a job – or rather the beginnings of an entire career spent in the fairground and amusement park business.

Alice, at 16, was in the Sophomore Class (second year) at Salina High School. One area of study in which she clearly excelled was art. The previous year, Alice and the other girls in Miss Friola's art class had received praise for their work making Christmas cards for soldiers in a local military hospital and posters for Salina merchants. A June 1922 edition of *The Habit* (the school magazine) includes a full-page illustration by Alice as title page to the magazine's 'Humor' section. Alice's drawing shows four fairies (two blonde and two dark) dancing gracefully in the woodland under an ornate blossoming tree. It is an attractive and proficient piece of work and the dance poses have an authentic feel to them. The juxtaposition of dance and humour in this drawing couldn't be more apt for her future career.

She was also emerging as a talented performer. Since the age of 4 she had given short recitations. Aged 8, she recited the patriotic poem 'Our National Colors'. At 13, she danced as one of the Sun-bonnet Girls in the operetta *Polished Pebbles*. At 14 she was Winter in *Dance of the Seasons*. ('Probably the most popular dance number of the evening.')

In February 1922, the Elks (a men-only charitable club, with much of the mystic ritual of the Freemasons but less shrouded in secrecy) presented its annual fundraising musical *The Little Lady*. An advertisement in the *Salina Evening Journal* made it clear that Alice was one of the show's three leading females:

> See the 'Dance Comique' by Elmo Barnes and Alice Peden, and hear Janette sing 'April Showers' in 'The Little Lady' at the Grand theatre tonight.

Yet again that combination of dance and comedy was proving the key to Alice's success.

The previous year, her father's grocery had run into financial difficulties, and he'd been forced to sell the business to avoid bankruptcy. Ever since Charles Peden Junior had been fatally struck by a motor trailer outside the store, it had become a place of bad memories. When Alice helped out in the Peden Grocery, as locals remember her doing, she would only have to glance out of the shop window at the traffic to be reminded of this family tragedy.

Elder brother George was now working away from home for much of the year, so she spent little time in his company. On the other hand, she could act and she could dance. Many performers go on stage to be someone else – and the stage would allow Alice to be an attractive, fun-loving, joyful young woman, at a time when her home life wouldn't. Plus she was starting to win the attentions of the opposite sex.

In October 1965, the *Salina Journal* carried a column of local nostalgia under the heading 'I can remember'. One reader recalled:

> A local girl, Alice Peden, acting at the New Theater. All the boys were there.

This incident from forty or so years earlier had clearly etched itself into the memory of at least one Salina resident. Not only did Alice Peden possess a charismatic stage presence, she was attracting a great many male admirers. Though her stage career was in its infancy, she was already an assured and confident performer. It seems that her family, as a whole, did not approve. Whether her mother or father gave her any form of encouragement is less certain. The fact that she had to run away from them suggests they didn't. But Alice was doing what she'd always wanted to do – and was doing it rather well.

The notion of fleeing a forbidding family for the footlights is more than just good alliteration – it's a journalist telling a great story. But the adult Betty never told the press of the biggest adventure of her teenage years. And it had nothing to do with her theatrical ambitions.

October 1922 was a time of great excitement for Alice. Salina was hosting the spectacular American Legion Aviation Meet, and Alice had thrilled to a stunt-packed programme, neatly summarised by the *Salina Evening Journal*:

> … a triple parachute leap, automobile races with airplanes, trick flying, wing walking, changing planes in mid-air and an effort by at least two flyers to better the world record for looping the loop, which is 125 consecutive loops.

A week later, Alice and her friend Vivian Vinzant went missing.

The *Salina Evening Journal* of 20th October attempted to piece together the chain of events, which began when:

> … J. McCloud, renting a car from the Donmyer taxi station, let the girls use it. They drove to Wichita in the machine, returning home, however, night before last. Alice Peden did not go home that night but telephoned to her mother that she was in town. Yesterday morning she returned home, but left again, only to sneak back in the afternoon, take her clothes, and meet the waiting automobile …

By the 1920s all vehicles were licensed, but there wasn't yet any testing or licensing of drivers. So the only remarkable part of the story was that Alice succeeded in persuading J. McCloud to lend her his rented vehicle. A letter she left for her mother said she was going to Kansas City to enter art school. Her parents suspected the involvement of Bob Reiman, a youth from Abilene (a city about 27 miles east of Salina). Bob had recently become very friendly with Alice, and the young lovers had devised an ingenious plan to deceive her parents, with the aid of Alice's friend Vivian Vinzant:

> The two girls have been chums for some time and for weeks, according to Mr Peden, the Reiman youth has been coming to Salina, getting the Vinzant girl and bringing her to Peden's as his sister. Mr and Mrs Peden did not know the difference, the father said. The deception, the young man is said to have admitted this morning, was practiced because Mr Peden would not allow Alice to go with him from the house unless there

was a third person along and the Vinzant girl posed as the sister for the benefit of her two friends.

Bob Reiman admitted the girls were with him the previous night, but believed they were currently heading for Kansas City. So George Peden, Alice's older brother, set off in that direction to enquire about various rumours surrounding the girls – one of which concerned an art teacher whose company they were seen enjoying at the recent Salina air show.

Nothing was heard of them for nearly two weeks. Then, on 1st November, the *Salina Evening Journal* carried a report from Monroe, Louisiana – some 700 miles south:

> Misses Alice Peden and Vivian Vinzant, members of prominent families at Salina Kan., were being held by authorities here today on the charge of vagrancy, following their flight to Louisiana from their homes from where they were frightened away through fear of arrest. The girls, who gave their ages at 16 years, declared they hoboed their way to this city on freight trains coming through Kansas, Oklahoma and Arkansas.
>
> The girls told authorities here they ran away from home after they were told a warrant had been issued for their arrest in Salina, on the charge of stealing an automobile. They said they took the car for a joyride, but it broke down and they were late in returning it.

The *Salina Evening Journal* contacted the county attorney, F. C. Norton, who was anxious to reassure its readers that there were no plans to issue a warrant charging Alice and Vivian with car theft – though he admitted there might have been some basis for the girls to be under that impression:

> Charges were they stole an automobile from the Donmyer garage. They state, however, according to the county attorney, that the car had been given them to drive by a young man, and they returned with it from Wichita. As this was evidence of their good faith in not intending to steal the car, no charges were contemplated, Mr Norton said.
>
> Charles Peden, father of the Peden girl, left last night to go after the two girls.

On the same page as this report is a profile of Frank C. Norton, who would shortly be facing the electorate in a bid to secure a second term as county attorney for Saline County. He was promising to take a tough stance on law enforcement – though being tough on two distressed teenage girls would hardly be a guaranteed vote-winner. So the girls were to be set free, while he concentrated his attentions on the growing menace of bootleggers. Yes, illicit alcohol continued to be a big deal in Salina.

The newspapers of several nearby states covered the story of the runaway girls. A Mississippi paper carried the headline: GIRLS FEARING ARREST TURN HOBOES IN FLIGHT – and the *Kansas Star* reported that 'a wide search had been made for them'.

The Monroe News-Star in Louisiana had all the details. The girls had been arrested after being spotted getting off a freight train at the Vicksburg, Shreveport and Pacific railroad depot. But the story they initially told the police was utter invention. They said they were 17 years old and had been hiking since May from Nashville, Tennessee to Denver Colorado 'on a wager' (in other words, to win a bet). However, when cross-questioned separately, the two girls' accounts of their adventures wildly differed.

By now Alice's mother had sent a telegram, instructing police officers to hold the girls until their arrival. This prompted Alice to offer a version of events that was closer to the truth, though she was now so proficient in the arts of lying and persuasion that nothing should be taken as gospel:

> Alice declared that she and her friend had hired a Ford car from a local garage at Salina to visit friends at Abilene. The car, she stated, broke down on the way back and being without funds they could find no way of having it repaired or towed back to Salina.
>
> Returning home, they were confronted with a bill for over $50 and threatened with arrest if they failed to pay. The girls declared they were afraid to inform their parents because of the consequences and decided instead to leave Salina and go on the road.
>
> At the home of a friend they were equipped with clothing and food and set forth. On the first day out, they were given lifts by passing automobiles and reached Topeka, from thence making their way to Emporia, and 'hopping' a freight to Ottowa, Kan. During this time, declared Alice, they slept out doors, in haystacks, barns, or on freight trains, where the 'hobo fraternity,' chivalrous to the extreme, gave up their soft berths on the bottom of box cars to the vagrant girls.

To the contemporary reader this may seem a bit of a lark – hopping on a train without a ticket. But, in the 1920s, the problem of hobos (itinerant tramps) sneaking on to freight trains – a practice known as 'freighthopping' – was commonplace. The railroad security staff, nicknamed 'bulls', had a reputation for dealing violently with anyone they caught. The safest place to avoid detection was the totally enclosed boxcar, used to transport general freight including coal, grain and sometimes livestock.

To see this experience through the eyes of Alice Peden, it's worth watching the 1928 silent movie *Beggars of Life* (based on the experiences of real-life hobo Jim Tully). Louise Brooks plays Nancy, on the run after killing her abusive stepfather. She disguises herself as a boy (as Alice is said to have done) and lives the life of a hobo. The only methods to board a boxcar unobserved are to wait in the rail yard until the crew changes shift, or to jump onto a moving train. In the movie, Louise (without the aid of a stunt double) makes the jump. But there are other perils too, notably the lascivious glances and unsavoury advances of a mob of drunken and quick-tempered hobos travelling in the same boxcar.

When Alice and Vivian weren't freighthopping, they hitched rides with local tourists, taking them through Oswego, Blue Jacket, Fort Smith and Oklahoma:

> Throughout their two weeks of 'hoboing', declare the girls, they never went hungry, although their supply of funds were as low as fifteen cents. At a farm house in Arkansas, they said, they managed to secure a good meal by offering a derelict Ford car which was found a mile down the road as security.

Policewoman Celeste Magness, the first female police officer ever to be employed in Monroe, Louisiana, won considerable praise for her sensitive handling of the case, having succeeded in gaining the girls' confidence when all others had failed:

> Mrs Magness today declared she was sorry to have them leave, and spoke highly of their conduct during their detention.
> 'The facilities for handling similar cases,' she stated, 'are inadequate. I have no way to insure their safety and no place where they might be placed during investigation. I have had several cases of young girls hoboeing about the country, and am always anxious to try and help

them. The problems which confront me in these cases are very serious and affect the future of the girls who have misguidedly left home.'

Alice and Vivian faithfully promised Mrs Magness that they would be 'good girls in the future' and anxiously awaited the arrival of Mr and Mrs Peden.

It made fantastic newspaper copy, but was not quite the thrilling caper it may have seemed. For Alice and Vivian, what started as the 'borrowing' of a car had rapidly escalated into a situation from which there was no easy escape. For Alice's parents, having already lost one child, there was the real fear that their daughter would also turn up dead. A few days later *The New Orleans Item* reported on the reunion with Alice's parents. The girls' ages are wrong (they were still 16) but the headline would make any tabloid editor proud – HOBO FLAPPERS TO BE SPANKED:

MISSES ALICE PEDEN and VIVIAN VINZANT of Salina, Kan., both 17 years, who hoboed their way from Salina to Monroe in box cars and on foot, are threatened with a spanking when they get back home, according to Mrs C. E. Peden, mother of one of the girls, who came for them. 'That's just what they need and what they will likely get,' said Mrs Peden, as she boarded the train with the fair young women on the way back home. The girls said they guessed Alice's mother was right.

The article included photos of both girls which, judging from their faces, were taken soon after the police had caught them. Few photos of Alice Peden exist and this is a rare chance to see Alice as a teenager, her hair bobbed *à la* Louise Brooks. The onstage Alice would have been very different, but this was a girl facing possible arrest and criminal charges. There is a reassuring hand on her shoulder and, at first glance, she looks much tougher, much colder, than Vivian. But there is real sadness in her eyes. This combination of repressed emotion, resilience and fighting spirit would be the key to her survival over the coming years.

When a parent spanks a child, there are injured feelings on both sides, and the actual pain of the slapping can be almost incidental. If the threat of the spanking was carried out, and if it did any good (if it ever does any good) we can't be certain. Alice may not have seen it as an expression of parental love and concern. Alice could well have been spanked before. And, far from turning her into a well-behaved dutiful daughter, it may have toughened her defences and made her all the more determined to seek escape and glamour.

There was scant evidence of a reformed and repentant Alice in the *Salina Evening Journal* on her return. She was still full to bursting with tales of her travels, including some that hadn't previously been mentioned in the Louisiana press, either through lack of space, or because Alice was still inventing them. Perhaps she was starting to believe her own fantasies:

> Tales of hoboing, of bumming their way from one place to another and of house boat trips along the Mississippi to New Orleans and back again up river are included in the adventures the two young girls have had. In Monroe when they were found several days ago the girls told of bumming their way on freight trains. Today in Salina, Alice Peden reiterated that story and added accounts of two trips on house boats secured after acquaintance with the owners of the boats.
>
> The two young girls, in two weeks' time, covered more area than the average tourist covers in two months. They admitted having had a 'regular trip'.

One thing was for sure. Alice would never be the same again. The past fortnight had been a heady mixture of thrills and danger. She may have promised Policewoman Magness that she'd be a 'good girl', but that was just an act. And, if there was one thing Alice excelled at, it was acting. From now on, if she wanted anything badly enough, she knew she could charm her way into achieving it. She'd charmed her way with boys, with boat owners, with hobos and with the law. Of course, if charm didn't work, there was always friendly persuasion. Or, as a last resort, a combination of outright lying and outrageous flirting. The big wide world had suddenly got smaller. And Alice had it in the palm of her hand. Anything was possible!

Enter Donald Ednell Knox. He wasn't Mr Showbiz, he wasn't rich, but he was more or less the same age as Alice, male, and good company. Donald was the eldest son of Edward Knox, a house painter, and his wife Nellie. The family, seven children in all, lived in Chapman – eleven miles beyond Abilene, the home of Alice's previous boyfriend. Donald and Alice must quickly have become very close because, in late June 1923 (only eight months after Alice's last escapade), she ran away again. This time with Donald at her side.

Last time Alice had fled southwards. Now it was in the opposite direction, northwards to Nebraska. On 30ᵗʰ June, in Omaha (Nebraska's largest city), Donald Knox and Alice Peden obtained a marriage licence. The *Omaha World Herald* published a list of those who had recently been granted licences, along with their residences and ages:

> Donald Knox, Chapman, Kas. Age 22. Alice Peden, Salina, Kas. Age 21.

In fact, both Donald and Alice had just turned 17. And Alice was the older of the pair – by 17 days. But, if they claimed to be over 21, they would not need parental consent. Whether the Alice pictured at age 16 could convincingly pass for 21 just a few months later would be utterly dependent on her acting abilities. It goes without saying that she did.

It's to be hoped that love was the driving force behind this whirlwind marriage, but there was another factor. Alice was two months pregnant. As a *Newsweek* article from January 1944 succinctly summed it up:

> On the stage at 14, married at 15 (since divorced), and a mother at 16.

Obviously all the ages are wrong, as we've come to expect. But, like Marcel Wallenstein's *Kansas City Star* article, it seems to be the result of a personal interview. For instance, in *Newsweek* Betty Knox is described as 'five-foot-four, brown-eyed'. (The five-foot-four-and-three-quarters Joe Keppel must have towered over her!) The *Kansas City Star's* version of events is:

> Eluding pursuit, she fled to Omaha where in desperation she married a young man named Knox. Her daughter was born. She divorced Knox. Not a novel story. It's been happening since Noah's brood shoved off from the Ark.

Not a novel story – but is it a true story? Well, if this article had Betty's blessing, it confirms the tale that she ran away to get married. It's possible she did so, as the postscript to the *Kansas City Star* article claims, 'dressed in overalls and posing as a boy' (though this was more likely her costume for the previous freighthopping adventure). Their marriage certainly happened before the birth, though not before the conception. But two months into a pregnancy is quite an early stage to feel you 'have to get married'. Maybe they were head over heels in love and couldn't wait to be man and wife. But (if young Alice had so far managed to conceal her pregnancy from her family) she may have decided to elope so that the first shock her parents had to deal with was her marriage. Then, a few weeks after they'd recovered from that bombshell, she announces the joyous news of her impending motherhood. Possibly the best means at her disposal of softening the blow.

So the order of events is correct. But there is one slight question mark. Obtaining a marriage licence is not quite the same as being married. The licence was signed by Donald and Alice, dated and witnessed, but the rest of the form is blank, with no details of either residence or parents' names. Halfway down the form is this instruction:

> … you are required to return this License to me within three months from the celebration of such marriage … under the penalty of five hundred dollars.

Five hundred dollars is a hefty fine – but that would be for failing to return the licence within three months of a marriage ceremony. Not for failing to have a marriage ceremony at all. The bottom half of the form, which is only to be filled in after the ceremony, is also blank. No marriage means no need for divorce – and no records have been discovered of either event. This appears to be confirmed by Donald Knox's subsequent marriage in February 1929. The form requires him to state 'Number of Groom's Marriage'. Donald's reply is: 'First'.

The suspect validity of Donald and Alice Knox's marriage would have been a well-kept secret, and with good reason. Even later in life, she was hardly going to reveal to the world that her child's parents were never actually married.

Alice gave birth to Jean Patricia Knox on 22nd December 1923. The big surprise on the birth certificate is Donald's current occupation. He is a clerk at the store once owned by his father-in-law, and still known as Peden's Grocery. So Alice the teenage runaway was no more. She had a husband working for the family business. They were just one big happy family.

As a further indication of family closeness, in little over a year, Alice, Donald and baby Jean Patricia are all living with Charles and Lizzie Peden at 611 Park Place, Salina. Donald is now a mechanic and Alice's profession is listed as 'housewife'.

So Alice was back where she started – with her parents in Salina. But with the addition of a husband and a young child. Her dreams of showbiz stardom had never seemed less achievable. If she had a career plan, then love, lust and bad luck had firmly put paid to it. She had heard the phrase 'I told you so' a thousand times. But now the voice saying it was her own. If, in her wildest fantasies, she'd ever pictured herself as a globetrotting celebrity dancer, she was going to have to forget it. It just wasn't going to happen.

5

Picking 'Em Up and Laying 'Em Down

(America 1920–1928)

'… they dance every minute, every second, they are on the stage.'
(*Bridgeport Telegram*, 1925)

THE RMS *NIAGARA* DOCKED AT VANCOUVER, British Columbia, Canada on 12th September 1920. On board were Wilson and Keppel, vaudeville artists. They'd put together some kind of act during their time in Colleano's Circus – but had never performed as a duo in Australian vaudeville. So this was a real leap into the unknown.

But, before we go any further … a very important question. Which was Wilson and which was Keppel? To their audiences it probably didn't matter that much. They spent their whole career endeavouring to look virtually identical. And, today, few people seem to know who was who. Some get it the wrong way round. Some are even under the impression that (despite the different surnames) the two are brothers. So take a moment to look at the photos in this book, or watch some of their routines. It's worth getting it clear in your mind.

Irishman Joe Keppel pours out the sand. Although both frequently assume deadpan expressions, Joe has the more expressive eyes. They will leer at Betty, or fix Wilson with a hypnotic stare during the sand dance. If anyone seems to be taking charge when they dance together, it is Joe. In some ways, when it comes to the comedy moments, Joe is the bigger ham – whereas Wilson's face, for the most part, remains an impassive mask.

Liverpudlian Jack Wilson is the musician. He plays the clarinet, the penny whistle, the accordion and the harmonica. And, during Betty's dance of the seven veils, when Keppel finally loses patience and attempts to rip off a veil for himself, it is Jack Wilson who admonishes him. So, onstage, it would seem that Joe Keppel is the more extrovert figure. Offstage, as we will see later, it was a different matter.

But the sand dancing and the seven veils are several years away. Jack and Joe's early American vaudeville act was about as Egyptian as … well … an Englishman and an Irishman clog dancing in the USA.

In late October 1921 they were at the Cataract Theatre, Niagara Falls, New York. As was customary in vaudeville shows, the stage acts alternated with the movie attraction, giving two or three performances a day. In the era of silent film, live performers and big-screen epics co-existed very amicably. It was only when the talkies came in that vaudeville suffered.

This particular week the motion picture was *The Lost Romance*, directed by William de Mille (Cecil B's older brother). Wilson and Keppel shared the bill with Janette (a girl saxophonist), Cantor's Minstrels (four singers and a pianist) and Devitt & Gunther ('little entertainers'). Jack and Joe were still using Keppel's Australian billing: 'Wizards of the Wooden Shoe'. Later they called themselves 'The Dancing Wonders' and even 'England's Champion Clog Dancers'. (In those pre-Internet days, who could disprove the claim?)

By the end of the year they informed theatrical newspaper *The New York Clipper* they were 'rehearsing a new act which is to be seen shortly'. In June 1922, they came to the attention of American theatre magazine *Variety*, which carried regular reviews of new acts:

> Wilson and Keppel. Male hard shoe dancing team attired in gray suits and black and white shoes. Routine consists of single and double hard shoe work of a fast order.

In the same month *The New York Clipper* took us through their act in more detail:

> Two men, neatly attired in checkered suits doing a straight hard shoe dance routine. They opened with a double number and then alternated

with a series of singles and closing with another double. The dances were varied and the taps consistently good. Being a dumb act, the routine is fast and an excellent one of its kind for any house on the circuit, where it can give either a fast start or a snappy finish to a bill.

So, at this early stage in their career, they were little more than high-energy hoofers in grey check suits. But this 'dumb act' didn't stay dumb for long. As the years went on they started experimenting with comedy patter – not always totally successfully.

'Judging by the accent of the talk and song hits used by this two-man combination they are recent arrivals from England,' began *The Billboard*'s reviewer in May 1925, obviously unaware that they'd been touring America for the past four years. He didn't dislike the act – except when they opened their mouths:

> The gags are very old and poorly delivered for the most part. Their forte is clog dancing, and a concertina adds a bit of novelty to the offering. In fact, if they could routine their bits omitting most of the talk used at present they would give a much better account of themselves than they did when reviewed at this house.

They continued to tinker with their billing matter. This catchy little epithet, reported in *The Bridgeport Telegram* (Connecticut) of October 1925, lasts them for the next couple of years:

> Wilson & Keppel, who open the bill in great style have an act they term 'Picking 'Em Up and Laying 'Em Down'. They are dancers and they dance every minute, every second, they are on the stage.

'Picking 'Em Up and Laying 'Em Down' was a slang phrase for fast footwork on the dance floor, or the ability to make a speedy getaway! It neatly described their act and was a popular dance number that had been written and recorded the previous year. Described as a 'hot Chicago foxtrot' it was a hit for the Benson Orchestra of Chicago, so Jack and Joe fairly certainly danced to it:

> Just pickin' 'em up and layin' 'em down,
> The dance that'll be the talk of the town ...
> You hold her and glide, you step to the side,
> And then kinda let your conscience be your guide,
> And honey, when your feet get real hot, steppin' all around
> You're pickin' 'em up and layin' 'em down.

Up to now Wilson and Keppel had worked on vaudeville bills which alternated with a silent movie main feature. Although there were still plenty of these around, sometimes the big picture was just too big to need any support acts. Clog dancing would hardly be required between showings of Cecil B. de Mille's *The Ten Commandments*. As movies became ever more spectacular, they began to be the sole attraction in many movie theatres.

But other initiatives were being tried. Wilson and Keppel returned to Connecticut in October 1926 in an all-live extravaganza: '*The Derby Winners* – a Real Snappy Burlesque Show'. *The Bridgeport Telegram* detailed the cast – very typical of the time, with talented kids, comics who 'blacked up', and a bevy of chorus girls:

> Among the leading participants are Charles 'Slim' Timblin, black-face funster; Charles 'Happy' Cook, tramp comedian; Walter Deering, baritone singer; Billy Highly, dancing juvenile; Al Ridgeway, in character roles; Miss Val Russell, black-face comedienne; Helen Harris, blues singer; Olive de Claire, prima donna and Vivian Kent, a miniature Pavlova.
>
> Wilson and Keppel show the 'last word' in stepping stunts. The 18 comely chorines are much in evidence.

Burlesque had a long thriving history in America and – if you weren't going to offer your patrons a movie – the next best thing would be a large number of attractive and decorous chorus girls. At this time, partial nudity on stage was becoming increasingly common, particularly on Broadway – but there's no suggestion that this show was unduly 'adult'. It was merely a horseracing adventure interspersed with song and dance numbers by 'a Chorus of 18 Thoroughbred Beauties'.

Jack and Joe spent more than six months in the company but, if they were ever tempted to get overfamiliar with one of the Thoroughbred Beauties, *The Bridgeport Telegram* provided a word of warning:

> Here's a secret! Apparently there are eighteen pretty girls in 'The Derby Winners' on view at the Park Theatre today. But there are only seventeen. And the prettiest 'girl' in the chorus is a boy!

The unnamed youth had specialised in female roles at university but, having failed to find work in the professional theatre, he'd taken the bold decision to break into showbiz in a somewhat unconventional manner:

... by hiding his personality 'neath a chorine's raiment, donning blond wig and squeezing his waist into the small size habiliments of a 'perfect 16'.

We can only imagine what would have happened if Wilson and Keppel had chosen that moment in history to become a trio, and plucked the prettiest girl from the chorus line!

By early 1928 they were no longer Picking 'Em Up and Laying 'Em Down. They were The Bus Boys. The *Toledo News-Bee* (Ohio) gives a brief summary of the act:

Wilson and Keppel arrive on the scene in a sight-seeing bus of miniature proportions, sing a little, create a number of laughs with their radio burlesque and then indulge in some classy tap dancing, part of which is up and down a flight of stairs. They are good.

Faint praise, but a fascinating snapshot of their 1928 show. By now, comedy was central to the act. They had gained confidence in their abilities to get laughs through physical comedy, music and singing. Plus a radio burlesque – which must have involved all three. Those stairs will dominate the act for a good few years to come. Apart from Wilson and Keppel's growing talent as performers, another of their invaluable skills was in devising and building their own props. The bus and stairs are early examples of how their skilled craftsmanship would often enhance their routines.

At the end of June 1928 they played the Ogden Orpheum, Utah. The big screen attraction – Monte Blue in *Across the Atlantic* – played at 12:30, 3:30, 6:00, 8:30 and 11:00 pm daily. The vaudeville shows were at 2:30, 5:00, 7:30 and 10:00 pm. An exhausting four performances a day.

Upping the number of daily shows was one indication that vaudeville was struggling to hold its own against the movies. This situation is reflected in Lorenz Hart's lyrics to the 1936 musical *On Your Toes*:

It's two a day for Keith, and three a day for Loew;
Pantages plays us four a day, beside the supper show.

During their career, Jack and Joe played all three of these major vaudeville theatre chains and, right now, were being represented by agent Arthur Silber who booked exclusively for the Pantages circuit. Earlier in 1928 they'd travelled vast distances, playing Pantages theatres across the west coast of America, from Los Angeles, California to Portland, Oregon to Seattle, Washington – plus a couple of trips over the Canadian border to Toronto, Hamilton and Vancouver.

Now, in June 1928 at the Ogden Orpheum, Utah, *The Ogden Standard Examiner* gives a rundown of the entire bill, starting with the main attraction, which must have taken Jack and Joe right back to their circus beginnings:

> The feature of the bill is the wild animal act billed as Richard Havemann's Kings of the Forest and Desert. The lions roar, the leopards snarl and Havemann mutters German to the great delight of the audience. Realistic anger scenes, in which the trainer seemed to be in imminent peril, please the crowd immensely, especially the children.

Wilson and Keppel present, of course, The Bus Boys 'which is well received', followed by mind reader Marjah the Mystic, and a touch of feminine glamour:

> Mabel McCane gives a delightful skit combining comedy and pathos in a girl's struggle to attain the bright lights and the admiring glances of men.

Meanwhile, one girl is undergoing that struggle for real. And it's time we caught up with her.

6

The Average Life of a Chorus Girl

(Kansas and Broadway 1925–1927)

'They either get fat and lazy, or their nervous systems go to pieces.'
(Allan K. Foster, 1926)

IN JUNE 1925, DONALD EDNELL KNOX AND HIS WIFE Alice Elizabeth (both aged 19) were still living with Alice's parents at 611 Park Place, Salina. Their daughter, Jean Patricia, was 18 months old. Both mother and daughter were now known by their middle names – Elizabeth shortened to Betty, and Patricia shortened to Patsy.

Right now, Betty Knox, housewife, had been forced by circumstances to put all showbiz ambitions to the back of her mind. But they never quite went away.

What if? That must have been the question that constantly buzzed round her head. Somewhere out there, in a parallel universe, there must be a husbandless and childless Betty Knox just going out there and achieving her dreams.

And there was. But not in a parallel universe. Much closer to hand. In Nebraska, the state directly north of Kansas. In the city of Lincoln (about 50 miles from Omaha, where Betty had eloped to pick up her marriage licence) lived a girl about the same age, without husband or offspring, called Betty Mae Knox.

Unlike Betty, her namesake had stayed at high school long enough to graduate. Betty Mae then auditioned for Maryon Vadie, an experienced ballerina, who was in Nebraska recruiting a troupe of keen but non-professional dancers to tour the Orpheum vaudeville circuit. Pretty soon Betty Mae came to the attention of Broadway impresarios the Shubert brothers, and on 10th May 1926 (the very day of wife-and-mother Betty Knox's 20th birthday) was high-kicking in the chorus line at the out-of-town opening night of lavish revue *The Great Temptations* at the Shubert Theatre, New Haven, Connecticut.

The New York Sun of the previous month described life as a *Great Temptations* chorus girl:

> Rehearsals at top notch speed for hours without end. Concentrated effort made possible by the knowledge that this is business and not practice. No periods of laughter and small talk, but endlessly: one, two, three, four, bend, turn, kick, eight. And when a rest is called every 'chorine' takes it seriously and rests. 'The Great Temptations', the latest revue to go into rehearsal, follows the general rule. The chorus go through a number almost endlessly until it passes the approval of the entire board of judgement, producer, director, supervisor and the several dancing teachers and assistants. And still that means little, for after days spent in synchronising a number, it may be discarded. Hard lines? Yes, but that is what makes it the greatest dancing class in the world.

The Great Temptations was a big show. Rather too big, judging from reviews of its Broadway opening night at the Winter Garden Theatre. J. Brooks Atkinson, of the *New York Times*, had watched the curtain go up at 8:30 pm:

> By 11:30, it was still in spirited progress with four of the thirty-four numbers yet to come, the brasses still resonant and the drummer skipping nimbly from one drum to another, as he had been doing all evening.

By and large, the critics found the show to be a mixed (though stuffed-to-bursting) bag. *Time Magazine* declared it 'an exceptionally dull revue'. Burns Mantle of the *Springfield Daily Republican* provided this succinct summary:

> Hazel Dawn has so much of a leading role as there is to be had. Charlotte Woodruff and a tenor named Halfred Young do the best of the singing. Billy B. Van and Ray Flippen are the tougher of comedians and seldom

funny. There are lots and lots of dancers. The music is by Maurice Rubens and pretty good. The book is by Harold Atteridge and pretty sad.

Mr Mantle fails even to mention a young comic, at the very start of his career, named Jack Benny. At one point during his crosstalk act with 'dumb girlfriend' Dorothy McNulty, Jack says, 'You know, I actually met a girl today who *wasn't* in this show.' The newspaper ads proclaimed 'a company of 150' – and a quick tot up of the names listed in the programme suggests that at least eighty of these were chorus girls. There were the Little Temptations (a line-up of high-energy hoofers that included Betty Mae Knox), the Great Temptations (tall girls), the Koster & Bial Temptations (fat girls) and the Foster Girls (an exceptionally well-drilled troupe who performed as entangled flies on a giant spider's web). Hence the show's strapline: 'A Revue of Feminine Loveliness'.

Which brings us to the matter of costume, and the distinct lack of it at times. This was frequently given artistic justification by setting the scene in a bygone age, or by presenting a visual representation of a work of art. However, some of the other nudity was harder to justify. Burns Mantle, in *The Springfield Weekly Republican*:

> Being a statue on a pedestal or an undraped Bacchante on the side of a heroic vase is one thing. Being an undraped goddess on parade and viewable from all geographical angles is another. There are 10 of these 'Great Temptations'. They march down from Mount Olympus at the call of Jupiter and start for New York with instructions to liven up the old town. And again I say they are the nakedest of all the walking ladies I have ever seen upon the stage.

Much like London's Windmill Theatre a few years later, the author-ities found motionless nudes easier to tolerate than those that had any tendency to jiggle. Japanese critic Dr Noritake Tsuda, writing in the *Bakersfield Californian*, had one valuable insight to offer:

> I have seen for the first time an American 'revue' where the chief attraction is nude women placed on public display for private profit. The performance which I chose because I was told it was typical, is aptly called 'The Great Temptations' ... a series of sensual scenes offered under the hypocritical name of 'Art' ... I am told such performances increase in number in New York during the summer, when wives are away on their vacations and husbands remain alone in the city. It is

surprising to me to hear that this condition is regarded as stimulating a demand for more art.

It was not only audience members who had misgivings. A decade or so later, Alexandria Wasilewska, evangelist and former *Great Temptations* chorus girl, spoke to *The New York Sun*:

'I saw many things that shocked me,' she says, 'and yet I was unconsciously learning not to think much of them. When I look back, I can see that's how Satan blinds us. That's how sly and deceiving he is.'

Several other *Temptations* chorus girls cast aside their reservations (and clothes) to promote the show in *Artists and Models* magazine, which offered a series of photo studies expressly pitched at the connoisseur of the naked female form – or anyone else with 25 cents to spare.

Over the summer of 1926, Betty Mae was mentioned several times in *Variety* magazine's regular column of chorus girl tittle-tattle:

Betty Knox, 'Great Temptations', claims the wild west as her home but has reached the conclusion that New York is just as wild.

Betty Knox is being blessed, if that's what you'd call it, with freckles from the summer sun.

Gloria Swanson has let her hair grow so Betty Knox of 'Temptations' has decided to follow suit.

In hindsight, it's easy to confuse the two Bettys. But, at the time, there was only one Betty Knox in the showbiz columns. And that was Betty Mae from Lincoln.

Betty Knox from Salina had been the family disgrace, running away from home to disport herself onstage in a tacky chorus line. The only time she ever made the headlines (as Alice Peden) was when she fled arrest for joyriding.

Betty Mae from Lincoln, on the other hand, was everyone's golden girl. Each fresh triumph was eagerly documented in the local press, and newspapers and theatrical publications further afield. Perhaps being a trained ballerina made her dancing ambitions more acceptable than those of Salina's Betty – although *The Great Temptations* would have been a great deal more risqué than any show that Betty ever appeared in.

A much trotted out piece of trivia claims that Betty Knox was once

Jack Benny's vaudeville partner – though, even if true, again it would refer to Betty Mae from Lincoln. It's most likely an exaggeration of the undeniable fact that Betty Mae Knox shared a stage with him for half a year in *The Great Temptations* – as did at least eighty other girls.

For several years after *The Great Temptations*, Jack did a double act routine with a dumb girlfriend character called Marie Marsh, inspired by the *Temptations* routine he had done with Dorothy McNulty. An unknown actress played this character for a while. Then Jack's wife Mary (known in those days as Sadye) took over the role and did it much better. Although it's vaguely possible the unknown actress could have been Betty Mae, there's no reason to believe that Betty Knox of Salina ever met him, let alone partnered him.

So while (in the parallel universe of Lincoln, Nebraska) Betty Mae Knox was on the fast-track to stardom, Betty Knox from Salina was fated to take the slower path. However, what had stayed constant, through all the emotional and physical upheavals of the past few years, was Betty's talent as a performer, her undoubted stage presence, and her determination to follow a career in show business. She may (quite possibly inadvertently) have become a young mother stuck in a small city, with a small-town mentality, far away from the vaudeville circuit. But that was one role she was not happy playing. She had been blatantly miscast.

But, if Betty Knox hadn't fundamentally changed, what had? Up to this point in her life she has been portrayed (by herself and others) as the perpetual runaway, the family embarrassment. But her family hadn't disowned her – she was living with them. And when she finally returned home, it wasn't in disgrace. It was with a husband. And – after a decent interval – a baby daughter. Betty may not have been, by nature, particularly maternal – but granny Lizzie surely was. Having endured the death of her youngest son, Charles Junior, Lizzie would have been the most doting grandparent imaginable.

So there were no major obstacles in Betty's way. Husband Donald had stuck by her, but the great romance – if that's what it ever was – had cooled off. Whether Betty grew disenchanted with Donald, or Donald with Betty, or their falling out of love was mutual, Betty's mind was now fixed firmly on her career. By 1927 Donald had moved away and settled in Des Moines, Iowa. In February 1929 he married Emily (his first marriage, according to the marriage register). His obituary of 1975 lists the four children he and Emily had together, but gives no mention of his first child – daughter Patsy. Once Donald had moved out, he would play no further part in the lives of Betty or Patsy.

With Lizzie taking care of young Patsy, it left Betty free to start auditioning for theatre work. If Charles and Lizzie didn't wholeheartedly approve, at least they indulged their daughter for a while. And, it seems, she found success before they had a chance to change their minds.

Initially, Betty may have trod the stage not as a dancer but as a straight actress, possibly in local theatre. A teenage Patsy, interviewed in 1938, said:

> ... you know mother was in repertory for a while ...

From small time drama groups to big city chorus line auditions may seem a massive step, but it was only a matter of hopping on a train, and Betty had been no stranger to train travel over the past few years. So she bought a train ticket and, like the title character in the 1920s-set musical *Thoroughly Modern Millie*, set off on her exciting journey. The action in this retro stage musical (based on the 1967 Julie Andrews movie) takes place around the same time that Betty was embarking on her own career. But there's another close connection. Aspiring flapper Millie Dillmount's home is also Salina, Kansas. She boards the train for New York with her return ticket in her pocket, singing of her confused emotions about leaving home ('a one-light town where the light is always red'). By the end of her journey she has torn up her ticket, determined never to return to Salina. Of course, there was one significant difference. Betty had a baby daughter. But she also had a burning ambition to succeed, and to show all those disapproving neighbours with their small-town attitudes that she had what it takes to make it big.

Theatrical papers were always advertising for chorus girls. Betty may have performed in touring revue, in a vaudeville act, or in one of the larger vaudeville theatres that boasted not only a house band but a resident chorus line as well. But, even if work was pouring in, there's no reason why Betty should ever have become a 'name'. At best, a line of dancing girls would be known collectively, often by the name of the choreographer (like the previously mentioned Foster Girls from *The Great Temptations*). It's part of the job description that you don't stand out from the crowd – so Betty would have had several years of successful anonymity. For most girls that would be the situation for their entire career.

It's tempting to wonder if Betty collected press cuttings of her Lincoln namesake's Broadway triumphs and used them to enhance her own CV. But she wouldn't have got a single job without auditioning, and she wouldn't have passed a single audition if she hadn't been a darned good hoofer.

Returning to *The Great Temptations* one last time, in August 1926, *The World Magazine* asked Allan K. Foster (choreographer of the Foster Girls) for his opinion on the longevity of a dancer's career:

> Now the average life of a chorus girl, and by that I mean the time she can successfully appear in public, is about three or four, and at the most five years. Their bodies cannot stand the strain of dance work and fast living together. They either get fat and lazy, or their nervous systems go to pieces.

Any potential Foster Girl had first to sign a contract, containing such clauses as 'Smoking and drinking are specifically forbidden,' and 'A Foster dancer must retire at 12 o'clock, shortly after the final curtain of the show.' However, in the long term, this abstemious lifestyle would prove itself a shrewd investment:

> I estimate that my girls, with their regular work, regular exercise, good plain food, and plenty of sleep, will last for the stage an average of fifteen years.

The Great Temptations closed in November 1926, and Betty Mae Knox of Lincoln went on to be a featured performer in a number of small scale touring revues, taking her well into 1927. And that, judging by her press coverage, would seem to be that. Perhaps her three to four years was up?

On the other hand, Betty Knox of Salina went on to achieve a stage career well in excess of fifteen years as a dancing glamour girl. And this was through a lifestyle supplemented by no end of 'fast living.' Smoking, drinking, late nights … everything that Allan K. Foster claimed would be the downfall of your average chorus girl. But, then again, since when had Betty Knox been average?

Betty Mae of Lincoln may have reigned supreme up until 1927. But, from 1928 onwards, there was a new Betty Knox in town.

7
Oodles of Sex Appeal

(America 1928–1932)

'The girl is everything in America.' (Joe Keppel, 1959)

In July 1928 Wilson and Keppel, now known as The Bus Boys, were playing the Pantages Theatre, Kansas City, Missouri. Top of the bill was Marjah the Mystic, the mind reader, with whom they'd been touring for some time. If Jack and Joe had asked Marjah to predict their own future, they might not have believed what the next few years had in store. Because, as *The Billboard* reported, radical changes were afoot:

> Wilson and Keppel, an English act, on this week's bill at the Pantages, will go from here to Memphis, where they will close the act and will form a trio.

And so, by the end of July, Wilson and Keppel the double-act were no more. Back in 1922, *Variety* had reviewed their smart-suited clog-dancing frenzy. In November 1928, they took a fresh look at the two Bus Boys and noted a significant addition:

> WILSON and KEPPEL, Dancing, 10 mins. Formerly a straight dance team and now a nut dance act in nut makeup and with semi-comic dancing. Third member, girl, there on looks and fairly good stepper. She has a pair of solo chances and joins the name players in the stair dance finish.
>
> The novelty opening now used could be elaborated for added strength. It's a miniature bus, pedalled by one of the men, with a seat on the top deck, upon which the other gent does a sitting-down tap routine. Double comedy dance number leads to the stairs finale.

A novelty dance act that misses topnotch classification because a topnotch routine is needed. In any event the gal should be retained, if only for her appearance.

Fortunately they did retain the gal – who would go on to contribute far more than just 'her appearance'. The review on the opposite page is even more dismissive of her talents:

Sweet looking girl dancer, more sweet than a dancer, is also new.

So the act now consisted of Wilson and Keppel, a model bus, a set of stairs, and a girl. But who was that girl? A few days later, Mount Vernon's *Daily Argus* (New York) revealed her name:

Wilson, Keppel and Betty present 'Off a Fifth Avenue Bus'

Late in their career (in 1959) Wilson and Keppel spoke to the *Manchester Guardian* about their beginnings in American vaudeville:

Some years later they noticed an extremely pretty girl in the company, observed the success she seemed to be enjoying, and wondered, in Mr Keppel's words, 'what the hell we were doing. The girl is everything in America.'

We don't know for sure which vaudeville turn Betty was part of. But, of all the acts Jack and Joe met on the Pantages circuit in the first half of 1928, the most likely was Jack DeSylvia's *Broadway Vanities*. This was a stage musical compressed into ten minutes and designed to slot into a vaudeville bill of half a dozen acts. (In other words, a 'tab show' – like the one Betty bluffed her way into five years earlier at the Kansas Globe.) In early March, Wilson and Keppel had worked with *Broadway Vanities* in Toronto, Canada. Joe Bigelow from *Variety* reviewed them later that month:

This is a flash turn, with a sweet-voiced and nifty-looking prima and half a dozen competent and various styled dancers. Although there on talent, act is most notable for its mounting and costuming. One number included costumes that would fit into any $4.40 revue. An eye-filler and clicked.

It seems that the two Bus Boys, waiting in the wings, were immediately struck by a classily attired (but certainly not overdressed) Betty. This was the very first example of Jack and Joe plucking a girl from the chorus (which later became their preferred method of recruitment). It's pretty clear she knew how to make an impact onstage and had an equally outgoing personality offstage. The trio quickly hit it off, and it may be debatable who talked who into joining the act.

Within months they visited the photographic studios of Theatrical Chicago and posed for a couple of group portraits. All three were smartly attired in jackets, with Wilson and Keppel in shirt and tie, and Betty wearing a large-collared white blouse. Such is the quest for eternal youth amongst the showbiz fraternity, these publicity shots were still in use in the mid-1940s.

In their 1947 publicity, they say they made their debut as a trio in Des Moines, Iowa. An intriguing location, because Donald Knox (Betty's ex-husband – if he ever was her legal husband) was living there at the time. It's unlikely she was still in contact with him, as he was to marry Emily (his first marriage, so he claimed) in a matter of months.

So how much did The Bus Boys double-act develop when it became a threesome? Very little. Betty did a couple of solo tap-dancing spots – giving the other two the opportunity to change costumes, move props, or just catch their breath. All three of them only danced together during the final moments of the steps routine. It was still basically Wilson and Keppel's act – with the welcome addition of a pretty girl. Particularly welcome, because (as the critic's 'nut makeup' comment indicates) the other two had already started dipping their hands into the makeup pots of grotesquery.

For a while they tinkered with the billing. There were the odd experiments with a hyphen: 'Wilson-Keppel & Betty' and even 'Keppel-Wilson and Betty.' But the order was fairly standard, even if the spelling of Keppel wasn't. During his vaudeville years, the American press variously referred to him as Kepel, Kepple, Kappel, Kippel and Kuppel. One early listing calls them 'Wilson and Kepple and Bettye' – which would seem a fairly bizarre mistake to make, had this book not already encountered both a Rubye and a Sadye.

Twisted typography apart, the trio of Wilson, Keppel and Betty had arrived. And that particular combination of names carries its own inspired logic. Wilson, Keppel and Knox sounds like a firm of solicitors – but putting 'Betty' at the end gives it a good rhythm, an unexpected twist and a neat final flourish of frivolity. Somehow the names alone are enough to make you smile. The male psyche says: 'Dull, Dull and ... Oh yes?'

It's doubtful whether the act alone would have held such a place in our affections, if it hadn't been coupled with that grouping of names. It says it all – two morose old men and a young female stunner.

Talking of ages, at the time the trio was formed, Wilson and Keppel were both 34 and Betty was 22. Whether that made them father figures or dodgy uncles became the subject of much speculation. The fact that the act endured as long as it did with the same trio would suggest that, by and large, everyone behaved in a highly professional manner.

With Betty on the scene, the *Variety* reviewer was not the only person to sit up and take notice. *Vaudeville News* said 'a most exacting critic would declare that, if need be, each could easily make the grade alone'. A talented team they certainly were, though Betty was repeatedly singled out for her looks and dancing prowess. However, as *Variety* had said, 'a topnotch routine is needed'. And, in early 1929, they premiered a totally new act. *The Times-Picayune* (New Orleans) and the *Rockford Republic* (Illinois) provide some detail:

> How 'Flaming Youth' frolics around on the college campus is very wittily portrayed in 'Collegiate Co-Eds', a comic skit by Wilson, Keppel and Betty. Their act is the last word in collegiate wit.
>
> The trio presents a bird's-eye view of college life as it is not. They present a short, intensive course in fun and song entirely too limited for such a talented troupe.

The Waco News-Tribune of Texas, who titled the act 'Two Collegiates and a Co-ed', carried a photo of a beaming Jack and Joe in top hats and wide Eton collars (probably an old publicity shot from their double-act days).

It can be no coincidence that the arrival of Betty triggered a complete rethink of an act that had, up to now, evolved gradually over several years. Wilson and Keppel had tried their hands at a number of novelty items, including songs and a radio burlesque, in the past. But this was the first time in their career that they'd devised a complete themed act from scratch.

In their later careers, Jack Wilson and Betty Knox would each dash off the occasional song, so these two would have particularly enjoyed crafting some new words and music – or fitting new words to old music. As something of an all-rounder, Betty would have had no hesitation in chipping in with the vocals. She was now truly part of the team, both as writer and performer.

In May 1929 they shared the bill with all-girl band The Happiness Girls at the Uptown Theatre, Detroit, Michigan. The journey involved taking the night boat from Cleveland, Ohio, recalled Ann Williams, the pianist of the outfit (in her memoirs *We Opened in One*, recorded and transcribed by her son). The vaudeville life meant constant travel, from theatre to theatre, from state to state, over vast distances. So it was often necessary to journey through the night, usually by train. Ann remembered a typical train ride:

> There were so many of us that we really took over a Pullman car. I saw a rerun of the Tony Curtis/Jack Lemmon *Some Like it Hot* not long ago, and it reminded me of our traveling days, or nights. This happened fairly often, that we would get on the sleeper after the show and be picked up during the night. You have heard the term 'sleeper jump'. That means far enough away to have to take a Pullman overnight.

Before the first show of the day (in the early afternoon) the performers ran through their acts with the house band:

> The standard routine for vaudeville acts was for the leader of the stage band, or of the act, whatever it was, to come to the theatre as early as possible on opening day in the morning, and put his music case as near the conductor's stand, or center stage, as possible. When it was time for rehearsal with the pit band, the leader would take the case nearest the center first, and rehearse the acts in order. Those pit band leaders were absolutely remarkable! Usually they were perfect for the first matinee.
>
> The pit bands usually had a piano, a couple of fiddles (actually a fairly complete string section), two trumpets, a trombone, and a string bass. The trap man [pit percussionist] was terrific. He usually sat up higher than the rest so he could see what was going on to catch various breaks and comedy bits. The rest of the players were low in the pit, where they couldn't see much.

Not only was the 'trap man' the rhythmic pulse of the band, he was also sound effects man for acrobats and slapstick comics – crashing cymbals, whacking woodblocks and sliding the swanee whistle with all the slickness and precision of a Tom and Jerry soundtrack.

Before each performance, Ann (like Betty Knox) would apply her elaborate stage makeup:

> We all wore full grease makeup for all shows. After removing street makeup with theatrical cold cream (which I still use) we used a greasepaint base, rouge, and a rather heavy eye makeup of shadow, liner, and a cosmetic mascara which came in a little pan, to be melted over a candle and put on with toothpick or matchstick. This could be beaded at the ends of the lashes, and was very effective. The beads could be pulled off and put back in the pan to be used over.

Although Collegiate Co-Eds served Wilson, Keppel and Betty well enough, we can only guess that the *Rockford Republic* got it right, and the routine was 'entirely too limited for such a talented troupe'. It was clever and original, but it lacked the enthusiastic response that The Bus Boys received – and, once again, their attempt at vocal comedy had misfired. After no more than three months Collegiate Co-eds was dropped for good and Wilson, Keppel and Betty became 'Dancing Entertainers', presenting 'a melange of dances'. If Betty felt disappointed that her initial creative input hadn't scored a hit, their next *Variety* review (July 1929) chose to single out Betty for a bit of a telling off:

> … Wilson, Keppel and Betty opened pleasantly enough. Betty might don more clothes for her taps. Strip dressing doesn't mean anything that early and taps, as well as kicks, can be enhanced as skirts swish around.

As can be seen from later film routines, Betty largely ignored this advice. And Wilson and Keppel were hardly going to encourage their attractive young crowd-pleaser to cover up. What she did instead was to vary her outfits, slipping on trousers or a long semi-transparent dress for some items, and saving her skimpiest costume for the finale.

Betty was more than a good-looking girl with a great figure. Her skill and stage presence were winning her rave reviews again and again. For many critics she wasn't just part of the act – she was the best part of the act. Writing in New York's *Syracuse American*, while reviewer Franklin Chase's comments were typical of many, his last sentence was most definitely not:

> Now, everybody knows that tap dancing is good, but a little goes a long ways unless there is genuine novelty to it. Well, these three have injected the novelty, both in entrance and all through the act. That blonde is a

graceful girl, isn't she?

While they were still experimenting with the act, Betty was clearly experimenting with her hair. In fact, ten months later another review talks of a 'comely blond Betty'. When the trio made a return visit the following year (by which time, perhaps, she had washed that blonde right out of her hair), Franklin Chase was still just as struck on her: 'You will like them, especially Betty.'

In March 1930, at Trenton, there was a double treat for the audience: Wilson, Keppel and two Bettys. At several theatres they shared the stage with 21-year-old impressionist Mae Questel, billed as a new entertainer. Among her singing impressions were movie star Helen Kane, known as The Boop-Boop-a-Doop Girl. The following year, Mae would use those same extraordinary vocal tones for animated cartoon sex siren Betty Boop, whom she voiced throughout her career.

In September a huge one-third-page ad in *Variety* announced the trio's appearance at New York City's premier vaudeville house, the RKO Palace. (RKO stands for Radio-Keith-Orpheum and was the result of several mergers between major vaudeville theatre chains over recent years. But the future lay in talking pictures and, over the next decade, RKO would emerge as a leading movie company responsible for *King Kong* and a whole string of glitzy romantic comedies starring Fred Astaire and Ginger Rogers.)

The *Variety* ad also informed us that the trio had recently completed one hundred weeks' work for RKO and had been signed up for a further sixty weeks through their current agents Arthur Blondell and Bill Mack. *The Billboard* said, of their performance at The Palace: 'The boys are spry and neat, while their girl partner is an able dancer and easy to look at.'

At the end of the year, there was another write-up in *Variety*. Betty Knox, again, got the lion's share of attention, and had obviously taken note of those previous tut-tuttings about her costume. The rest of the review is surprising, but only in its total lack of surprises:

> Wilson, Keppel and Betty are the opening trio. They offer some robust and vivid hoofing atop a toy bus, something new which was appreciated. Betty, as the solo feature in a torso twisting number, clad in men's garb, brought out a few new difficult steps and added more hand warmers to this trio's following. Closed with excellent stair dancing.

The bus act may have been new to this reviewer, but it wasn't to anyone who had seen them over the past two years – and neither were the stairs. In fact, they'd reverted to the old Bus Boys routine they'd been hawking round the vaudeville circuit years before Betty even came on the scene. It must have been a little soul-destroying. With the arrival of Betty came innovation and enthusiasm. They'd experimented with new material, but it didn't get the same level of laughter and applause as their tried-and-tested old routines. So they ditched the new and went back to the old. The audiences loved the Bus Boys – and the audiences loved Betty – so why change a winning formula? The work was certainly pouring in; but, in their hearts, the three dancers must have felt they'd lost their way.

Another contributory factor was the economic depression that followed the Wall Street Crash of October 1929. When business confidence is at rock bottom (and, when money is short, that includes show business confidence) it's not a good time to take risks with something that is far more than your act – it's also your meal ticket.

A review in *The Billboard* a few months earlier confirms the impression that Betty had been more or less crowbarred into the Bus Boys act:

> Betty is perched in a chair on the top deck, while one of the boys is in the driver's seat. The other fellow comes out to replace Betty on the bus. He sits in the chair and taps to the concertina accompaniment.

She sits there while the bus comes onstage, then almost immediately has to vacate her seat before the tap-dancing can begin. It all sounds a bit of a muddle and, most likely, was. They still didn't quite know what to do with Betty. She had a couple of solo spots in which she really shone, but little chance to interact with Jack and Joe. However, the act was steadily evolving. At the New Palace, Chicago, *The Billboard* (positively gushing with praise for Betty) spots a new ingredient:

> Betty has oodles of sex appeal and in addition lets loose a barrage of clever dance steps. The sand dance of the boys and their stair-dance finish, in which Betty also worked, put them over solidly.

The sand dance of the boys – the most significant addition they ever made (apart from Betty) and the key to the act's development over the coming months. It would eventually transform them into the most instantly recognised speciality act of all time.

In March 1931, having spent more than ten years in the States, and foreseeing many more years of steady work, Joe Keppel became a US citizen. He gave his address as Raleigh Hall, West 47th Street, New York. Neither Wilson nor Keppel had a permanent home for their entire working career. Raleigh Hall rather grandly described itself as a 'residential club for men who live well' and offered 'light, attractively furnished rooms, with tub or shower; writing, smoking, lounge, billiard rooms; comforts, conveniences of first class hotel'. It served as long-term lodgings for those periods when their vaudeville tours took them no further than the substantial New York theatre circuit.

The rave reviews continued ('They are clever steppers and she has a winning personality') but it was the sand dancing that was attracting more and more attention. *The Morning Oregonian*:

> Wilson, Keppel and Betty have a novel dance act which includes a new dance on sand, combining rhythmic sound with rhythmic motion most effectively.

Sand dancing was not unheard of in America. It was one of those seemingly effortless types of tap dancing, where the dancers would casually scatter a few handfuls of sand on the floorboards, then start shuffling their feet. It was particularly associated with both black and black-face performers. It probably hadn't been seen on stage that much, because of the practical matter of clearing the sand away at the end of the routine.

Fortunately, Wilson and Keppel were adept props makers, who had already constructed a miniature bus and a transportable flight of stairs, so a sand mat was a very simple matter. Something big enough to dance on, that would also contain most of the sand – only needing a quick brush round as they left the stage.

They told W. E. J. Martin of the *Buffalo Courier-Express* that they had been sand dancers at the very start of their career, but had abandoned it a dozen years ago and only recently put it back in the act. A claim that should perhaps be taken, not with a handful of sand, but with an excessively large pinch of salt. No early reviews, not even of Joe Keppel's solo act in Australia, mention sand dancing. However, they'd mixed with all types of dancers over the last decade and, after witnessing it from the wings, may have decided it was just the thing for their own act. As they told Mr Martin, they also quickly realised its comedy potential:

> And they also remember those comedians, who, following a dance turn which used sand, always stepped out with a handful of nails which the comics knew always would get laughs as the metal hit the stage.

The superlatives kept coming ('some of the best dancing seen here this season'). They'd regained the confidence to try something new – and it had worked. Suddenly things were back as they were when Betty first came along. Every new idea sparked off two or three more. The act was evolving. The act was taking shape. The act had stopped being a random assemblage of bits and pieces. It was rapidly turning into … an act. Okay, it was still a bit of a ragbag (and would remain so for several years to come) but it was a new ragbag, and it was a ragbag with a theme running through it. Joseph E. Greenidge's review in *The Daily Star* (Long Island, NY) of 12ᵗʰ November 1931 is well worth quoting in full:

> Wilson, Keppel and Betty pretty nearly covered the Western hemisphere – it seemed to me – in their act at the RKO Theater, Flushing, where they present the essence of the show for the second half of the week.
>
> At first it appeared to be one of those eye deceptions called illusions – but no – the sphinx was right there propounding the eternal riddle. It was merely that India had moved to Egypt, or rather had been moved by these 'Fifth Avenue comic dancers', who otherwise presented a neat, colorful and entertaining act.
>
> Betty appears in an Oriental number which was exquisitely executed. Betty has ability along this line and should not be so bashful in taking the vigorous applause that is due her.

For everyone who thought Wilson, Keppel and Betty were doing all that Egyptian stuff from the word go – this is how long we've had to wait for its first appearance. Egyptian, Indian, Oriental – it was a rich, highly spiced concoction they were serving up at the time. (The Indian ingredient may refer to Betty's dance, or possibly a surprise element provided by Joe Keppel which is detailed later but may have been part of their Egyptian act from the outset.)

The important fact is that at some point during the highly creative last couple of months, one of the trio had suddenly made a connection (a fairly obvious connection, once it's been made) between sand and the desert.

From that 'eureka moment' everything had quickly and neatly fallen into place. We know Wilson and Keppel were wearing comedy makeup. Perhaps the identical droopy moustaches and deadpan expressions were already in evidence. All they needed were Egyptian headdresses and some kind of shift or robe and they were primed for action.

Nearly ten years earlier, in 1922, Howard Carter excavated the tomb of Tutankhamen. This sparked great interest in Egyptian art and culture throughout the world. Fashions were particularly influenced by these newly discovered ancient Egyptian artefacts.

(Plenty of Egyptian-inspired architecture predates the Tutankhamen discovery. Grauman's Egyptian Theatre in Hollywood, California, opened several weeks *before* news of the excavation reached the US – though many subsequent buildings owed their existence to the King Tut craze.)

So Jack, Joe and Betty would only need a quick trip to a museum, or a glance at a book or magazine, to get some idea how to dress the act. And that may well have been the extent of their research. Throw in a Sphinx on a backcloth and – *voilà!* – the audience is transported to an authentic representation of old Egypt.

But let's return to Joseph E. Greenidge's final sentence. 'Betty … should not be so bashful in taking the vigorous applause that is due her.' Betty was an experienced hoofer. Her solo tap numbers had been in the act for the past three years. Why was she still 'bashful' about taking applause?

There was one vital piece of information that Mr Greenidge wasn't privy to. Around 1927, Betty's parents left their home city of Salina, Kansas. Despite Lizzie Peden having lived there all her life, she and husband Charles decided to retire to Flushing, Long Island. It seems an odd choice to move closer to the hustle-bustle of New York. But there was another factor: their granddaughter Patsy (remember her?). With Betty's travelling lifestyle – and three or four shows a day – Patsy had basically been brought up by her grandparents. If they moved closer to New York, there was more opportunity for Betty to see her own daughter from time to time. While Wilson and Keppel's New York base was Raleigh Hall, Betty would have stayed with her family.

So that night – premiering their brand new act at the RKO Theatre, Flushing – Betty was almost certainly dancing in front of her parents, her (nearly) eight-year-old daughter Patsy and numerous friends and neighbours. She was the local celebrity – and the local audience surely gave her a rousing reception. Was it any wonder she looked a little embarrassed?

Next month, the Christmas 1931 edition of *Variety* carried a full-page ad by agents Blondell & Mack, who booked exclusively for the RKO circuit. All Blondell & Mack's clients were listed, including:

Wilson, Keppel and Betty presenting our new comedy act 'Arabian Antics.'

Now, as they entered 1932, they had a new act – and a new name for their new act. Admittedly Arabian and Egyptian aren't quite the same thing, and the later addition of a Moroccan fez confuses things even more – but for most American theatregoers (geographers excepted) it was all suitably far away and exotic.

There were two aspects to the sand dance that were probably in place by now. One was the classic 'Wilson and Keppel' pose – dancing in profile, shuffling along, one man close behind the other, one arm in front and one behind, palms upwards. This was their masterstroke, to take the stylised attitudes from the wall paintings in Egyptian tombs and animate them with such seriousness and conviction that, to this day, many people (The Bangles included) are convinced Egyptians actually walked like that.

The other aspect was the extreme shortness of their tunics and the vast expanse of bare leg. Had it been Betty wearing the costume, the crowd's reaction would have been quite different. But just the sight of those four decidedly unsexy skinny legs was enough to provoke waves of hilarity. The story they gave later is that they had been working in a stage camel suit, and it was so hot inside that they wore nothing but short singlets. As their fellow performers watched them clambering out of the camel, there was so much laughter, they decided those singlets would be the ideal outfit for the sand dance. A great story – and a superb way to make an entrance. But maybe it was too cumbersome, too difficult to get in and out of, or just too hot and sticky – because no reviewer ever mentioned a camel.

The Wisconsin State Journal of February 1932 confirms the content of their act:

> Wilson, Keppel and Betty burlesque old Egypt quite satisfactorily in their dance act. Wilson and Keppel, with a matting strewed with sand, have a highly amusing dance. They also use some stairs, after the manner of Bill Robinson.

So they hadn't revamped the entire act. They were still hanging on to the old staircase routine they'd been doing since at least 1926. It's hard to see how it fitted in with the 'Arabian Antics' theme – though we can be pretty sure ancient Egyptians didn't live in bungalows. And this was not the first review to draw comparisons with Bill 'Bojangles' Robinson.

Bill Robinson's stair dance routine was an acknowledged classic. He later featured it in *The Little Colonel* (1935) with Shirley Temple. (This performance is claimed to be the first cinematic example of an African-American male dancing with a Caucasian female.) His stage version used a two-sided set of steps that went up and down – whereas Wilson and Keppel's went in just one direction. There were a few common elements – such as slapping the steps with the palms, and standing stock still while the feet tapped out a complex rhythm – but there was no serious suggestion that Bill Robinson had a monopoly on this act, or that Wilson and Keppel had stolen his routine. Bill Robinson was also a sand dancer, but so were countless others.

In March 1932, to herald their appearance in the revue *Novel Notions*, the *Long Island Sunday Press* published that rarest of things – a photo of the trio. Or rather, two-thirds of the trio. It wasn't a current photo (not a fez or knobbly knee in sight) but it's an exquisite glimpse into the earliest days of Wilson, Keppel and Betty.

For a start, Jack Wilson (blowing a simple musical pipe) is in top hat and tails. The men kept up their smart, stylish appearance throughout most of their US career – despite the gradual introduction of comedy routines and comic makeup. So their subsequent Egyptian makeover created quite a culture shock. A wind of change that blew away the elegant attire while creating a cold draught around Jack and Joe's lower portions.

The other person in the picture is Betty. Her right leg is totally straight and points upwards, almost vertically. Her right arm reaches up, her hand gripping her right ankle. This is very like the *port d'armes* pose of can-can dancers. It is one more reminder that Betty was a dedicated and accomplished dancer and – at this point in her career – exceedingly bendy.

The following month, Jack Wilson demonstrated an amazing lack of foresight by following Joe Keppel's example and applying for naturalisation as an American citizen. Like Joe, he gave his address as Raleigh Hall.

Jack obviously had no idea what was round the next corner. In fact it was London agent Harry Foster, over in the States on a talent-spotting trip. Wilson, Keppel and Betty were making one of their frequent appearances at The Palace, New York City. Having seen them in action, Harry Foster quickly snapped them up for three or four weeks' work, touring English variety theatres. The trio readily accepted. For the men it would be a brief return home. For Betty, it was her very first trip abroad.

There was nothing to lose and every possibility of gain. It was 1932 and American vaudeville was in terminal decline. Since the 1920s, vaudeville artists had made a good living by playing the picture houses between movie showings. Movies had been silent (though with musical accompaniment) and the vaudeville acts provided something different. By 1932, movies talked. Theatres were wired for sound. Vaudeville houses became movie houses. And, with advances in sound recording, the all-singing, all-dancing big screen extravaganza was the coming attraction. The vaudeville performer was literally dwarfed in comparison.

Those who have tried to pinpoint the exact moment that vaudeville died usually opt for 16th November 1932. It was on this day that New York City's Palace Theatre – one of the few remaining jewels in the vaudeville circuit crown, and the very location where Harry Foster had engaged the trio – became a full-time movie house. Jack and Joe were all too aware that the touring life they'd enjoyed over the past decade was unlikely to continue throughout the next. They weren't exactly rats leaving a sinking ship; they were just taking a mini cruise on the Good Ship Great Britain, where variety was buoyant and sand dancers had a better chance of keeping their feet dry.

In June and July, Wilson, Keppel and Betty fulfilled their remaining commitments in America, playing weeks in Chicago and Detroit and one final trip across the border to Montreal, Quebec. The *Motion Picture Herald*, which carried a regular column of vaudeville reviews for the benefit of the dwindling number of picture-house managers who were still booking acts, gave an untypically harsh write-up of the trio's Detroit appearance:

> Although this is billed as comedy, the laugh sauce is mild, to say the least.

Right now, they couldn't have cared less. In August 1932, Betty Knox boarded the *Ile de France* at New York and set sail for Plymouth. Daughter Patsy was well accustomed to waving goodbye to her mother. Betty had spent the past four years on the road and, this time, they would only be separated for a matter of weeks. Four weeks. Maybe five.

Patsy would not see her mother again for more than five years.

8
The Sultan of Zanzibar

'… before she took granny's place in the act …' (Patsy Knox, 1938)

WILSON AND KEPPEL TOLD COUNTLESS FIBS about their early career. Despite what they've often said, there is no evidence that they worked together (or even knew each other) before that 1920 meeting in an Australian circus. But there's no such thing as bad publicity. So, at a time when they'd no past career to speak of, perhaps it's understandable they'd spin a few extravagant tales of past triumphs that had never happened. The newspapers would lap it up, and there was little chance of them ever being rumbled.

Several months before they and Betty got together, Jack and Joe told the press they'd first worked as a pair in Liverpool, aged 10, as members of J. W. Jackson's Eight Lancashire Lads. This famous clog-dancing troupe was where Charlie Chaplin started out, so it was a claim to fame well worth repeating. After moving to Britain they never mentioned it again.

They also claimed to have toured India and survived several mutinies (which occurred around half a century earlier) and performed in South Africa in front of the Sultan of Zanzibar and his three hundred wives, receiving five hundred bunches of bananas in payment, before finally arriving in the United States.

But once they teamed up with Betty they completely changed their story, saying they started their career in America, meeting 'in San Francisco in 1902 as youngsters in a minstrel show'. Another interview states they made separate stage debuts in the US – Jack Wilson at Bristol,

Connecticut in 1909 (although, according to the 1911 Census, he was still living with his mother in Liverpool and working as a tanner) and Joe Keppel with Van Arnheim's Minstrels at Albany, New York in 1910 (three years before John R. Van *Arnam*'s minstrel troupe was actually formed).

But then, in 1933, there's another bizarre claim. A whole new story, which they stick to for more than a decade, and which many people today believe is true:

> After five years in America, they formed a partnership with a Miss Betty Knox, the mother of the present Betty, and soon after the newly formed trio went to Australia on a long contract. They then toured South Africa with their own show. A trip to the Far East, with engagements in India, China, Java, Japan and the Philippines, followed ... At the finish of the war, Wilson and Keppel rejoined their lady partner, and the act resumed its place in American vaudeville. Some seven years ago, the former Betty retired and the present Betty took her place.

A fourteen-year-old Patsy confirmed this version of events in a 1938 interview:

> ... you know mother was in repertory for a while before she took granny's place in the act 11 years ago ...

So that's the story. Betty Knox was not the first girl in the act. Fifteen or so years earlier, Wilson and Keppel had teamed up with Betty Knox senior and toured America and the world – then, after the First World War, resumed their American tour for another half-dozen years before exchanging her with her daughter-in-law.

Highly unlikely. Every American newspaper listing and review between 1921 and 1928 calls the act Wilson and Keppel, and makes no mention of a female partner. Betty's mother-in-law was actually called Nellie. She had six further children after Donald Knox and died (rather than retired) three years before Betty joined the act. Juggling a large family with a vaudeville career and world tour would have been challenging, to say the least.

Or maybe it wasn't Betty's mother-in-law, but Betty's mother who was Jack and Joe's original partner. Elizabeth Peden (known as 'Lizzie') was eighteen years older than Wilson and Keppel. If she retired in 1928 (to be replaced by Betty) the men would have been 34 and she'd have been 52. And why would young Alice Peden have needed to run away from home to become a dancer, when this was precisely the same profession her mother was following at the time? An intriguing tale, but the facts don't fit.

All the best constructed farces begin with a single lie, progressively elaborated upon, ending up with a preposterous and barely credible chain of events. Wilson and Keppel's CV is much the same. At a time when they had very few past triumphs, they started to invent them. They were a double act stretching right back through the mists of time, travelling round the world and finally ending up in America. But, when Betty came along, they decided to reinvent the whole story and pretend they'd gone to America much earlier, met up with Betty, and then toured the world as a trio.

But this version of events didn't quite work. They were two middle-aged men with an attractive young girl. If Wilson, Keppel and Betty had been touring together since before the war, she'd need to be of a similar age to them. Hence the need to invent Betty Senior.

Although Betty's daughter Patsy seems to join in with the deception initially, it's interesting that this story is completely dropped in later years. It's never referred to in any of Betty Knox's own interviews. Even Jack and Joe in 1959 refer to Betty Knox as 'the first Betty'.

Let's be quite clear. Wilson and Keppel the double-act began in Australia in 1920, and Betty came along and made it a trio in the USA in 1928. And, throughout their long career, Jack and Joe were cheeky little fibbers.

And now to Plymouth, where the *Ile de France* has just appeared over the horizon.

9

The Gandhi Bit

(Britain 1932–1934)

'... the kind of limbs that make you understand why sleeves and trousers were invented.' (*New Zealand Evening Post*, 1933)

BETTY KNOX SAILED INTO PLYMOUTH HARBOUR on 5th August 1932. According to the incoming passenger list her occupation was Theatrical Performer and her destination was the London Palladium Theatre. All those years of auditioning, learning routines, jettisoning routines, trying, failing and trying harder, had paid off. Here in Britain, Betty was starting at the very top of her profession. They were fifth item on a bill of thirteen, and the theatre programme summarised their act in just three words: Comedy in Dance. Three days later *The Performer* reviewed their British debut:

> Making their initial appearance in England here, Wilson, Keppel and Betty presented a slick and novel dance routine – distinctly away from the stereotyped. The skilful stepping of the two male members included fine staircase work and a humorous sand-dance, while Betty – an attractive artiste – was responsible for solo dancing of merit. The act was vociferously applauded.

The Stage reviewer, who was in the audience on their first night, remarked on 'an unrehearsed spill out of a rickshaw'. The rickshaw (of which more later) had superseded their Fifth Avenue bus, being slightly more in keeping with the pyramids and fezzes. So it seems that Joe Keppel marked the occasion of his first British performance by falling on his arse.

Betty must have heaved a sigh of relief on reading that *Performer* review. In a show packed with acrobats, jugglers and big names, such as singers Layton and Johnstone and bandleader Roy Fox (with vocalist Al Bowlly), Wilson, Keppel and Betty had made an impression. In fact, if you were sad enough to count the words (and, after reading it for the twentieth time, why wouldn't you?) they had more coverage in that review than any other act. Though, coming a close second, was another turn making its British debut: Dixon and his 'Pal' ('the seal with the human brain').

But Harry Foster hadn't brought them all this way for a Palladium residency. A second week only, then it was up north to the Manchester Hippodrome. Newspaper reviews of British variety acts are seldom hugely detailed affairs but, on this occasion, the *Manchester Guardian* critic details a whole section of the act which hadn't previously been mentioned – and never would be again:

> … Wilson and Keppel, who are one theme with variations, sit on a box of snakes playing mournfully, and with long rests, upon the tin whistle, while Betty does some remarkable tap dancing. As soon as she has gone the snakes spring out of the box and try to bite Wilson and Keppel. Their faces, their attitudes upon the whistle, their rapt attention to Betty: these are all good to see. Their sand dance before the Sphinx is another excellent affair: and so also their dance upon Wilson's bier. He was shot in the snake affair.

Here was another demonstration of their ingenuity with props, and an indication that they no longer felt the need to pack the act with high-energy hoofing. The laughs were becoming as important as the dancing. And the laughs were coming from Wilson and Keppel's deadpan faces and their subtly lustful glances at Betty. It is also evident that Betty was far more than a diverting interlude between the sand and the stairs. She was an integral part of the comedy, featuring in the final dance (even if it was over Wilson's dead body).

Two months later they crossed the channel for their European debut – first the Scala Theatre, Berlin, then on to L'Empire Music-Hall in Paris. The critic of *La Rampe* concluded that some people would find their antics amusing – whilst others would take fright. In December, at the Glasgow Empire, they were reunited with someone from Jack and Joe's Australian circus days – tightrope virtuoso Con Colleano. A few weeks later, *Variety* reported that the Colleano family and Wilson, Keppel and Betty had been 'making whoopee' at London's West End nightspot The Kit Cat Club.

Their month's trip to Britain had already lengthened to three or four. Betty may have been a little homesick, but there were so many new places to visit that the weeks were whizzing past. It was Christmas when she boarded ship once more. Not for home, but across the Irish Sea, for a Boxing Day engagement at the Theatre Royal, Dublin.

It soon became obvious that Betty wouldn't be returning to America in a hurry. Work was plentiful and the diary was filling up for months ahead. Wilson and Keppel had the advantage. They were home already. Joe Keppel would travel to his home in Ireland from time to time – and Jack Wilson, who never really had a home, was still surrounded by his countrymen. But Betty had always been friendly, outgoing and keen to learn. She wanted to know everything about the British – all those little things that made Britain and America so different. The food, the drink, the vocabulary, the regional dialects. And everyone she met was eager to explain it all to the pretty girl with the broad Kansas accent.

Most importantly, in British variety theatres they were the main event – not the sandwich filling between movie showings. Wilson, Keppel and Betty were getting good billing at the best variety houses. Each night, as they left the theatre, excited crowds would be waiting at the stage door with their autograph books. Joe Keppel, who had the neatest, most ornate handwriting Betty had ever seen (far better than her and Jack's scrawled efforts), usually signed for all three of them. Pretty soon they had picture postcards ready to hand out, with their signatures (or Joe's collective signature) already printed on. All that was needed was a hastily scribbled dedication.

At the start of 1933 they played a few weeks at the Manchester Hippodrome, then the Liverpool Shakespeare theatre, then several weeks in London – The Pavilion, The Leicester Square Theatre, Victoria Palace – and finally back to The London Palladium, where their British tour had begun. They spent the 'crazy month of May' there. That was the name of the show. They were support act to the entire Crazy Gang – Flanagan & Allen, Eddie Grey, Nervo & Knox, Naughton & Gold and

Caryll & Mundy (Hilda Mundy being the sole female member of the Gang).

The Crazy Gang had a reputation for playing pranks and for popping up unexpectedly throughout the show – sometimes in a theatre box, heckling their fellow performers. Amongst the supporting acts were The Ganjou Brothers and Juanita with their 'Romance in Dresden Porcelain'. This classy acrobatic act featured the three Polish brothers in elegant 18th century ballroom attire, topped off with powdered wigs, on a set resembling an antique mantelpiece clock. Juanita would initially be seen swinging on the clock's pendulum, before joining the men for a series of gracefully posed balances, in which she was spun, swung and flung from brother to brother to brother. Their act was then totally burlesqued by the Crazy Gang, with one of them (probably the petite Jimmy Nervo) dragged up as Juanita and thrown implausibly high by the others – achieved with the aid of a crew of burly stage hands in the wings, hauling him up on invisible wires.

If Wilson, Keppel and Betty managed to escape the practical joking onstage, Jack and Joe might easily have found a whole line-up of gyrating Bettys suddenly bursting into their dressing room. But, even if the Crazy Gang was on its very best behaviour, it would still have been a hilarious month backstage.

Newspapers as far away as New Zealand commented on Wilson, Keppel and Betty's popularity in London. The *Evening Post* memorably described Wilson and Keppel as 'having the kind of limbs that make you understand why sleeves and trousers were invented'.

On 20th May (ten days after her 27th birthday) Betty attended a combined birthday party at London's Plaza Hotel, with four other American performers currently working in the capital. Nearly every American act in town was there, plus just one newspaperman working for US magazine *The Billboard,* who wrote: 'The party will certainly be remembered – by those who could remember.'

Two days later, on 22nd May 1933, in the middle of that crazy month, and on that same stage, came a reminder of how quickly Wilson, Keppel and Betty had achieved recognition. Nine months after their arrival in Britain, they were participating in their first Royal Variety Performance in front of King George V and Queen Mary. The Crazy Gang formed the backbone of the show, interspersing songs and sketches between other big-name acts, including singer Evelyn Laye and bandleaders Geraldo and Roy Fox.

Wilson, Keppel and Betty were item 14, in the middle of the second half. As reported in *The Performer*, the presentation they gave that night demonstrated Betty's knack of matching her outfits for the occasion, a knack possibly not shared by Joe Keppel:

> Wilson, Keppel and Betty began with the Gandhi bit, and then went into the sand dance number, which at once placed them in fine standing. They followed this with Betty's smart wooden-shoe tap dance (Betty attired in full-length trousers for this instead of the customary 'shorts', which added to her height), and the act concluded with the greatly liked staircase dance, in which the many and varied antics of Wilson and Keppel in dancing gained many big laughs.

The 'Gandhi bit' was the extraordinary sight of a tap-dancing Joe Keppel briefly transforming himself into Mahatma Gandhi, the charismatic and influential campaigner for Indian independence. Strange that this crass impersonation of a controversial political figure was considered entertainment fit for a King (whose job description also included Emperor of India) – though, throughout history, it has been common practice to portray a perceived threat to stability as a figure of fun. In the same year, the movie *42nd Street* featured Bebe Daniels singing 'You're Getting to Be a Habit with Me'. After being wooed by a succession of young male suitors, she is finally whisked off the stage by a singing Gandhi. If the Kissagram business had been big in 1933, top of the request list would surely have been the Gandhiagram.

Interviewed by the *Manchester Guardian* in 1959, Wilson and Keppel remembered another Palladium show in which they narrowly escaped causing offence:

> … two sheikhs, who were solemnly making for their seats … were transfixed by the performance. So was the audience watching the sheikhs' reaction until, when they were finally won over, everyone was laughing at everyone else.

According to Jack and Joe, even King Farouk of Egypt (a few years later) 'roared' at the sand dance. Hopefully in a good way.

Programme notes in the Royal Performance issue of *The Performer* are packed with all those highly dubious claims about Wilson and

Keppel's early career. Betty's artistic talent, as evidenced in her school magazine illustration, is also blown up out of all proportion:

> Besides her stage work, she is an accomplished dress designer and artist, for which she is well known in the States, having held contracts to design exclusive models for some of the best-known American establishments.

But one statement, being much closer to their present home, was undeniably true:

> At present, the act is appearing with great success at both the Palladium and the Trocadero Restaurant – at the latter place in Chas. B. Cochran's 'Revels in Rhythm'.

One of the advantages of working in London was the capital's thriving nightlife. Plenty of restaurants would stay open to the early hours of the morning and provide cabaret for their patrons who wished to party the night away. Many a big name performer could complete their evening performance and then move on to a restaurant and do the whole show again at around midnight.

So Wilson, Keppel and Betty were back doing three shows daily (four on matinee days), much as they did in American vaudeville, except they were now working far later into the night. But, with digs in London, it didn't matter if they slept through most of the morning. Dawn would frequently break before they'd even gone to bed.

The cameras of Pathé, the cinema newsreel people, captured a potted version of this midnight cabaret at the Trocadero, in which (according to *The Performer*) 'the splendid dancing of the attractive Betty vied for popular favour with the laughable sand dance and comedy evolutions of the two pseudo-Arabian gentlemen'. It's a rare chance to see Wilson, Keppel and Betty when 'Arabian Antics' was comparatively new, both to them and their audiences.

We start off with the sand dance, to the sound of Alexandre Luigini's *Ballet Egyptien*. As usual, Wilson and Keppel are dressed in short tunics and long headcloths – which is what they wear throughout this filmed performance. Other routines featured the fez, but it isn't in evidence here. Even in this early version, with cutaways to diners seated round tables, most of the familiar moves are there. Wilson and Keppel stare glumly upwards while rhythmically shuffling forwards, one behind the other, without lifting their feet, to audience laughter. (In later years, the humour would come from Keppel's very close proximity to Wilson's hindquarters.) Every now and then, the slithering footwork is broken up by some good old-fashioned tap-dancing.

The next extract is a brief flavour of the steps routine. The brightly painted set of six steps is sideways on to the audience. (The majority of Wilson and Keppel's work is sideways on, in true 'Egyptian wall-painting' style.) Wilson taps busily and noisily up and down the steps in a bravura display. Keppel copies him, but on tiptoe, not making a single sound. The accompanying music is a cakewalk dance straight out of an American minstrel show. Apart from their attire, the Egyptian theme is getting somewhat tenuous.

The 'Tiger Rag' heralds Betty's entrance, in a daringly brief outfit that sparkles and shimmers. Her skirt is little more than a row of tassels. Her top covers her where she needs to be covered, with a good amount of bare flesh above and below, and she just about succeeds (with one minor strap adjustment mid-dance) in keeping it on. The conclusion of their act is delightfully ragged. Betty does some high kicking, clapping and wiggling, while Wilson and Keppel jump from step to step. Betty then races up the steps with Wilson and Keppel in hot pursuit. Finally, they dance hand-in-hand down the steps and along the stage, with their arms flailing round in circles, in one of the messiest and most enthusiastic finales ever performed. As the music finishes, they fling their arms in the air (as they did throughout their career) as if to say: 'That's your lot. Now applaud.' As ancient as Wilson and Keppel often looked, this was a rare sight of three youthful hoofers (youthful in attitude, at least) having a ball together.

Back in America, *Variety* reviewed the Royal Variety performance. They singled out three acts as the outstanding hits of the second half – two American acts and one English. Wilson, Keppel and Betty was one of the American ones. They may have been a Liverpudlian, an Irishman and a Kansan – but, remember, Jack and Joe were both naturalised Americans.

The same edition of *Variety* carries a full column ad announcing that the trio were 'playing our 40th consecutive week in England and the Continent'. After thanking George and Harry Foster, their European representatives, there was a reminder that RKO representation was still by Blondell & Mack.

The Billboard also revealed that the trio had requested to be released from Blondell & Mack, but the Artists' Representatives' Association had refused their application. It seems Wilson, Keppel and Betty had theatrical impresarios across the world fighting to get a piece of them. Almost literally, judging from this piece a month later in *Variety*:

> Wilson, Keppel and Betty out of the Wallace Parnell new revue, due to Charles Cochran not releasing team from Trocadero cabaret.

Wallace Parnell was the brother of Val Parnell (who had a long association with the London Palladium and with many Royal Variety Performances, including that of 1933). Wallace was about to produce the touring revue *Once in a Blue Moon* – and it was the touring aspect that was the problem. They could only honour their late-night Trocadero commitment if they were playing the London theatres. The two stubborn negotiators eventually hammered out some kind of deal and *Once in a Blue Moon* was on again. Until:

> Joe Keppel (Wilson, Keppel and Betty) latest appendicitis victim.

The London gossip column of *Variety* for 29th August 1933 had a fair smattering of ill health. And Joe Keppel wasn't the only celebrity to be struck with this condition. Earlier in the month they'd reported that 'Bud Flanagan's appendicitis cut is bigger than his salary cut'. Joe Keppel's condition became more serious and developed into peritonitis. Jack Wilson knew there was no choice but to pull out of the show. Retired variety performer Billy Shenton Junior takes up the story:

> And Wallace said, 'Now, hold your horses. What if I can get you a man who can fill in, who can take over?' And Jack said, 'You can't get somebody who can take over an act like this, over the weekend.' And Wallace said, 'Well, yes I can – Billy Shenton.' Because Dad was one of the finest dancers in the country at the time.

Billy Shenton Junior got to know Wilson, Keppel and Betty very well during their British career. I first interviewed him in January 2012, when he described to me how Wallace Parnell brought Billy along and introduced him to Jack:

> So they got chatting together. 'Well, we're both okay for build and look and so forth. Here we are on a Saturday. We've got Saturday, Sunday –

we've got to open on Monday.' They had the stage to use all over the weekend, and they worked day and night all the way through. And my father went into the act on Monday. And Jack said, 'I never thought it would be possible.' However, they did. And they worked like brothers together – perfectly.

While Joe Keppel was recuperating, *Once in a Blue Moon* – with Billy Shenton deputising – toured Birmingham, Sheffield, Leeds, Hull, Glasgow and Newcastle. They travelled between theatres by train. (Only the most prosperous top-of-the-bill acts would have a car in those days.) As members of the Music Hall Artistes' Railway Association they were entitled to travel on Sundays at a discount. This was mutually beneficial, as fewer members of the general public used the trains on Sundays, but (being the variety performers' day off) this was when the pros took themselves and their props to whichever town they were playing the following week.

The box car would be packed with everything needed for the show – and, for Wilson, Keppel and Betty, that was plenty. It included their 'flat packed' staircase (with its maple steps particularly suited for vigorous tapping), their carrying platform for Betty (which also doubled as a receptacle for musical instruments and smaller props), their Sphinx backcloth, the sand mat, and a hundredweight or two of Bedfordshire deep-river sand. Having experimented with many varieties of sand, once they hit upon the perfect coarse-grained variety, they made sure they took it everywhere with them. After several years carting sackloads of the stuff around the country, they came up with the sensible idea of storing large quantities in centres which they frequently visited – such as Leeds, Glasgow, London and Cardiff – so they could dip into their supply once they'd arrived. (They were so scrupulous in tidying the sand away after each performance, they'd return pretty much every last grain by the end of the week.) On Monday mornings they'd turn up at the theatre to rehearse with the band and the technical crew.

Having weathered the potential storm of Joe Keppel's absence, *Once in a Blue Moon* continued on tour throughout the remainder of 1933. Their advert in the *Hull Daily Mail* described them as 'The World's Funniest Dancers'. The reviewer didn't quite go that far, but was still pretty impressed:

Dancing extraordinary is forthcoming from Wilson, Keppel and Betty, who step it out in weird stages of dress and undress – Betty's 'Nautch dance' is something of a sensation.

Nautch dancing derives from India, with its emphasis on skimpy clothing and alluring arm and body movements. Despite the absent Joe Keppel, Betty Knox was doing her utmost to ensure they still got rave reviews. But their problems weren't quite behind them. In early December, *Variety* had one more bombshell to drop:

Betty Knox (Wilson, Keppel and Betty) seriously ill, with English girl temporarily replacing. Joe Keppel has been out of the act for months, recovering from appendicitis operation.

Although *Variety* kept its stateside readers fully informed of every fresh episode in this backstage drama, there is no evidence that British theatregoers were ever put in the picture. As far as they were concerned, they were watching Wilson, Keppel and Betty, even though Wilson was the only true original still present. In fact, this so-called 'American' act was currently one hundred per cent English.

One actress who auditioned for them during Betty Knox's absence was Jean Kent. She had recently celebrated her 90th birthday when I visited her in 2011. Known subsequently for playing a succession of 'wicked ladies' on screen in Gainsborough melodramas, Jean had started her career in childhood as an acrobatic dancer. When work was hard to find, she borrowed the birth certificate of a cousin who was a couple of years older, and got herself a job at the Windmill Theatre (though, being a dancer, she was considerably more covered up than the strictly motionless nudes). It was at this early stage in her career that she tried out for the role of Betty:

I was a good little acrobat. I could do all the 'overs' and the back bends and the splits. They had me up on the stage and they looked me up and down, and one of them said, 'No, I think you'd be a little too heavy.' And then he looked at me closer and said, 'And you're very young – you'll grow.' Anyway, I didn't get the job. Somebody else got it.

It's probable that Betty had a number of short-term replacements, including the multi-talented Jean Bamberger. Born in Devon in 1913, Jean was a professional dancer from her early teens, incorporating ballet, acrobatics and buck dancing into her act. Buck dancing (an American-style clog dance) was also in Joe Keppel's repertoire during those early solo appearances in Australian vaudeville. At 16, she was one of theatre producer C. B. Cochran's 'Young Ladies', appearing in two Jessie Matthews shows: *Wake Up and Dream* and *Ever Green*. And, in 1933, she even danced on TV! This may seem faintly ridiculous, but the BBC had started making experimental television transmissions using the Baird process (only 30 lines, compared with the 405 lines of later years).

In December 1933, the *Nottingham Evening Post* review of *Once in a Blue Moon* said:

> Wilson, Keppel and Betty are just two more reasons why one's evening is a glad one. Wilson and Keppel are humorous with their feet, and Betty is a supremely graceful acrobat.

Of all the plaudits Betty Knox received over the years, she had never once been described as an 'acrobat'. Jean Bamberger, on the other hand, most definitely was. Her death certificate describes her occupation as: 'Acrobatic dancer (retired)'. It would seem highly likely that Jean was being encouraged to portray the role of Betty in her own style.

A few months into 1934 (in a report dated 'London, March 31') *Variety* finally had some good news, under the heading 'Back Together Again':

> First Joe Keppel was out of the act for six months, due to appendicitis, and then Betty contracted some internal trouble, necessitating a lay-off of 16 weeks. At one time, the act only had Jack Wilson playing, with the other two recruited locally. For the first time in six months, act is now the same outfit as originally came over.

The nature of Betty Knox's 'internal trouble' is never specified, but it was certainly serious enough to require a lengthy convalescence, possibly following an operation. And there would be more hospital trips to come. It may seem unfair that Billy Shenton's contribution to the act was never publicly acknowledged, but privately Wilson and Keppel did all they could to express their gratitude for Billy's involvement, which lasted a total of eight or nine months.

It took some time for Joe Keppel to be fit enough to work again, but when that day finally arrived they made Billy a proposition – he should stay on as their manager, and deputise for either of them should they fall ill. Billy politely declined the offer. He was a young dancer with a young son and he wanted his own career. As Billy Shenton Junior (the young son in question) recalls, that was not the end of the matter:

> So they said, 'Right, we're going to give you an act – give you a living.' So for the next month they then rehearsed and worked on this act with the Billy Shenton Trio: 'Cairo Capers'. It was a damn fine act, it just smacked of Wilson, Keppel and Betty. And Dad worked it right through till 1939, when war broke out, then after that for a while. Then we went Chinese and carried on from there.

Once they made that change from the Billy Shenton Trio to the Shen Tun Trio, with its oriental theme and costumes, at least it was an act that Billy Shenton could call his own. Maybe they were slightly misguided, but it was exceedingly generous of Jack and Joe to share their expertise and to devise an act that was every bit as ingenious as 'Arabian Antics', even down to the similarly alliterative name: 'Cairo Capers'.

'Cairo Capers' began with Billy Shenton and partner making their entrance riding a camel, using a technique that would be adopted many years later by Bernie Clifton and his out-of-control ostrich. In other words, the dancers' legs would be the legs of the camel, while four short dummy legs, looking as if they belonged to the riders, hung over the sides of the animal. Jack and Joe constructed the basketwork frame of the camel, while Betty embroidered the head, complete with 'winking' eye. It would have made a great opening to Wilson, Keppel and Betty's own act, but they were unselfish enough to give it to Billy Shenton.

By May 1934, *Once in a Blue Moon* had reached the end of its 36-week run. Wilson, plus the original Keppel, plus the original Betty were, as *The Stage* announced it, 'back in Vaudeville' – that is, back touring the variety circuit.

After leaving, Jean Bamberger resumed a busy and varied career. Along with Eta Nelson and Joy Beadell, Jean formed female dance group The Three Redheads, who toured variety theatres during the 1930s and 1940s, throughout the war and beyond, including many ENSA (Entertainments National Service Association) concerts for the troops in France.

With the original trio reunited, a hectic schedule of British and European appearances lay ahead. Not just on stage – in cinemas too. In vaudeville they'd danced between the movies. Now, at long last, Wilson, Keppel and Betty were the big screen attraction.

10

Expressions That Would Make a Mummy Laugh

(Movies 1934–1936)

'Corn in Egypt – It's Wilson, Keppel and Betty!' (Kenneth Western, 1936)

BETWEEN 1933 AND 1936, Wilson, Keppel and Betty made three visits to the studios of British Lion to preserve their act on celluloid. *On the Air, In Town Tonight* and *Soft Lights and Sweet Music* (all directed by Herbert Smith) were movies in which a minimal plot provided the framework for a whole host of variety acts. Jack, Joe and Betty were the only performers who appeared in all three movies, providing a surprisingly varied set of routines. Until recently, *On the Air* and *In Town Tonight* were thought to be lost. They still are. But, somewhat miraculously, Wilson, Keppel and Betty's complete segments from both movies have turned up in the most unlikely of places.

On the Air (1934)

On the Air was filmed in 1933, shortly before the indisposition of Joe and Betty. The plot concerns a group of holidaying variety stars coming to the aid of the village vicar by staging a concert. And, with that premise established, all the director had to do was point his cameras at a succession of acts trotting out their traditional turns on a mock-up theatre stage. Although the movie has since vanished, various sequences (including band leader Roy Fox, rotund xylophonist Teddy Brown, and Wilson, Keppel and Betty) were borrowed to beef up the 1934 Danish movie *København, Kalundborg og -?* ('Copenhagen, Kalundborg and -?'). It's another flimsy plot constructed around a parade of variety acts. A fictional Danish radio station, bogged down in bureaucracy, provides its listeners with an unvaried diet of cultural, educational and exceedingly boring programming. Eventually it changes its ways and broadcasts a hugely successful variety show.

Wilson, Keppel and Betty's four routines commence with Betty's nautch dance to Ketèlbey's 'In a Persian Market'. Her Egyptian-themed costume consists of headdress, bikini top and (in this routine) a full floor-length semi-transparent skirt. She clicks the finger-cymbals, swaying her arms from side to side – and sometimes high above her head. She sways her hips, she spins round. As the music doubles in tempo, she spins faster and faster, her skirt billowing out. It has been ingeniously weighted, creating a delightful pattern of waves.

Next is Joe Keppel, in Egyptian headdress and a long robe. He is seated on a long-handled two-wheeled rickshaw, doing a sitting-down clog dance on a small platform at the front. This is their American vaudeville Bus Boys routine given an Egyptian twist. He lifts his robes slightly, showing his fast moving thin legs in black tights and his light-coloured clogs. He continues to lift his robes higher and higher until they obscure his head. On the inside of the robes is a caricature of Gandhi – so the impression is that Gandhi himself is doing the dancing. (The 'Gandhi bit' from the previous year's Royal Variety performance.) Jack Wilson, in fez and shift, accompanies all this rhythmic footwork on the accordion.

Now Jack Wilson takes over the dancing while Joe, still seated on the rickshaw, plays the harmonica. Again the emphasis is on rhythmic clog dancing. He kicks one leg out in front of him – he turns his back on the audience and, grasping the handles of the cart, repeatedly leaps in the air, clicking his clogs together. Finally, as Joe plays the traditional Scottish air 'Miss McLeod's Reel' (despite their costumes, the music in this section is firmly rooted in British and American folk tradition), Jack pushes the rickshaw offstage, to the sound of his own galloping footwork.

(When Billy Shenton Junior saw this recently discovered footage, he immediately recognised the rickshaw as the same one the Shen Tun Trio subsequently wheeled all round Australia in their Chinese Parody. When Jack and Joe dropped the rickshaw routine from their act, shortly after Joe's convalescence, they had passed it on to Billy.)

We return to Betty Knox, hands on hips, her right foot tapping repeatedly. The camera pans up from foot to head, and we see she is clad in white short-sleeved (and even shorter-skirted) tropical explorer's outfit, topped off by a pith helmet. Betty's own clog dancing, frequently on tiptoe, is accompanied by Jack and Joe on penny whistles. While continuing to tap, she begins to spin in circles with arms outstretched. She is slim and petite, her arms particularly slender, and she somehow manages to rotate rapidly without the customary dancer's trick of 'spotting' (focusing the eyes on a fixed point during the majority of each rotation). She, and the pipers, conclude with a 'how's your father' rhythmic flourish, and she raises her pith helmet to take her applause.

Their segment of the movie concludes with the much-filmed sand dance, with Alexandre Luigini's *Ballet Egyptien* heavily featured in the musical accompaniment. Actor and comedian Richard Murdoch (who specialised in tongue-twisting songs to classical melodies, right from his early days partnering Arthur Askey in radio's *Band Waggon*) would later perform a version that went like this:

> My Aunt's name is Ella Wheeler Water-Butt and she lives down at Burton-on-Trent.
> When she goes out shopping on her bicycle she always gets her handlebars bent.
> Steak and kidney, seven-and-a-tanner's-worth,
> A little bit of chicken and a marlinspike.
> Hutch and Ted Ray at the Metropolitan are doing even better than at Heckmondwike.
> Sabotage at Poole in Dorset. Camouflage my uncle's corset.
> Sunday, Monday, Tuesday, Wednesday … and the rest of the week.
> Plastic pyjamas – are never quite what they ought to be.
> Gentlemen farmers – are never quite what they're taught to be.
> Seventeen fiddles in a second-hand suitcase.
> Semolina pudding in a very old flute-case.
> Cabinet Ministers shout: 'What a very silly song.' I'm out!

Other melodies often woven into the music include 'Vision of Salome' by J. Bodewalt Lampe (apparently written to accompany Isadora Duncan's own fluidly expressive 'dance of the seven veils') and Schubert's 'Moment Musicale'. An oft repeated claim is that the music for the sand dance was arranged for them by Hoagy Carmichael, and that they used the same band parts for three decades. Although the second statement is highly probable, the first (like many of their stories) is impossible to authenticate.

But, however the sand dance sounded, most people agree how it smelt. This is a bigger compliment than it may seem. Betty Driver, who had a long career in variety as a singer before she became *Coronation Street*'s hotpot queen, worked on the same bill as Wilson, Keppel and Betty several times. In *Betty: the Autobiography* she recalled the aroma of sandalwood that wafted from the stage during the sand dance. There was good reason for this. They applied a layer of sand to the sand mat (and another layer to the bottom of their shoes) with Le Page's glue, which had a particularly pungent odour. To mask this, Joe Keppel forked out a considerable sum of money on gallons of sandalwood perfume from a Scottish company, which he liberally mixed with the sand that he sprinkled at the start of the dance, making their show a treat for almost all the senses – apart, of course, from any sense of historical authenticity.

The sand dance begins to the strains of 'Vision of Salome'. Jack and Joe wear flowing Egyptian headdresses (never the fezzes for the sand dance!), pale sleeveless tunics with very short skirts (split down the side, with dark shorts underneath) and, between those and their black-and-white clogs, they display an incredible expanse of bare leg. Wilson follows Keppel across the sand. Both have one arm in front and one behind in 'Egyptian' pose, and are shuffling in profile. After a quick tap step, they turn and now Keppel follows Wilson. They are spooning, with Keppel close behind Wilson, both staring solemnly to the heavens. They face the audience, lift one side of that already brief skirt and lazily slide one leg from side to side. They repeat the process with the other leg.

Other classic moves follow, some of which would be remembered and copied by Morecambe and Wise (and not just in their Cleopatra send-up with Glenda Jackson). Keppel faces the audience (elbows out and one hand placed on the back of the other in a vaguely Native

American Indian pose) and shuffles from right to left, repeatedly bending his right leg and lifting his knee high, while Wilson grasps hold of that knee. There is rhythmic shuffling, there are long foot slides. Then Keppel stares wide-eyed at Wilson, waving his arms hypnotically, as Wilson shuffles towards him in a trance-like state. The last section is pure vaudeville, with a few shuffles but plenty of old-fashioned hoofing, until Keppel gives the cue for them to fling their arms high in the air – their traditional way of inviting applause.

We can be pretty sure they performed the same collection of routines for George V and Queen Mary the previous year (though, as the reviewer remarked, Betty wore 'full-length trousers' for the tap dance). But the clog dancing content harks back to their earliest days in America – and Wilson and Keppel's bus-cum-rickshaw act originated many years before they met Betty.

In Town Tonight (1935)

Late in 1934, Wilson, Keppel and Betty slotted another day of filming between variety engagements, for the movie *In Town Tonight*, released in January 1935.

The plot, such as it was, involved comedy actor Jack Barty as a self-appointed talent spotter, seeking out new recording stars for gramophone company boss Finlay Currie. Once again, a succession of acts (including 'Albert and the Lion' recited by Stanley Holloway, and ventriloquist Arthur Prince and 'Jim') gave up a few hours to shoot their contribution, before leaving for their evening theatrical engagement. And, once again, the resultant movie seems to have vanished. But, by a strange quirk of fate, Wilson, Keppel and Betty's own contribution recently resurfaced. Of the various copies of later movie *Soft Lights and Sweet Music* held by the British Film Institute, one has their entire contribution to *In Town Tonight* spliced into the movie, midway through their *Soft Lights* routine. Why anyone thought it necessary to double the length of their segment in an otherwise fast-moving variety bill, I've no idea. But it contains some absolute gems.

Jack Barty discovers Wilson, Keppel and Betty in a music shop. We first see the caption 'An Egyptian Fantasy' above an image of the trio on a nifty bit of artwork resembling a sheet music cover. Then Wilson and

Keppel carry Betty, who is seated cross-legged on a low platform also containing two large drums, to centre stage. This is an exact match to their most famous costumed photo, which was taken on the set of this movie. Jack and Joe are 'befezzed' and in long shifts. Betty wears a headdress, bikini top and short tasselled skirt. She is noticeably more buxom than in other movie appearances – her cleavage possibly enhanced by some discreet padding. As she dismounts, Jack and Joe efficiently slide out the carrying poles of the platform, enabling it to be separated into two halves. Jack picks up a clarinet and Joe a tambourine. Betty is about to perform her solo nautch dance but, as this featured in the previous movie, a diagonal wipe moves us swiftly to a later section of the act.

The platform is now in two halves, either side of Betty, who plays a rhythmic beat, using two large padded sticks, on the drums each side of her. It is both a dance and a showcase of her percussive skills. She twirls the sticks and spins round without ever missing a beat. In contrast to Betty's resonant thudding, Jack and Joe play tiny tin dishes with small hard-headed sticks – alternately striking the dishes and tapping them on their bottoms. To the strains of Grieg's 'Hall of the Mountain King', the two men indulge in some haughty posturing, circle each other and do some hip thrusts, then turn their back to the audience and wiggle their bottoms. The routine becomes even more infantile, as Jack and Joe go into 'pat-a-cake' hand-clapping followed by 'ring-a-roses'. Betty strides forward and sits with her legs straight out in front of her. As she rapidly opens and closes her legs, Jack and Joe, pulling up their shifts to reveal black briefs, do a series of squat-jumps either side of her legs, slow at first, then doubling in speed. They finish with a flourish, arms aloft, and Betty waves the drum sticks in the air.

Next up is a real treasure – Jack and Joe's famous staircase routine. This belongs firmly to their pre-Betty clog-dancing days of American vaudeville, when they would have been attired in suits, rather than the sheik headdresses and vertically striped mini-togas they wear here (with a pattern closely matching the decoration on the set of six steps). Initially they dance together, up and down the steps, with Jack close behind Joe. Their arms are straight down by their sides, their bodies stock-still – except for their feet, tapping out complex rhythms in the 'pedestal dancing' tradition. The music weaves between an exotic Jewish tonality and an old-fashioned Dixie number.

Jack Wilson does a couple of solo spots, with breathtaking speed and dexterity, tapping noisily up and down, or facing front and weaving his legs in and out, so he is frequently dancing with his feet crossed. Joe Keppel, on the other hand, is the lazy clown of the outfit. He holds one hand out in front of him and, with the other, alternately claps and slaps his buttocks. (The whole act is weirdly bottom-fixated.) Later he grabs one leg and plants it heavily on three ascending steps, then grabs the other and repeats the process.

As the music doubles in tempo, it is Jack who provides most of the frantic finale, with Joe egging him on from below. Jack runs upstairs and high-kicks his way down, then hops one-legged all the way to the top. He descends speedily on one foot with the other leg bent, the toe tapping the top of each stair behind him. From Betty's high-kicking entrance, the end is the same as the version filmed at the Trocadero – every bit as ragged and chaotic but, as it's totally identical, obviously meticulously rehearsed.

The final routine is the only one they repeat from *On the Air* – the one everyone expects, nay demands, to see – the sand dance. The action starts a little earlier, so we can appreciate how incredibly speedily they set it up. When they first carried Betty on, they almost instantly detached the platform, containing the drums, into two sections. At the start of the sand dance, the sand mat is tightly rolled (later in their career they would replace it with a hinged wooden board). Jack Wilson flicks the mat, unrolling it across the length of the stage then, with a single tug, unfolds a raised back section that helps prevent the sand spreading everywhere, while Joe moves back and forth sprinkling the sand from an appropriately ceremonial two-handled brass urn. The whole procedure, from the unrolling to the first shuffling step, takes little more than ten seconds. Lesser performers would have covered the setting up of equipment by chatting to the audience, but this famously mute trio always designed their props with speed and efficiency as top priority.

After the movie's release in Australia, *The Australian Women's Weekly* rated Wilson, Keppel and Betty second only to Stanley Holloway, adding:

> As eccentric dancers they take a lot of beating, combining, as they do,

snappy dancing with postures and facial expressions that would make a mummy laugh.

Soft Lights and Sweet Music (1936)

Soft Lights and Sweet Music, the only other British movie made during Betty Knox's time in the act, was released in February 1936. Yet again it's a succession of variety big names given the freedom to perform their act, with the very minimum of plot to encumber them. The cast is headed by Ambrose and his orchestra with American-born vocalist Evelyn Dall ('England's Original Blonde Bombshell'), and comedians Harry Tate and Billy Bennett. The droll monocled musical duo The Western Brothers appear as somewhat mature graduates of Harry Tate's Cowbridge College. The Brothers have hatched up a scheme to 'see and hear everything for nothing ... the best show in town for the price of a twiddle' via their latest invention – a high-tech (by 1930s standards) television set. As the movie camera zooms in on the rudimentary glass-fronted wooden box, a succession of acts burst into full screen monochrome glory. We are treated to three more dances from our trio, announced by Kenneth Western as if he's uttering a mild expletive: 'Corn in Egypt – it's Wilson, Keppel and Betty!'

Their segment opens with Wilson and Keppel, cross-legged on the floor, in peakless caps and long striped robes, playing drums with their hands while singing wordless chants. Betty moves to centre stage. She wears a long polka-dotted dress with full sleeves, in the sheerest, most transparent material imaginable. Under the dress is a sparkly two-piece costume. After some suitably exotic high kicks and arm movements, accompanied by her rhythmic footwork, she begins to spin on the spot. From here on, apart from the costume, it is much the same as their earlier Danish movie. The spinning, tapping, and drumming seem to go on forever, crescendoing to a full stop. Betty ends stock-still, arms in air, panting heavily with just the hint of a 'phew' expression on her face.

We then cut to the stairs, with another take on Joe Keppel's Gandhi routine, accompanied by Jack Wilson on mouth organ. Once again we return to the touchy subject of 'blacking up' – and there's hardly a square inch of Joe's body that is still its natural colour. He wears the dhoti, his wooden clogs, and large round glasses with white frames to contrast with his dusky makeup. His skinny top half is completely bare –

as far as physique goes he's a pretty good match for the Mahatma. Cringe-making as it is to a modern audience, it's a slickly executed comic routine. Joe sometimes slaps the stairs with his palms, he descends by rhythmically slapping one leg then lifting it down, and concludes with some comedy jogging up and down the stairs, sideways on and facing the camera. If Gandhi had ever taken up clog dancing, who's to say he wouldn't have looked like this?

(One last thought on the whole Gandhi business. An old American slang term for workers who lay railway tracks is 'Gandy Dancer.' Is it possible that Jack and Joe heard the phrase, joked about what a dancing Gandhi would look like, and ended up putting this weird visual pun into their act?)

Their final routine is, surprisingly, not the sand dance. All three start by poking their heads through some wooden cut-out Egyptian mummies, while shuffling from side to side. Then Betty goes into some slightly jerky belly-dancing moves. Her skimpy sparkly two-piece gives more emphasis to her bare midriff and legs. Apart from her headdress there is nothing Egyptian about Betty's attire, though Wilson and Keppel now sport fezzes and long shifts. As Betty gyrates from hip to hip, the two men poke their heads forward for a closer look. Standing in line, the three of them do the classic Egyptian arm movements, but it's Betty that catches the eye. While the men play it straight-faced as ever, Betty does it like a bored American chorus girl going through the motions for the hundredth time. She may as well be chewing gum, the attitude she's giving it. Anyone who thought the men were the funny ones, and the girl was there purely for her looks, may think again after seeing this routine. A quick ring-a-roses, with Betty in the centre, before the men gesture for her to sling her hook.

By now the music has lost its Arabic flavour and sounds more like a Scottish reel. There is much fancy footwork with one man extremely close behind the other. Then a two-man version of the Scottish sword dancing (or rather leg dancing) they'd done with Betty in the previous movie – this time with Wilson opening and closing his legs and Keppel skilfully jumping to avoid landing on them. Finally Keppel drags Wilson off by the leg, with his other hand shielding his eyes, as if looking out to sea.

Wilson, Keppel and Betty, more than any other variety act, have a reputation for doing the same old thing, year in year out. Yet in these three movies there have been nine different routines. Certainly, in this period they were still developing new ideas, some of which gradually replaced those routines that predated their Egyptian look. The rickshaw (which derived from the Bus Boys) was on its way out by the time it was filmed, as was Betty's pith-helmeted explorer. The Egyptian mummy cut-outs belonged to their current stage act. Keppel's blacked-up Gandhi was probably devised especially for the movie – their quick-moving act wouldn't allow for such an elaborate costume change. But Betty's drumming was a comparatively recent addition.

It's difficult to make direct comparisons over the three movies, but Betty's style seems to have changed the most. There is still some brisk and demanding tapping, but there's a definite feeling that she's playing up the humour in her performance rather than the sexual allure.

It's worth remembering that by the last movie Betty was close to her 30th birthday, and that she'd been seriously ill a couple of years before. She would continue to provide the glamour in an otherwise distinctly unglamorous act for many more years to come. But, as Allan K. Foster had said back in 1926, the average life of a chorus girl was 'about three or four, and at the most five years'. Betty Knox had been on stage professionally for around ten years, and up to five years before that as an amateur. Each night she would share the stage with chorus girls a decade younger than herself. It would be understandable if she took the decision to play the role of the saucy seductress with her tongue planted firmly in her cheek.

11

Bad for the Nazi Youth's Morals

(Britain, Europe and America, 1935–1937)

'In an audience, anyone could shoot ...' (Betty Knox, 1943)

THERE IS A MUCH RELATED TALE concerning Wilson, Keppel and Betty's pre-war appearance in Germany. It's probable it took place in February 1935 (just weeks after the release of *In Town Tonight*) – the month Wilson, Keppel and Betty played the Berlin Wintergarten.

The Wintergarten was Germany's leading variety house – and Wilson, Keppel and Betty shared the stage with an assortment of clowns, jugglers and acrobats. Top of the bill was singer and comedian Else Elster, one-time girlfriend of the chief of Berlin Police. The trio's bill matter on that occasion (and that occasion only) was '*Im Schatten der Sphinx*' ('In the Shadow of the Sphinx'). Their wordless act effortlessly transcended the language barrier – but the Germans did have one problem with it.

This story was often related in later years by Wilson and Keppel – but the fact that it is told by Betty Knox herself as early as 1943, and in an interview she gave to respected journalist Hannen Swaffer, suggests it is largely correct. It would not enhance either of their reputations to make something like this up. So this is the story of Wilson, Keppel and Betty's performance at the Berlin Wintergarten, as described in the *World's Press News* of October 1943:

... Goebbels arrived with Goering to see the act, for everything had to be approved 'in case it offended the Reich'.

They took exception to the bare legs of the men.

'It would be bad for the Nazi youth's morals,' said Goebbels. 'You must put on trousers.'

The joke is that the two men have skinny legs and bony knees, which are part of the act's humour.

'I won't put on trousers for anyone,' said Wilson, with typical British obstinacy.

He knew that perversion was so common in Germany that anything that, in the slightest degree, showed nudity was regarded as a peril to Hitler's 'make-them-tough' ideas. But he couldn't see any harm in his bony knees.

It's a wonderful story, and this is the most accurate version of it that you are likely to read. This 'no knees please, we're Nazis' attitude seems pretty ludicrous. If anything got the SS hot under the collar, it is far more likely to be the sight of Keppel getting perilously close to simulating sexual intimacy with Wilson's rear end. Whatever the reason behind the complaint, Betty Knox almost certainly danced for an audience that included propaganda minister Joseph Goebbels and Luftwaffe commander Hermann Goering. All the more intriguing when one sees where her future career takes her.

In the same interview, an account of the trio's visit to Italy is given in Betty's own words. Hannen Swaffer sets the scene:

And so, in Rome, they found themselves helping Mussolini. There, it seemed, the act had been booked for an exposition – the Mostra di Minerale – really a war exhibition. It was right next to the Colosseum.

'When Mussolini came in, which he often did,' says Betty, 'the entire place was cleared. We did a show for the Duce, and then we went home. "To hell with the public."

'The general feeling was that it wasn't safe for Mussolini to be in a big crowd. He had no objection to appearing in public parades, but in those he could be easily guarded, of course. In an audience, anyone could shoot ...

'Outside, the crowd waiting to see him was always so big that we would have to fight to get in to play. As we didn't speak Italian, it was hard to explain who we were to the man at the door. The easiest way was to do a snake dance. Then, he understood.'

Speaking to the *Manchester Guardian* in 1959, Joe Keppel recalled their performance for Mussolini being so hastily arranged that they had none of their trusty Bedfordshire sand to hand. They had to make do with a curious mixture of salt, sugar, 'and I don't know what'.

In April 1935 they were back in London for *Coliseum Vaudeville*. The lavish London Coliseum (now home of the English National Opera) was originally built as a variety theatre. By the mid-30s it was offering a programme of plays and musicals, with just the odd week of variety. But the Coliseum's idea of letting its hair down was not quite the orgy of song, dance and laughter one might expect. Wilson, Keppel and Betty had played many a vaudeville engagement, but possibly never one which opened with a full symphony orchestra playing Wagner's *Tannhäuser* overture. Or with a Corps de Ballet dancing to the final movement of Beethoven's Seventh Symphony.

But, scattered amongst these cultural highlights were Bobby 'Uke' Henshaw (Broadway's merry mimic) and, just before the final choral-orchestral-balletic extravaganza:

Wilson, Keppel and Betty, famous burlesque dancers, in 'Cleopatra's Nightmare'.

Those last two words (and this is the earliest example I've discovered of this particular billing matter) perfectly summed up their unique combination of glamorous girl and grotesque geezers. Its origins are probably in the previous year's Cecil B. de Mille movie epic *Cleopatra*, starring Claudette Colbert, with its sumptuous Art Deco vision of ancient Egypt. Much like the influence Tutankhamen had on fashion in the 1920s, again women wanted to emulate Hollywood's take on the great queen. Cleopatra was everywhere and was the ideal finishing touch to their act. Two minions pay homage to their beauteous queen in a dance, the recollection of which would disturb the sleep of the serenest of sovereigns. Theatrical posters from late 1935 onwards would invariably proclaim: 'Wilson, Keppel and Betty in Cleopatra's Nightmare'.

In July 1935 a concert on a far smaller scale was taking place at the St Michael's Auditorium, Flushing, Long Island. The Lindsay and Mason School of Dancing was putting on its annual student recital – and among its young performers was 11-year-old Patsy Knox. Husband and wife Cedric Lindsay and Hazel Mason were a former vaudeville singing and dancing double-act and their school offered tuition in tap, acrobatic and ballet. If Patsy harboured any ambition to follow in the tap-steps of her famous mother, she couldn't be in better hands. Regrettably, and not for the first time, the audience of admiring parents lacked the presence of Betty Knox.

In November, Wilson, Keppel and Betty made a return visit to the Theatre Royal, Dublin (now a brand new 3,700-seater in a new location), where they topped the bill. 'Direct from New York City,' said the publicity. Indeed they'd taken a lightning trip there the previous month – most likely to finally sever their connections with US agents Blondell & Mack.

While in Dublin, they were interviewed by the *Irish Independent,* and Joe Keppel was the natural choice of spokesman for the trio. There was so much he could have said about their experiences touring America, Britain and Europe. Instead he dug out that old anecdote about the Sultan of Zanzibar paying them in bananas – and talked of a command performance in India before the Rajah of Rajputana. Both highly inventive tales that not only predated Betty Knox, they even predated Jack and Joe's meeting up in Australia in 1920.

All of which suggests that, given the choice between a true-life anecdote and some exotic sounding piffle, the piffle would win every time. It may be no coincidence that Joe Keppel was born just a few miles from the location of the Blarney Stone.

1936 was an exceptionally busy year, touring Britain (and briefly popping over to Paris) with no long-standing London residencies or revues. Tiring though it was, it was a great opportunity to socialise with an ever-changing line-up of performers, and for Betty to broaden her knowledge of Britain and the British. Towards the end of the year there was a show with a transatlantic flavour: *America Calling*. But Boxing Day brought a welcome chance to relax a little and call Blackpool home for a few months. Not a holiday, but the pantomime *Aladdin*, with experienced principal boy Betty Huntley-Wright in the title role.

It's probable that Betty Knox already had some knowledge of the peculiarly British phenomenon of panto. One might expect it to be a total contrast to the nightly routine of 'Cleopatra's Nightmare', but it was nothing of the sort. Speciality acts would normally be called upon solely to provide their speciality, whether it fitted in with the plot or not.

There is a well-known anecdote about a production of *Cinderella*. The Fairy Godmother grants the first two wishes of a beautiful dress and a coach. 'And for my third wish, I'd like to hear Issy Bonn sing "My Yiddisher Momma".' Issy Bonn walks on, does a handful of songs, walks off, and the plot resumes.

It didn't matter that *Aladdin* was set in a totally different part of the world from 'Cleopatra's Nightmare'. Wilson, Keppel and Betty were the perfect frontcloth act – they were practically two-dimensional, like shadow puppets, with their sideways-on emulations of wall-painted figures. The frontcloth came down and, while the next lavish change of scene was set, they would go through their routine on the front part of the stage. Then the sand-mat or steps would be cleared away, the curtain was whisked skyward, and we were back once more on the bustling streets of Peking.

On New Year's Day 1937, the trio had its first experience of broadcasting, when an excerpt from *Aladdin* was transmitted live by the BBC. Admittedly it was only Northern Region radio, though keen wireless listeners might have spotted the odd swoosh through the sand from Jack and Joe, or tippety-tap from a rapidly rotating Betty.

In June, when they topped the bill at Derby's Grand Theatre, the *Derby Evening Telegraph* treated its readers to an explanation of the act's evocative title – 'Cleopatra's Nightmare':

> Two brothers dreamt simultaneously that Cleopatra performed fantastic dances. When they awoke and tried to explain to each other the weird movements they had seen they were struck with their humorous possibilities ...

This description fairly closely matches what became the regular opening to their act. Betty tempts the two men by clicking finger cymbals. They stand impassive until she wanders off, then mimic her movements in their own dance. A review in the same Derby paper gives us another highly revealing glimpse of the act's current content:

> Wilson, Keppel and Betty have made a most successful burlesque out of the dance, and, in addition, Betty gives an attractive interpretation of the dance of the seven veils, which has a surprise ending.

So it seems that Betty Knox (at the age of 31) had decided to spice things up a little. The act needed a new gimmick and she was going to be the one to provide it – striptease! Is there any red-blooded male whose heart wouldn't beat a little faster at the Eastern promise of total exposure? And would Keppel (whose own dodgy ticker had cut short his naval career) be able to survive the whipping off of Veil No. 7?

Inspiration had struck once again. It fitted the act like a glove. If later filmed versions are anything to go by, it was a chance to brush down those snakes, which made a brief appearance in 1932 and hadn't been heard of since. This was what Betty did best – artistry combined with comedy. The number one priority for this new piece of business was the laughs. But the laughs weren't going to come without a cleverly executed dance routine, and a bit of gentle teasing en route.

Evidently the trio still enjoyed inventing brand new routines. It's an important reminder that most (if not all) of their set pieces were devised while Betty Knox was still in the act – even if her version of the veils wasn't captured on film. In October 1937, a detailed review in the *Devon and Exeter Gazette* of their show at Exeter's Theatre Royal gives a clear acknowledgement of the skill behind all the clowning:

> Betty, an active young lady, with a pleasing personality, combines grace with comedy in several artistic numbers, and concludes with a new version of the veil dance. Her two colleagues present all manner of weird contributions – of the comedy type it is true, but characterised by certainty and precision.

The previous week *The Stage* had reported:

> At the Shepherd's Bush Empire this week Wilson, Keppel and Betty are making one of their final appearances in England prior to a short visit to America early in November, where they have arranged to play a few dates. They will, however, be returning to this country early in the New Year.

They boarded the SS *Queen Mary* from Southampton to New York, and were soon back on stage in vaudeville, where their Egyptian-themed act had originated. By now, the majority of movie houses had ceased to provide live entertainment – except the larger theatres, which offered a vaudeville bill of fewer acts but starrier names. They first played The Oriental, Chicago, Illinois, where both audience and *The Billboard* critic welcomed them like returning heroes:

Wilson, Keppel and Betty stopped the show with a novel dance routine and proved once more that an audience will buy an act that has something refreshing to offer. Doing their first stint here in several years, their Egyptian movements and odd bits of comedy were as funny as ever. Atmosphere of turn afforded the house line to do an interpretive number to 'Caravan'.

(In other words, the house band and chorus line entered into the spirit with this current desert-themed hit, first recorded by Duke Ellington.)

It was just like old times for the trio, sand dancing between screenings of the big movie. In Chicago, appropriately enough, it was Edward G. Robinson in *The Last Gangster*. In Detroit, at the Michigan Theatre, they were alongside James Stewart and Robert Young in *Navy Blue and Gold*. According to *Motion Picture Daily* the gross takings for the week were a magnificent $25,000, a full $5,000 higher than average. At the Metropolitan, Boston, Massachusetts, *The Tech* rated them the best of the vaudeville support acts 'with their sundry bits of dance, slapstick, and plain tomfoolery'.

But Wilson, Keppel and Betty hadn't gone all the way to America just to 'play a few dates'. That wasn't the main reason for their visit. They were going to collect something of Betty's. Something far more precious to her than people may have imagined. She was going to fetch her daughter Patsy and bring her back to England – in Betty's own words: 'so that she could see the war'.

12
Not Keen on Dancing

(Britain 1938–1941)

'Be mad about music and not at each other.' (Betty Knox, 1939)

BETTY RETURNED TO ENGLAND, along with daughter Patsy, on 20th December 1937 – two days before Patsy's 14th birthday. Though each had chosen to adopt their middle name, formality dictated they appear on the *Queen Mary* passenger list as 'Alice' and 'Jean'. But what did fellow entertainers make of this young American teenager frequently seen tagging along with the trio? Well, privately, many believed that Patsy's father was none other than Jack Wilson.

An article from the *Daily Mail* of 5th January 1938, which I've already quoted from, is a rare example of both mother and daughter being interviewed. The headline is *SHE GAVE HER MOTHER STAGE FRIGHT*:

All through her schooldays in New York Patsy Knox, dark haired, 14-years-old daughter of Betty Knox (of Wilson, Keppel and Betty, the burlesque dancers), has longed to see her mother on the stage far across the water. And last night at the Prince's Theatre, Manchester, her dream came true.

Mother and daughter travelled to England together, but Patsy spent Christmas with friends and last night was her first opportunity of seeing Wilson, Keppel and Betty on the stage.

Said Patsy: 'Mother was grand, but I'm not keen on dancing. I want to be a straight actress; you know mother was in repertory for a while before she took granny's place in the act 11 years ago.

'I'm over here for good now.'

Said Patsy's mother: 'Yes, I'm sending her to a school of dramatic art over here and turning her into a real actress. There's more scope today in drama than there is in dancing, and I'd hate her to follow me just to oblige.

'It's grand to have her with me again after all this time. I hadn't seen her for six years when I went back to America with the act for a three-week season just before Christmas.

'I've never been so nervous in my life as I was when I saw Patsy looking hard at me, waiting for me to be funny.'

Other than that puzzling claim about granny being the original 'Betty' (the current myth the trio was telling about its origins) everything else rings true. But it was the beginning of 1938, and a war with Germany was looking increasingly likely. In Hannen Swaffer's 1943 interview, he talks of Betty's attitude to this:

> She had long been a fervent Anglo-American. She acquired a quickly-developed love for our people while touring the provinces.
>
> It grew so that, just before the war began, she went back home to bring back her daughter – 'so that she could see the war'.
>
> And it was because she had worked and lived with the Germans that, years ago, she knew that war was inevitable.
>
> 'They talked freely to me,' she says. 'You know what vaudeville performers are …'

But, however strong the bond between Patsy and her absentee mother, was it really the act of a loving parent to pluck a young girl from the relative safety of a New York suburb and deposit her in what would become the prime target for Hitler's Luftwaffe?

It's possible that Patsy initially refused to go – causing Betty to contemplate splitting from the act and remaining in America with her daughter. This version of events would seem to be confirmed by another Betty – Betty Bryant – who says she auditioned for the role of a replacement Betty in her teens.

Betty Bryant was a Pennsylvania-born clog dancer, who performed from the age of 6 on the family showboat, which sailed the Ohio and presented shows and plays wherever it was moored – doing particularly good business in Pittsburgh and Cincinnati. In the off-season they would tie up the boat and often visit New York or Chicago, to either watch the shows or perform. Betty Bryant was 15 when Wilson, Keppel and Betty came to New York in late 1937. According to Betty Bryant, she passed the audition but her mother wouldn't let her take the job, because she wasn't happy about her daughter travelling to Europe at such a young age.

A similar tale comes from British dancer Nita Carroll, who later became one of Phyllis Dixey's 'Varga Models' in the *Peek-a-Boo* striptease revues. Nita's stage career began in her very early teens with dance troupe Terry's Juveniles – the training ground of many a musical star over the years, from Jessie Matthews to Melvyn Hayes. During the 1939-40 pantomime season both Wilson, Keppel and Betty and Terry's Juveniles were speciality acts in *Aladdin* at Streatham Hill Theatre, South London. It's believed that, at some point during the run of the panto, Jack and Joe approached the leader of the troupe asking if Nita could be released to join their act. However, it was considered that Nita was too young (she was 14 at the time) and she wasn't allowed to go.

These recollections from Nita Carroll and Betty Bryant both suggest that (for whatever reason) Betty Knox was giving serious thought to her future within the act – and plans were already under way to trade her in for a far younger model! If events happened as Betty Bryant described, then there was the real possibility that Betty Knox wouldn't make that return trip to England. Maybe Betty had to talk Patsy round. Or maybe she was thinking that, at the age of 31, her 'dancing girl' days were drawing to a close. Ultimately mother and daughter both wanted the same thing – to be together at long last. And the reasons why they finally picked Britain rather than America aren't too hard to fathom.

Firstly, the two of them had obviously succeeded in remaining close, and Betty's letters to Patsy conveyed the excitement of the life she was living and the people she was meeting. Secondly, it seems that Patsy shared her mother's ambitious streak and outgoing nature. And thirdly, never mind the war – she was going to drama school!

For someone who, up to now, had given every impression of caring little about her daughter, Betty was now the doting and attentive mother. And, despite the separate lives they would often lead, they remained close for the rest of Betty's life.

Just how close Betty had become to Jack Wilson is another matter. Billy Shenton Junior recalls:

Jack has always been very, very protective to Betty. Joe, I think, tried his luck – shall I say? – for a start but was, sort of, warned off by Jack. Whether anything went on between them or not, I don't know. But they were very, very close. It was Betty and Jack. Not Joe. Joe always went off on his own. Had his own digs. Betty always stayed at Olivelli's with Jack. Can't understand why, 'cos some of the rooms at Olivelli's were like cells, you know. But on tour, round the country, she always stayed with Jack. Not in the same room or anything like that! But always in the same digs. They were just very close.

Olivelli's (35 Store Street, London) was where the pros would meet up after the shows. It had opened in 1934 as a modest hotel and restaurant, run by Sicilian-born Rita and Enrico Olivelli (known affectionately to patrons as Mama and Papa). But it quickly became a favourite gathering place of showbiz performers. Noel Whitcomb of the *Daily Mirror* (writing in 1955) explained how this came about:

> Their first customer was a bareback equestrian girl from a circus, who ordered soup and nothing else.
>
> Mama took a look at this kid, sent over a plate of spaghetti. Papa quietly put a glass of Chianti beside her.
>
> 'Whaddayou think we are, Papa – millionaires?' roared Mama. When his back was turned she sent over a roll.
>
> The girl came back later with the rest of the circus – all hungry. 'We'll pay next week,' they said.
>
> And they did. Which was how it all began.

During the day, students from the nearby Royal Academy of Dramatic Art (RADA) would pop in for a coffee. It closed its doors to the public around 11:30 at night. But the downstairs restaurant remained open – though you had to be a pro, and known to Papa and Mama, to gain admission. Writing in *The Mirror* (Perth, Western Australia) in 1936, trick-cycling musician Bert Harding told of his recent trip to London where he 'had many a yarn' with former Australian vaudevillian Joe Keppel. He also told readers something of the nocturnal habits of the London pro:

> At Olivelli's I learned quite a deal of vaudevillians' night-life. Their chief meal commences about 1 or 2 am, and seldom do they retire till 4 or 5 am. At this theatricals' rendezvous congregate a dozen different nationalities, and to enjoy the gaiety one must be a first-class linguist.

As time went on, Papa and Mama Olivelli bought a couple of neighbouring properties and expanded the hotel side of the business. Variety performers working in London knew they could find affordable food and accommodation there, plus good company to while the night away. Many big American stars would drop in, such as Danny Kaye, Mickey Rooney and Liberace. Signed photos festooned its walls, including one from Groucho Marx which declared, 'As long as there is an Olivelli's, there will always be an England.' But, as Ralph McGill fondly recalled (in the *Miami Daily News* of 1952) the majority of patrons were the humble speciality act:

> More often than not they would be in costume. There would be acrobats in spangles, comedians in foppish or cockney dress, and singers in evening attire. Almost always there would be someone at the ancient and out-of-tune piano, playing with others singing.

And the most frequent tickler of the Olivelli ivories was none other than Jack Wilson. Joe Keppel visited Olivelli's occasionally, though he usually stayed at 'digs' in Wood Green. But Jack would hold court at the piano way into the night, treating his fellow pros to hilarious and outrageous song parodies. In 1947, when the hugely successful Rodgers and Hammerstein musical *Oklahoma!* opened at the (supposedly haunted) Theatre Royal, Drury Lane, Jack penned the following parody (to the tune of *California, Here I Come*). The lyrics were displayed on large cards, and sung by the entire restaurant, led by comics Jimmy Smeddle and Joe Young, with Jack at the piano:

> Oklahoma's here in town
> It sure turned things upside-down
> They came to our city, to give us a treat
> The audience adores 'em, you can't buy a seat, and when he
> Hears those songs of sweet refrain,
> That old ghost will walk again
> Bidding welcome to the 'Lane'
> Oklahoma's here in town!

Max Wall, the acrobatic dancer and supreme exponent of the funny walk, was a regular patron of Olivelli's and great pals with Betty Knox. 'A wonderful girl with an enormous sense of humour,' he wrote in his autobiography *The Fool on the Hill*. It's hardly surprising that Betty gravitated towards Jack. They were markedly similar in outlook. Billy Shenton Junior met her several times:

> I always remember she was terribly American, and I tried to ape the American accent right from the time I was a very junior kid, you know, eight or nine years of age. I'd go all American when I went over to see Betty. Offstage she was always very smart. I've seen her wear a suit a few times, which was not quite done so much in those days. She could mix. She could drink. She could smoke. Anything else, I don't know. She was a lovely woman. Very outgoing. Very American.

And, in many ways, very like Jack. But does Billy think there's any truth in the rumour about Betty, Jack and Patsy?

> Many times in the business people have said, 'Oh, that was Jack's daughter.' But Jack has never said so. And, I think, with my father and Jack, they were such lifelong friends, I think, at some time or the other, it might have come out if it had've been. So I'm pretty sure it wasn't.

If there's one thing that showbiz folk enjoy, it's a good gossip about fellow pros. Perhaps they brought it upon themselves by inventing this tale that they'd been a trio for much longer than was actually the case. Whatever Jack and Betty may have got up to together at one time or another, 1923 would have been several years before they met. Betty became pregnant when she was still 16 and hadn't properly entered the profession. As Donald Knox married her so promptly, we must assume he was the real father. There is no evidence that Jack and Betty's paths crossed before 1928. But, as Betty had suddenly returned to Britain with a previously unmentioned daughter, it was inevitable that Jack would be the number one suspect.

It's amazing that two people like Joe Keppel and Jack Wilson, who looked virtually identical on stage, were so different in both appearance and temperament offstage. Although Irishman Joe Keppel preferred to socialise away from the act, he was in no way a shrinking violet. Billy Shenton Junior:

> Joe Keppel was as Irish as Guinness. 'Woah, Bill, got to get some of that concentrated carrot juice, boy. That'll get you going, you know.' That's the only bit of Americanism that came in. But it's Irish-American, you know. 'And the little black pills. Keep you healthy and strong and give you plenty of oomph.' Because he was a hell of a boy for the girls, was

Joe. He really was a terror with the girls. But he treated them very well.

But Jack – no, he never wandered on to anybody, you know. He was always around with Betty. And he was typical Liverpudlian. 'Aye, very funny.'

Joe may have been 'as Irish as Guinness' but he never drank the stuff – nor any other kind of alcohol. Neither did he smoke. Possibly as a result of his earlier health problems he was quite fastidious about his diet, supplementing the carrot juice and little black pills with nuts, cereals, radishes and honey. Jack smoked, drank rum and Guinness, ate what he liked – and, despite all that, remained a close match for Joe in both weight and physique. (Though you'd hardly call either of them the picture of health.)

Billy described to me how the men's contrasting personalities were reflected in their offstage appearance:

Joe always wore a very smart, dapper suit. Very smart trilby hat. Rimless glasses. And he was immaculate. A Windsor knot on his tie. A young girl, she could look very nice out with Joe.

Jack, he'd got this battered hat. He'd got this one suit. The waistcoat. Watch chain. And the embarrassing thing was – he always carried the money, for the act I think, in a body belt, underneath his trousers. So if he went to go anywhere, he'd have the embarrassment of saying, 'Well, just a minute.' He'd undo his flies. Then he'd got to get down into his money belt to get some money out.

He'd had his wallet stolen out of his hip pocket years ago – they'd cut the pocket out altogether. And he said, 'Never again.' And he carried this thing. And, as I say, he looked like a tramp. My mother always used to knit him pullovers, which he'd wear underneath his waistcoat. Because he always looked as if he was bloody freezing to death.

Many people have recalled meeting Wilson and Keppel in their dressing room, and observed how the two barely communicated with each other. This has often been interpreted as a bitter long-standing feud – perhaps the unhappy result of a love triangle involving Betty Knox. Billy Shenton Junior never saw any evidence of a rift between the two men:

They were on good terms, but they could sit there and not talk to each other. Joe would sit there and do a crossword puzzle. And, of course, this is why they always got separate digs as well, because they'd learned – this is how acts do split up. Because they live in each other's pockets.

Joe always found very good, comfortable digs. If they were recommended by Joe, they were bloody good digs. I don't know if he was knocking off the landlady or what, but they were very good digs. Jack, well, he would go wherever he could be recommended, but with Betty. But they did not mix socially.

Wilson, Keppel and Betty played the Ipswich Hippodrome in Suffolk several times in the 1940s and 50s when, once again, Jack and Joe went their separate ways. Jack Wilson stayed at the Great White Horse in the town centre, while Joe Keppel booked into a private guest house on the town's outskirts, where he insisted on using his own silver teapot and silver butter dish.

On 28th March 1938, Betty kept her promise to daughter Patsy, and enrolled her as a junior drama student at RADA. Together with the expert dance tuition that she'd received at the Lindsay and Mason School in America, Patsy was well on the way to achieving her stage ambitions.

In May, small ads in *Variety* informed readers that both Betty Knox and Joe Keppel were dressed by Sidney Fisher of Piccadilly, London, who not only paid for the ads but certainly offered a substantial discount to two walking advertisements for his stylish garments. He wisely declined to make a similar offer to scruffbag Jack Wilson.

In November 1938, the trio appeared at the ABC Paris. A display ad proclaims them '*les célèbres comiques Américains*'. Below their names are a couple of minor support acts, one of whom is comparative newcomer Edith Piaf. Early in the New Year they were in Nice at the Tabarin Variety and, in spring 1939, they toured South Africa. By June, they'd returned to the London Palladium in a mainly American bill, featuring the slapstick movie team The Three Stooges and ventriloquist Señor Wences. In August, at Portsmouth Hippodrome, they supported three grand old ladies of the Music Hall: Hetty King, Lily Morris and Ada Reeve.

And then, on 3rd September 1939, Britain declared war on Germany. A crucial event for so many lives, not least those of Wilson, Keppel and Betty, because the British government ordered the immediate closure of all theatres and cinemas. *Variety* magazine makes the situation very clear. In America nothing has changed, but there is not a performer in their regular column of London news whose life has not been turned upside-down. Comedy actor Naunton Wayne has become a policeman, Winston Churchill's daughter Sarah (aka Mrs Vic Oliver) is an ambulance driver, and Beatrice Lillie has scrapped plans to star in a New York musical in order to stay in London. Wilson, Keppel and Betty, and a few other American acts, are setting up home on the Somerset coast:

> Nelson and Night, Billy Vine, Tracey and Hay, and Wilson, Keppel and Betty staying at a rented house in Weston-Super-Mare, where they intend organizing concert parties for duration of war.

At this stage no-one knew for sure how long the war would last, how severe it would be, or how to go about everyday life. In a matter of weeks it became clear that everyday life would be (wherever practically possible) the order of the day. The theatres reopened and Wilson, Keppel and Betty were back on tour. Over the coming years they'd often be singled out for honourable mention in the US press as one of few American acts who'd chosen to stay in Britain throughout the war.

Patsy Knox (who had gone to Weston-Super-Mare with her mother) joined the local repertory company at the Knightstone Theatre – her first professional engagement, just a couple of months before her 16th birthday.

At Christmas, Wilson, Keppel and Betty had the usual panto residency – their third *Aladdin* with Betty Huntley-Wright – this time at Streatham Hill Theatre in South London. It was here that Jack and Joe unsuccessfully offered the role of Betty to 'Terry's Juvenile' Nita Carroll. It was only a few months into the war, but Betty Knox clearly wanted to move on. For the moment she would continue in the act. But she was getting frustrated. Bombs were falling all around, and all she could do was dance.

During the usual run of weekly engagements throughout 1940 they met Will Hay Junior, doing his father's famous schoolmaster act. They also encountered Bobbie Kimber who, on learning that female ventriloquists were a comparative rarity, put on a wig and dress and kept his true identity a secret for years. No end-of-year panto this time, but a couple of months touring in *Garrison Theatre*, a stage version of the radio hit starring Jack Warner and Joan Winters.

February and March 1941 saw them as resident performers in *Strike*

Up the Music at the London Coliseum – the first West End musical to open since the Nazi blitz. *The Stage* wasn't impressed:

> Spectacular productions are not unknown at the Coliseum, but it is something of a wartime surprise to find Sir Oswald Stoll permitting displays of near-nudity in some of the production scenes of his latest presentation. If there were much that were clever or novel to recommend them there might be some excuse, but the Coliseum has got along very well up to the present with a higher artistic outlook than the cheap allure of feminine underdressing.

The *Catholic Herald*, not surprisingly, had similar reservations. Though they had no problem with speciality acts such as:

> ... the ever welcome Wilson and Keppel (Eastern comic strip come to life) with the rather distracting Betty ...

(She may have been months away from her 35th birthday, but Betty had clearly lost none of her power to distract a Catholic!)

With the promise of acres of female flesh on view, one theatregoer smuggled a cine camera into a performance, hoping to get a few shots of the big production numbers in sumptuous 16mm colour. Sure enough, at the climax of an interplanetary ballet, when the golden chariot of the sun makes its entrance, a motionless topless beauty is in the driving seat. The amateur cinematographer also captured the final moments of Wilson, Keppel and Betty's staircase dance – the three of them, in a line, holding hands, in a perfectly synchronised display of fast steps and jumps. It's an impressive finish to the act, but a total contrast to the movie versions from the early 1930s. In those days, everyone was jumping, high-kicking, their arms flailing round in a wild (almost reckless) display of energy. The 1941 version is certainly not lacking in skill, but it's far less manic.

As a reminder of how the Blitz and the blackout were disrupting London's nightlife, *Strike Up the Music* was presented twice daily, at 2 and 5 pm. (No West End theatre started its second house any later than 6 pm.) The theatre programme listed the nearest public shelters but made it clear that, in the event of an air raid, the show would go on uninterrupted. Sirens wailed, bombs fell, but Wilson, Keppel and Betty still high-kicked their way to the top of the staircase – while countless Londoners dashed down their own stairs and huddled in the cellar beneath.

Next stop was Blackpool Tower Circus, for much of April. Of all the places they had performed, this 'English Eiffel' was one of the most bizarre. Somehow it succeeds in accommodating an entire indoor circus ring, plus an ornate ballroom (complete with rising and falling Wurlitzer organ) all in the same building, with a lift to transport you to its 518-foot summit. It was the customary circus line-up of acrobats, clowns, midgets, waltzing bears and a boxing kangaroo.

There had been plenty of shows where Wilson, Keppel and Betty were the maddest act by far. Now they had plenty of competition. Plus, as a frontcloth act, used to performing on an area of comparatively little depth, suddenly they were in a circus ring with the audience seated all around. For Wilson and Keppel, it was a trip back in time to their first meeting at Colleano's Circus. If nothing else, it certainly brought back the aromas – an indoor circus can't have had the most fragrant of atmospheres.

The following month they shared a bill with 22-year-old Beryl Reid, who later appeared on radio's *Educating Archie*, as schoolgirl Monica, opposite ventriloquist Peter Brough and dummy Archie Andrews. In Beryl's autobiography *So Much Love* she recalls spending time backstage with Betty Knox, and their mutual fascination with a feature in *Lilliput* magazine called 'Sillistrations', which were cartoons based on well-known sayings. These particularly appealed to Betty and Beryl's absurd sense of humour, and the pair would doodle their own, such as 'Pretty Kettle of Fish' – a beautifully decorated kettle, with fish bursting out of it. This is one of the first recorded examples of Betty's joy of puns and written comedy, but it was a world in which she was becoming increasingly involved. Beryl also remembers Wilson and Keppel working industriously in their dressing room between shows, surrounded by tools, busily constructing props and repairing shoes.

In June 1941, Wilson, Keppel and Betty began a prolonged tour of an eighteen-scene revue that would take them right through to July the following year. It was produced by impresario Bernard Delfont (the brother of Lew and Leslie Grade, whose family name was actually Winogradsky) and was called *Hello America!* It would not be too long before America would enter the war (in fact, about halfway through the tour of this show) and they were already offering much behind-the-scenes support to Britain, strategically and financially. So this was a highly appropriate time to salute our transatlantic allies. As critic Edward Graves (writing for *The Billboard*) explains, the true significance of the show's title only becomes clear as the entire company perform the stirring finale, in front of a backcloth depicting the Houses of Parliament:

> Peggy Stone sings 'America I Love You'; girls step out in Uncle Sam costumes; panels in cloth light up to reveal John Bull and Uncle Sam holding phone conversation.

Although the show was described as 'An Anglo-American Rhapsody' there were very few truly American performers in the show. Principal comic Nor Kiddie was Lancashire born, leading lady Eunice Roberts was from Newcastle-upon-Tyne, and dancers The Gordon Ray Yankee Clippers had (just the previous month) been known as The Gordon Ray Bathing Beauties. *The Stage*, in October, rates 'Cleopatra's Nightmare' as 'one of the revue's best incidents'. It also reports that several of the cast – including Betty Knox – 'help well in the amusing sketches'.

As Betty was a genuine American performer, it's not surprising that her acting skills were to be utilised in this Anglo-American entertainment. Although she hadn't previously spoken onstage in Britain, we know that singing (and possibly spoken patter) featured in their early vaudeville Collegiate Co-Eds routine. Until the end of their career, Wilson, Keppel and Betty would maintain that they never uttered a single word on stage – and, as far as 'Cleopatra's Nightmare' goes, that was certainly true. But this is a rare instance when the audience got to hear Betty's authentic Kansas accent.

A search through the extensive archives of the Ipswich Hippodrome produced a theatre programme for *Hello America*. Item 5 is a comedy sketch with a military theme, entitled 'On the Home Front', in which Nor Kiddie plays Private Everyman and Betty Knox is a Stranded Lady.

By item 15, the 'stranded' Betty was on more familiar territory: 'CLEOPATRA'S NIGHTMARE – Introducing the American Comedy Dancers: WILSON, KEPPEL and BETTY.' This particular week there were several northern comics in the cast, including a radio star from Sheffield renowned for his verbal punctuation. ('This is Stainless Stephen comma comedian question-mark.') So any act that could flaunt its US credentials was particularly welcome.

The Billboard noted a slight (but highly significant) alteration to 'Cleopatra's Nightmare':

> A spear combat dance, adhering to the team's principle of burlesque, replaces the staircase number now used in the show's opening scene, with Wilson and Keppel working as sailors.

The Spear Dance was their final addition to the act, and would remain a permanent fixture until their retirement. It was never filmed in its entirety, but some amateur cine footage and a few photographs (from later years) do exist. Perhaps its major appeal was its portability – they had been steadily jettisoning all their larger and bulkier props. All they needed for this was two spears and two shields.

Wilson and Keppel (never knowingly overdressed) are both stripped to the waist, wearing something resembling a baggy nappy that hangs down to their knees, with much bare leg on show. Their headgear is best described as a white bowler hat with an upturned brim (a weird hybrid of bowler and pierrot clown's headgear). They each carry a long spear and a small round shield and attack each other in mock-combat. In one photo, Wilson appears to be attempting to run Keppel through with his spear – the trick being that the spears (like a 'joke shop' knife) have an internal spring, so that the point, when pressed against the body, will retract into the handle. Playwright Peter Nichols recalled (in the foreword to this book) that 'one dancer got in a contortion with the other so that he finished by seeming to be holding his balls' – a bit of business that almost certainly belongs to this routine. At the end of their carefully choreographed carnage, Betty joins them for a final dance.

The Spear Dance, devised by Jack, Joe and Betty Knox, was now their finale – replacing the only routine that predated her. The most cumbersome piece of equipment they owned. It had been part of Jack and Joe's double-act, years before they met Betty. They had travelled all over America, Britain and Europe with it. And, as Billy Shenton Junior neatly put it: 'My father barked his shins so many times on that bloody staircase.' They may have charged madly up and down them at the Trocadero in 1933, but Wilson and Keppel were now in their late forties and that wooden monstrosity belonged to an earlier era. And besides, it was never, ever, not to the slightest degree, not even remotely Egyptian!

It had now been relegated to the back of the stage, as a brief episode in the show's opening, rather than the culmination of 'Cleopatra's Nightmare'. At the end of the run of *Hello America*, and with a huge sigh of relief, they would be dismantling those steps for the very last time.

At this stage of her career, Betty Knox was certainly branching out. First dancing, then acting; but it didn't stop there. In the 1943 article by Hannen Swaffer in the *World's Press News*, he tells of Betty's writing talent, which had steadily evolved since she first met up with Wilson and Keppel, aged just 16 (though she was actually 22):

> Although so young, she helped to build up a turn that soon became a 'standard act' – £75 or thereabouts, although now it gets more.
>
> It only changed in the sense that, every year or so, Betty wrote a new number to put in.
>
> In due course she began to write comedy scripts and songs for fellow pros. – and, more recently, she has written all Tessie O'Shea's material.

Although it's unlikely that Betty single-handedly shaped Wilson, Keppel and Betty's act over the years, it's clear that her input was significant, and that Wilson and Keppel probably trusted her comedic instincts as much as their own. Two brand new routines, the Spear Dance and the Seven Veils, had been introduced in recent years. The Seven Veils, more than any other, would only succeed with a skilful and inventive performance by Betty, so it must be assumed she played a major role in its creation.

As for writing Tessie O'Shea's material, it would be a foolish claim to make in print if it wasn't basically true. In her early days, Cardiff-born Tessie would sing slightly blue songs accompanying herself on the banjolele (a banjo-ukulele hybrid) in the style of a female George Formby. But increasingly she cultivated a transatlantic image – *Two-Ton Tessie from Tennessee*, first recorded in 1939, becoming her signature song. She worked extensively in the States from the 1960s onwards and died aged 82, in her Florida home.

Betty is never credited as lyricist on any of Tessie's recorded songs, because Tessie bought Betty's material outright for her own exclusive use. But one song is definitely hers, as revealed by *The Billboard,* back in December 1939:

Betty (Knox) is achieving new fame as a songwriter, having just given Tessie O'Shea her biggest hit for years in 'International Rhythm', written in topical vein.

'International Rhythm' wasn't just a huge hit, it was a huge song. Running at just over five minutes, it was the epic number that concluded Tessie's act throughout the war years and was penned only months after war was declared. The opening lines sum up its theme – the vital need (especially at this moment in history) for nations to work together:

Now music, it's international, it's just like the sun and the sky
And right from the very beginning, man has sung to keep his spirits
    hi-de-high
So why can't the world get together and conduct their affairs with a
    song?

This leads into the pulsating rhythmic chorus, peppered with clever internal rhymes:

And we'll sing an international rhythm, take the syncopation of every
    nation in swing
An international rhythm, it's a serenade and it must be played
On a trombone or a big bassoon, because a tom-tom beat keeps the
    world in tune

The next verse takes us on a brief musical tour of Britain, drawing together snippets from 'Killarney', 'The Campbells are Coming' and 'Sosban Fach' (pronounced impeccably by the Welsh-born singer with the Irish name) before travelling farther and wider:

To darkest Africa – a-boom-diddy-boom-ba, and on to Cuba to capture
    a Rumba,
Rio de Janeiro a gay bolero, and then from sunny Spain we'll take a
    Tango strain

We stop off at the USA for a burst of 'St Louis Blues', then home for a snatch of British marching song 'Soldiers of the King', before a heartfelt build-up to the final chorus:

Now put them all together and what have you got? You've got a musical
    melting pot
And every man that you meet, he's your musical brother
Be mad about music and not at each other …

Britain had plenty of patriotic songs to get us through the war, but precious few that acknowledged the spirit of international co-operation needed to secure that victory. You'd expect nothing less from Betty Knox, and this song always got a rousing reception. I'm told that Tessie loved the song and even sang it at home in her later years.

There is one published song (copyright 18th June 1942) which bears the name of Betty Knox as lyricist, alongside Charles Irwin and E. Whittam. 'I Saw a Robin' (far more modest in scale than 'International Rhythm') has a message common to many a wartime ditty – that better times are just around the corner. The lyrics make great play of the fact that 'chirrup' sounds a lot like 'cheer up', and the chorus goes like this:

> I saw a Robin in the snow today. As plain as day I heard the Robin say,
> Cheer up! Cheer up! Spring is on the way,
> Cheer up! Cheer up! I heard the Robin say.
> I asked the Robin if he had cold feet. As plain as day I heard the Robin
>   tweet,
> Cheer up! Cheer up! Winter's got to go,
> Cheer up! Cheer up! A Robin ought to know.

And a talent with words would be the key to Betty's future career. On 3rd June 1942, American newspaper *Variety* carried two succinct sentences:

> Betty Knox is quitting act of Wilson, Keppel and Betty to join staff of the *London Evening Standard*. Her daughter, Patsy, takes her place in the act.

13

Give Me Two Weeks

(Britain 1941–1942)

'... where the real hot-potters eat tripe and trotters ...' (Betty Knox, 1941)

BETTY'S COMPLETE CHANGE OF CAREER may have seemed like a bolt from the blue, but it was something she'd been considering for some time. The story, as Billy Shenton Junior remembers it, began one night in London. The show had finished, and the cast were gathered in the pros' habitual meeting place – Olivelli's downstairs restaurant:

> They were down in Olivelli's, during the blitz, and a bomb came down, right outside Olivelli's. And it blasted down into the cellar there and blew half the pictures off the wall. And Betty said, 'Godammit, I'm not standing for this any more. I'm going to get into this war!'

The editor of the *London Evening Standard* at the time was Frank Owen. He and Betty had met some years previously, as related in *World's Press News* of 1943 by Hannen Swaffer, who gallantly reduces Betty's age by a couple of years:

> It was not till she was 33 that Betty Knox became a newspaper woman. We must blame Frank Owen. He had gone to Rome to see his future wife, Grace, who had brought the first American 'glamour girls' to Europe – and there he met Betty, whose act was in the same show as Grace's.
>
> He was immediately struck with what has often astounded me – Betty's puzzling knowledge of Europe in general and her weird familiarity with the lives of the British masses.

'You know more about the British provinces than any reporter I know,' said Frank. 'You ought to join our paper.'

Betty, you see, had not only travelled a lot but acted and lived in the high-spots and the dumps, in first-class hotels and the cheapest of digs.

'And,' as she says, 'you don't know people unless you live and work with them.'

Grace Stewart, a former Miss America, was a showgirl who'd been dancing in European cabarets at the same time as Wilson, Keppel and Betty were touring abroad. She had initially turned down Frank Owen's proposal of marriage, but he had pursued her across Europe, with the blessing of the *Standard*'s proprietor, Lord Beaverbrook. Frank's interest in Betty shouldn't suggest any particular obsession with dancing girls. It was the fact that Betty had barely stopped travelling for the past fifteen years. This, plus her curiosity as an American abroad and her outgoing personality, all made her an instinctive, if untrained, newsgatherer. In 1944, Marcel Wallenstein, writing in the *Kansas City Star*, told how Betty got the job:

> The war unraveled its red skeins and Betty Knox danced in theaters while air raid sirens wailed a requiem for victims trapped under ruins. Bombs smashed West End stages. She danced between air raids. She danced in air raids with trembling legs.
>
> One night sitting with Frank Owen after her performance she said she wished she had been a journalist. Owen agreed she might have been a success.
>
> 'Then why don't you give me a job?' she asked him.
>
> 'How much are you earning?'
>
> 'Fifty pounds a week.'
>
> 'Well,' replied the editor, 'I'd give you a lot less than that.'
>
> She snapped back at him. 'Give me two weeks to break my daughter into the act and I'll take it.'

We last met Patsy aged 15, in late 1939, working in rep at Weston-Super-Mare. 'I'm not keen on dancing. I want to be a straight actress,' she had said. And Betty had helped her realise that ambition. However, the one area of performing in which she really excelled, even if she wasn't particularly keen on it, was dancing. A biography of Patsy in *The Performer* of 1947 says:

First stage appearance, 30 May, 1941 at the Hippodrome, Preston. First London appearance, August, 1942, at the Streatham Hill Theatre. Took her mother's place with the well-known dancing act and made an immediate impression. Learned acrobatic dancing and tap etc., with a view to doing a single act, but had no hesitation in giving up this idea in order to help in keeping up the name of Wilson, Keppel and Betty.

If the date of her stage debut is correct, Patsy had joined the chorus of a touring revival of the Noel Gay musical *Me and My Girl*, which originally starred Lupino Lane, and contained the show-stopping number 'The Lambeth Walk'. She makes a fleeting appearance in Marcel Wallenstein's interview with Betty in 1944:

Patsy Knox returned from the theater and told her mother she wanted to be a serious actress. She would be some day. She is pretty and hard working and knows what she wants.

But right now, Patsy was prepared to put her acting ambitions on hold and replace her mother in the act. 'Give me two weeks,' Betty had said. But when were those two weeks? The previously quoted biography in *The Performer* says:

Betty Knox retired from the stage in 1941 to take up newspaper work and her daughter, Patsy, replaced her in the act.

But *Variety* didn't break the news of the transfer of Bettys until June 1942. So which was it? 1941 or 1942? Had Betty Knox completed the year-long run of *Hello America* (ending in July 1942) and passed the role directly to Patsy? Or had she left in 1941 with Patsy not taking over until the following year?

By a combination of chance and detective work I managed to locate someone who knew for sure – the leading lady during the *Hello America* tour of 1941–2: Eunice Roberts. In June 2013, I journeyed up to Blackpool to interview a woman a few weeks away from her 92nd birthday about the events of 72 years earlier. It was a trip well worth making. Eunice was bright-eyed, eager to talk, with vivid memories of her early career:

I was a good tap dancer. In those days I could do wings and crawls and back-snatches. I was a terrific dancer. Well, my grandmother had thirteen children and the family were all dancers. I used to sit, as a little girl, and look through the bannisters and watch them all. And I picked all my steps up from them. I never had a dancing lesson in my life.

By the age of 15, Eunice had joined the Eileen Rogan Girls. And later she was one of the line-up of high-kicking Tiller Girls:

> Then I broke out on my own. And then Bernard Delfont picked me up, because I was very good with the patter as well, and made me leading lady. And that was when I met Wilson, Keppel and Betty.

Eunice was approaching her 20th birthday when the tour of *Hello America* began in June 1941. Wilson and Keppel were in their mid-40s and Betty Knox was 35:

> Betty was plumpish. She wasn't a slim, thin girl. But she was a smashing woman. We were great friends. She was terribly American. She was all-American really. She talked American. She had that accent.

Betty always dressed well in expensive clothes. She once took Eunice shopping and treated her to a new outfit:

> There's a football team here – they're in blue and purple. I'll always remember because afterwards, years after, I'd say, 'Well, there's my outfit.' It was blue and purple. There was a beautiful jacket, and a beautiful dress and a hat. And she dressed me up. She was wonderful. We were great together. She was lovely.

Betty even confided to Eunice how she felt about the show's dashingly debonair impresario, Bernard Delfont:

> Betty was in love with him, but he never looked her way. But she was silently in love with him. Nobody knew, only me. She told me. She loved him – she loved Bernard Delfont. But he was happily married I think.

In addition to her solo spot in the show, Eunice was also 'straight woman' to resident comic Nor Kiddie:

> He was one of these quiet comedians – they used to walk on the stage and crack a gag. I was a good feed for him – he liked me as a feed. I'd answer him back and stick in a little bit of my own. And he used to go bloody mad offstage. He used to say, 'It's my act!' 'Okay, alright.'

But, while Wilson, Keppel and Betty were onstage, Eunice would invariably be standing in the wings:

I used to watch the act from the side every night. I loved the act. I fell in love with the act.

Eunice told me that, between performances, Betty Knox would often be found writing plays or little sketches:

She loved writing. Writing was her life – she wasn't interested in the act really. She was just 'in it', you know. It was just a form of money, I suppose – just wages. She'd be writing. All the time.

Betty also wrote a musical number for Eunice's solo spot, making the most of Eunice's talent for accents and mimicry. Like 'International Rhythm', it was a world tour in a nutshell. It began with a take-off of sizzling songstress Carmen Miranda, known as the 'Brazilian Bombshell' and famous for her fruit-laden headgear:

It started off with, 'Ai, ai, ai – do you want to live in the tropics, in the crazy lazy Sowse American way?' And then I'd do it as, 'Ee bah gum – have you ever been to Blackpool, where the real hot-potters eat tripe and trotters the good old Lancashire way?' And then, 'Indeed to goodness, have you ever been to Wales … ?' And it finished up with, 'But there's no place like home, sweet home's the place to be.' And she wrote that because I was good at impressions when I was a kid. And I put that in the show.

It was exactly this local colour and ear for dialect in Betty's writing that so impressed *London Evening Standard* editor Frank Owen and prompted him to offer her a reporter's job a few months into the tour of *Hello America*. But when Eunice told me what happened next, it wasn't at all what I expected to hear:

And she got me in the dressing room and said, 'Will you take over?' She said, 'I know you know the act, because you bloody watch every night from the wings.' I could do the act backwards, I loved it that much. And I used to rehearse when they were rehearsing. I used to be rehearsing in the wings with them, you know. She said, 'I know you know the act. Will you do it?' So I said yes.

I asked Eunice how much time it took to perfect the routines:

Oh, it didn't take long. Two minutes, I think! No, it didn't take long. She trained me to do the exact movements that she did with the seven veils. The comedy one was the most important to them.

Onstage musical accompaniment to the seven veils was provided by Jack and Joe on hand-drums. Eunice also took her turn on percussion – and again it was Betty who taught her:

> I used to come on and play the drums at the back while they danced. I stood up at the back – dum-diddy-dum-diddy-diddy-dum-dum – while they were at the front.

But why didn't Patsy take over directly from Betty, as every biographical account maintains? Surely she was the logical first choice. I asked Eunice if Betty had approached Patsy:

> She didn't want it. She didn't want to know. She said, 'I don't want to know.' She wasn't interested in it.

It was perfectly understandable that Patsy, approaching her 18th birthday and at the very start of her career, didn't want to be saddled with the same old-fashioned act that her mother had trotted out non-stop over the past decade. So Patsy, with strong acting aspirations, continued to make her own way in the profession, while Eunice took on the mantle from Betty.

After Betty Knox had left, Eunice kept her solo spot in the show as well as being the new 'Betty'. They may have been billed as an American act, but the trio had now lost its only born-and-bred American. Eunice recalls that Jack Wilson came out with the odd Americanism from time to time, but Joe was totally Irish. There were other personality quirks too:

> Now Jack was mad about music and every time he went to a hotel, whatever hotel we went to, he used to go and find the piano and play. That was his hobby – he loved that. And there was Joe – he was like an old dad, you know, he used to walk about with a small purse, which everyone thought was comical, and he was a bit mean.

Of all the anecdotes about Jack and Joe, it's amazing how many are money-related. But, as the newbie of the trio, Eunice surely incurred the two veterans' displeasure if she didn't do things precisely like her predecessor:

> Oh, no. Not at all. We laughed more than anything. 'Cause I picked up everything. I'd been watching it for blinkin' months, from the side of the stage, you know.

There had been gossip about Jack and Joe's sexual conduct around Betty Knox, and they would be dogged by similar rumour-mongering for the rest of their career and beyond. Eunice was a quarter of a century younger than the men, shapely and leggy, so surely had to fend off the odd unwanted advance:

> Oh, they were wonderful. There was nothing rude or anything. No touchy-touchy or anything like that. Nothing. They were just like two old men. Like me dad.

Days before our interview, Eunice watched a TV programme featuring old footage of the act, and was surprised that her co-stars (who, at the time, she regarded as 'two old men') looked so youthful. She had clear memories of sitting cross-legged on the platform and being carried round the stage at the start, of the finger-cymbals, the sand dance, the seven veils, and joining Jack and Joe in a tap dance to conclude the act. She also remembered the less prominent position of the staircase for Jack and Joe's clog dancing routine:

> They were at the back of the stage, and they tap-danced down the steps, from the wings, you know. Dum-diddy-dum-diddy-dum down the steps.

After six months or so, Eunice took the decision to leave the show. She was young and wanted to try new things:

> I decided I'd had enough. I wanted to get away – entertain the troops. A girl on the show who was a contortionist, she says, 'Come on with me and we'll do a double act – go on ENSA and entertain the troops.' I said, 'Let's go and entertain the Yanks.' So we did, the two of us went. And then she met a feller or something – and I went and did it on my own.

Patsy Knox was again approached (there being no obvious replacement who knew the act as well as Eunice). By now either her attitude had changed, or perhaps her solo career wasn't going quite as well as she'd hoped. Whatever the reason, she finally agreed to take on the role of Betty. Eunice met her several times but wasn't involved in the training which was, once more, conducted by Betty Knox. Meanwhile, Eunice had found herself a new stage partner:

> He played the drums and I sang 'Drumming man, he's the drumming man...' His dad was a pianist, and his mother was a little Jewess who

used to travel with us to the digs. I was blonde then, all this blonde hair, loads of hair, and this figure, which was good then, and I used to do it all in front, and he used to be drumming at the back. And then I'd sing, 'Take it, take it, take it, Mr Beat' and then he'd do a drum roll and a drum solo. He was wonderful on the drums.

The name of that drummer was Peter Sellers. In later years Eunice changed her stage name to Melody Lane and entertained in the Blackpool clubs. But few people are aware that, between Betty Knox and her daughter Patsy, there was another Betty called Eunice Roberts.

So in 1942, aged 18, Patsy Knox became the 'Betty' of Wilson, Keppel and Betty. It probably never occurred to them to amend the name of the act to Wilson, Keppel and Patsy. There were plenty of advance bookings under the name which, over the years, the public had got to know and love. So Patsy, born Jean, became Betty. Initially she'd been highly reluctant (her claim in *The Performer* of 1947 that she'd 'no hesitation' in joining the act was far from true) but, as a career move, it made a lot of sense. Rather than a name well down the list in a theatre programme, Patsy was now one-third of a headlining act.

In 1944, *Newsweek* magazine made the highly chivalrous claim that Patsy 'looks so like her mother that orchestra leaders cannot tell them apart across footlights'. But the simple reason why Patsy did so well in the role was that she *wasn't* a carbon copy of her mother. She was an acrobatic dancer, not a tap dancer. And her whole style of performance brought something new to the act. Billy Shenton Junior had watched both Bettys from the wings, and was immediately struck by Patsy's approach to the part:

> She was more sinewy, if I can put it that way, than Betty. Betty was a great performer but, as I say, a hoofer. Patsy had this – allure with her, as well. Where Betty used to do this 'come on' business to Joe, Patsy would just do something different. And it was more sensual than it was from Betty. Patsy was playing it straight.

But there was a secret in Patsy's past that made her acrobatic prowess all the more extraordinary. While she was growing up in New York, some typical schoolgirl high spirits had led to a serious accident. Billy Shenton Junior:

The usual chasing through the corridors, you know, and she went to go through a swing door which was shut. It was a plate glass door. She went right through it. And cut herself all up the arm. And they whipped her into hospital there. And it was a weekend, of course. And all they'd got on duty were interns. And they said, 'Oh yeah, yeah, fine.' And they stitched it all up and cleaned it all up and that was it. And, of course, nobody thought of pulling down the sinews and eventually it was too late. It had all seized up. And that's why she'd got this semi-crippled hand – which was very difficult for her. But she then carried on, still doing the acrobatic work, but everything she did, she had to do one-handed.

If you watch any of Patsy's routines filmed in 1943 or 1944 you would not immediately be aware of any problem. But if you study her right arm carefully, it soon becomes clear that she is doing very little with it. The cartwheels and spins are all done one-handed. She moves both arms very gracefully but, at times, her right hand is bent at a slightly unnatural angle. Even when she has finger-cymbals attached to both hands, she only actually plays the ones in her left hand.

So Patsy's arrival brought significant changes to the act. She was more athletic, more energetic, more subtly erotic. And all these skills cleverly concealed her physical limitations. Like Betty, she was carried onstage sitting cross-legged on a platform. In Betty's era, the platform was separated into two halves, each with a drum on top, and Betty would thump out a rhythm on the drums either side of her. But Patsy hadn't the strength or control in her right arm to manage this, so the drums were dispensed with and greater use was made of the finger-cymbals. The audience would hear the regular tinkling rhythm and be quite unaware she was playing them single-handed.

Jack Wilson's extreme generosity and his close friendship with Betty Knox have already been mentioned, and Billy Shenton Junior cites a further example in relation to Patsy:

> During her career, once she was over here, both before she went in the act and afterwards, Jack spared no expense whatsoever in having her seen by all the finest orthopaedic surgeons in the country. He spent a small fortune on it. And they all said, 'Well, you know, if we'd done it at the time, fine. But this has been left too long.'

The tour of *Hello America*, which had seen three different Bettys during the course of its run, concluded at the Ipswich Hippodrome in July 1942. The following week Patsy made her London debut with the trio at the Streatham Hill Theatre. Betty and Patsy's respective roles were described thus by Hannen Swaffer:

> The daughter does a humorous snake dance at the Stoll Theatre every night – and the mother goes into the *Evening Standard* office every morning.

On 12th December 1942, Betty Knox made a radio appearance on the BBC Home Service. The programme was that long-running interview show *In Town Tonight* (also the title of her 1935 movie). Each week the strains of the 'Knightsbridge March' by Eric Coates were cross-faded to an effects record of a busy street. A voice shouted 'Stop!' and the buses and cars were abruptly silenced. The announcer dramatically intoned: 'Once more we stop the mighty roar of London's traffic …' and the programme began. The guests in this particular edition included Linda Chinn ('who has cycled across the Sahara Desert and the Alps'), Dame Sybil Thorndike ('the famous actress who has recently been touring Wales'), Chris Gibbons ('singing miner') …

… and Miss Betty Knox ('an actress who is now a journalist').

14
It's the Kind of World I Want

(Britain 1943)

'Even you wouldn't dare.' (Betty Knox, 1943)

AT THE TIME BETTY KNOX WAS ON ITS STAFF, the *London Evening Standard* had considerable Socialist leanings. Soon after she joined, Frank Owen was called up and joined the army's Royal Tank Corps. Owen's place as editor was taken by Michael Foot (who would later become leader of the Labour party). As is clear from her 1944 interview with Marcel Wallenstein, these were Betty's politics too:

> 'I like newspaper work,' she said, 'Also, I saw the English when they were up against it. When you see such things I suppose it binds you to the people enduring them. I listened to Michael Foot and Frank Owen and began to understand a little what kind of a world they want. They may not get it. Anyhow, I'd like to help. It's the kind of world I want.'

As a journalist who was not only new to the paper, but also new to journalism, Betty had much to learn. She was set to work contributing items to the Londoner's Diary – a page of short pieces about politicians and celebrities of particular local interest to the London readership. No journalists are credited on this page, so we have no way of knowing which items Betty was responsible for. All we do know is that the newspaper's proprietor, Lord Beaverbrook, was not pleased with everything he read there. Lord Beaverbrook, whose own politics were staunchly Tory, was a powerful press baron who also owned the *Daily Express* and *Sunday Express*. In his archived correspondence with the *Evening Standard* he doesn't appear to meddle excessively with his editor's decisions, but after reading one particular Londoner's Diary, he dashed off this fierce missive to Michael Foot:

> These Diary notes ... will not do. They contain phrases which would be quite inappropriate in the *Evening Standard*.

He goes on to quote some examples:

> 'Notable appreciation', 'Deserves to be preserved', 'Generations yet unborn', 'Bore his burdens bravely' (that is how I am bearing my burdens inflicted by these Notes), 'I would not be surprised to learn', 'Outstanding characteristic'.

This letter was written on 20th January 1943, a little over a year after Betty had joined the staff. Whether any of the offending phrases are hers, we don't know. It's likely she would have been picked up on similar verbal transgressions many times in her early days. Some of them don't even seem particularly wrong, but a 'style guide' to journalists working on the Londoner's Diary was issued from time to time (and doubtless shortly after 20th January) in a bid to stamp out lazy journalism – including such sound advice as 'Avoid clichés like the plague.' Those professors and pedants who got particularly distressed by sloppy journalese could be assured that there would be no lowering of standards at the *Standard*.

While Betty was watching her words, Jack, Joe and Patsy were touring the country in Jack Hylton's new show *Hi-de-Hi*. Flanagan and Allen topped the bill and joined the trio in a Middle East scene, which included a specially penned song 'The Desert's in my Hair' by Dickie Hurran. Later in the show, impressionist Florence Desmond provided a 'To Be or Not To Be' routine, imagining various celebrities' views on the controversial issue of Sunday opening. But perhaps the biggest controversy of the show was its title. *Hi-de-Hi* sounds innocent enough but, in the same issue of *The Stage* which heralded the production, there were two display ads by clearly disgruntled fellow pros. The first said:

> NOTICE Tony Legate's new show is 'HO-DE-HO' (Title Fully Protected)

The second, from comic Hal Monty (who, together with showbiz colossus Bernard Delfont, had once trod the boards as dance duo The Delfont Boys) proclaimed:

> On Saturday, April 3, from 'Music Hall', I Broadcast a Song entitled 'Hi-De-Hi, Ho-De-Ho'. Anyone infringing on Copyright, TAKE HEED

After all those apparent threats of hi-de-high court injunctions, the film studios would have been an oasis of calm for Patsy. In June 1943, *Variety Jubilee* hit the British screens. Quite a spectacular affair from the small-scale (and even smaller budget) studios of Butcher's Film Services, it told the tale of a music hall run by three generations of the same family. Gus Elen and Florrie Forde were portrayed by other artistes, Marie Lloyd by her own daughter, and music hall veterans George Robey and nonagenarian Charles Coborn appeared as themselves. Wilson, Keppel and Betty filmed four routines (probably their entire act). Fortunately all four routines survive, and may have featured in a longer cut of the film. The version most commonly available has only one routine – the sand dance, featuring just Wilson and Keppel. Apart from a rather splendid backcloth depicting the Egyptian pyramids, it differs very little from previous movie versions, although Joe Keppel is at times almost indecently close to the rear end of Jack Wilson, no doubt provoking waves of raucous audience laughter at their pokerfaced antics.

A couple of months after the release of *Variety Jubilee*, Wilson and Keppel made a rare appearance without Betty, but as a trio with George D'Ormonde (a comedy acrobatic cyclist who, like Wilson and Keppel, had extensively toured the States during the 1920s and 30s). It was a fundraiser staged by the Water Rats, that well-known showbiz charitable organisation. The turn they provided that night demonstrated talents that hadn't been publicly aired since those far off days of American vaudeville. *The Stage* of 16th September 1943 reported on the evening:

> Wilson and Keppel, the dancers, with George D'Ormonde followed with a burlesque of an old-time singing trio, 'Corn, Cob, and Corn', of which the joke was seen when they were told to go back to their usual acts.

A month or so earlier, Betty Knox had been partying with fellow journalists including a young American (ten years Betty's junior) called Walter Cronkite. In the 1960s and 70s he would become the highly respected anchorman for CBS News but, at the start of 1943, he had arrived in London to cover America's involvement in the war for the United Press news agency. A series of letters he wrote to his wife Betsy form the basis of the book *Cronkite's War: His World War II Letters Home*. On 4th August he wrote of events a couple of days earlier:

> Monday night things picked up a little bit. Betty Knox is going to the hospital this week (today, come to think of it) and so was throwing a Dutch Treat party for herself. I met her, Salisbury and Dickinson at the King and Keys pub next to the *Daily Telegraph* building in Fleet Street, we had a drink there with Jack Tait and Eric Hawkins of the *New York Herald-Trib* and Doug Werner of our office ...

Harrison Salisbury was Cronkite's boss, the London editor of United Press, and Bill Dickinson was another UP correspondent. Betty's 'Dutch Treat' (a night out where everybody paid their own way) then led on to the Savoy hotel where they met up with *Life* photographer Dave Scherman, Lee Miller from *Vogue* (a photographic model turned photojournalist) and Kathleen McCaughlan from *The Times*. In Cronkite's letter of the next day, he continued the story:

> Well, we sat at a corner table of the American Bar. Dickinson sat at one end of the semi-circular bench and I sat at the other end and Knox said it looked like a minstrel show, so you can guess where that went.

Betty was recalling the opening of the traditional American minstrel show, when the performers (in black-face makeup) would enter singing a popular song until, at the 'gentlemen be seated' command of the eloquent Mr Interlocutor, they'd sit in a semi-circle around him. Mr Interlocutor would then play straight-man to the slow-witted characters on each end of the row (Tambo and Bones) in a series of 'schoolboy howler' pun-based gags. Seated on that bench in the Savoy, Cronkite (rising to Betty's bait) proceeded to crack a succession of groaners with Bill Dickinson as stooge. After the Savoy, they set off for the White Tower, a Greek restaurant just off Tottenham Court Road, close to the Ministry of Information:

> So the whole gang piled into a couple of taxis and went to the White Tower and sat at a table outside in front of the place where the urchins in that somewhat bombed tenement district could lean over the rail and breathe into your food.

What Cronkite's account vividly illustrates is that Betty Knox was now keeping company with the very best British and American reporters. She had risen through the ranks at the *Evening Standard* and was as popular a companion in journalistic circles as she had been amongst variety pros. In the months following her hospital visit on 4th August, her diligence in speedily mastering her trade won further recognition. Editor Michael Foot offered her the chance to emerge from the anonymity of Londoner's Diary. Marcel Wallenstein:

> When Foot succeeded Owen as editor he asked Betty Knox to write a small piece daily about the American forces in Britain. She responded so liberally Foot gave her the column. It is, by any reckoning, ably done. The public likes it and the US army likes it even better. Her colleagues, American war correspondents in London, consider Betty Knox, small, determined, shrewd, hard working, a worthy member of their tribe.

And these two paragraphs come from a January 1944 article in *Newsweek*:

> A favorite of British and Continental dance halls for some fifteen years, Kansas-born Betty Knox by last week had become the favorite of the large wartime colony of Americans in London. But her transatlantic triumph was not on the stage. It was, instead, in the pages of the *London Evening Standard* where, thrice weekly, she conducts her column: 'Betty Knox's USA – Over Here'.
>
> Last October, Betty made a splash with her own idea, a breezy column about the thousands of American soldiers, sailors, Marines, Wacs, nurses and ordinary citizens below diplomatic rank who have been drawn to London by war service. Into her 600-word stint she packed their arrivals, departures, doings, difficulties, and deeds.

If ever there was a journalist perfectly equipped to educate the Americans about the British, and vice versa, it was Betty Knox. She had travelled throughout America, the UK, and a fair amount of Europe. And, wherever she had been, she had talked, listened and learned. And the best thing about this column, after the straitjacket that was Londoner's Diary, was that she could write in her own style. Americanisms wouldn't be frowned upon, they would be positively encouraged – as long as they were translated for the benefit of the British readership.

Betty's column 'Over Here' (a subtle allusion to the jokey British description of American servicemen: 'Overpaid, oversexed and over here') made an instant impact, commencing with an interview between Betty and novelist John Steinbeck. He was fluent in Italian, and had just returned from Capri, where he'd been working as a war correspondent with the American navy:

> He doesn't like to talk about his books and is shy about being an author, but he showed me his favourite piece of writing with understandable pride.
>
> On a ragged piece of paper were the surrender terms for Capri. Steinbeck helped to write them. The surrendering commanders obligingly signed an extra copy.
>
> He also wrote the stuff that was broadcast through the loudspeakers over enemy lines. He says: 'I guess I'm the only novelist who didn't go to Capri to write a romantic novel.'

That was the first item from Betty's first column, on Friday 15ᵗʰ October 1943. Next day's column included a review of an American self-help manual: 'Letter Writing in War Time' by G. A. Reeder:

> No matter what your type is Mr Reeder has sound advice in sample letters, which include everything from 'my enchantress' to 'sugar pie' and 'my hero' right down to 'super-duper lover'.
>
> If you think you are a great lover Mr. Reeder makes you think again. If you are pen tied, he shows you how to let down your hair.

And Betty was most definitely letting down her hair. Indeed, you can almost picture her applying a match to her copy of the *Evening Standard* journalists' style guide as she types. This column was going to be friendly, informal, and very, very American. In short – it was going to be Betty. And every Monday, Friday and Saturday there would be more of the same. The columns were sometimes headed by serious war news:

> The US Eighth Air Force destroyed 600 enemy airplanes in raids over Germany this month. The Schweinfurt raid alone accounted for 104. Fighters brought down 13 of these.

But, by the bottom of the page, the style would relax, and Betty would relate some quirky tale in language that would have Lord Beaverbrook weeping into his brandy:

Sergeant James Piccini gets more letters than anyone else. He has worn out the postman at an Eighth Air Force base, who has delivered 441 letters to Piccini in 13 months.

Piccini (a Damon Runyon fan) says they are all from his ever-lovin' wife Ellen, who lives in Quincy, Mass. He will bet anyone £10 he is the all-American-British champion letter-getter.

Such was the impact of Betty's column that, just two weeks (and six columns) into its run, Hannen Swaffer published his in-depth interview with Betty, including one tale far too hot for the *Standard*:

Betty goes about, as a rule, in rough tweeds and without a hat. She always rushes up with a new story that no one will print and the comment, 'Even you wouldn't dare,' chuckles in a husky contralto, and then wants to know what the hell the Government's going to do about Greece, or something.

A typical burst-in of hers was her recent story, which no one would print, about how John Winant came out of the Embassy one night, and, seeing two American soldiers outside, said, with his usual modest courtesy, 'Can I help you?'

When they asked, 'Are there any dames in this joint?' he knew they didn't mean stenographers.

'But this is the American Embassy,' said Winant, 'and I am the Ambassador.'

'Say, those limeys must have been pulling our leg,' growled one of the men.

And they wandered into the darkness.

Betty's 'Over Here' columns contained a fair smattering of celebrity and showbiz news. At the end of October she reported: 'Britain's theatre boom has reached such a peak that shows for West End consumption are exiled in the provinces waiting for a London home.' Fortunately, the revue *Hi-de-Hi* had been at the Palace Theatre in London since the start of June, so Betty saw a good deal of her daughter Patsy, and of Jack Wilson. Betty was still lodging at Olivelli's, 35 Store Street – where Jack also stayed whenever he was working in London. If Betty was any kind of 'night owl', which by habit and vocation she always had been, it gave her the chance to throw off her journalistic hat (not that she wore one) and party with all her old friends, who had now become her daughter's new friends.

Which brings us to the first of Patsy's 'deleted scenes' from *Variety Jubilee*. The curtains are whisked apart to reveal Wilson and Keppel dashing round the stage in a circle, carrying Patsy on the usual long, low platform with handles projecting from either side. This is the way they'd opened the act since adopting the title 'Cleopatra's Nightmare'. The platform was an ingenious prop which doubled as a tidy storage place for their various musical instruments – so they could slickly bring everything on at the start, and remove it all at the end.

Patsy sits cross-legged on the platform while the two men circumnavigate the stage. The men are wearing their fezzes and long dark-coloured shifts ending well below the knee. Patsy is wearing a bikini top and short flowing skirt. Her headdress is veil-like, though not obscuring her face. As she dismounts and starts her dance, the whole impression (in both costume and moves) is closer to a Hawaiian hula-hula dancer than an Egyptian queen – but it's foreign and exotic, so that's close enough.

Betty Knox had always been the flapper with the frantic feet, but Patsy (aged 19 at this time) succeeds in cooling the tempo while raising the temperature. In other words – those swaying hips and waving arms are pretty hot stuff.

The orchestra gives us a few bars from 'The Streets of Cairo' (otherwise known as the Hootchy-Kootchy dance) while Patsy sways and ripples. The men work themselves up into a musical frenzy. Wilson blows on some strident rudimentary oboe, while Keppel bangs a small drum against his hand, his stomach, his buttocks – in fact, pretty well everywhere – in quick succession. Then Patsy moves from one to the other, enticing them with the faint chink-chink of the finger cymbals (or the 'nudge bells' as the trio called them). The two men have now decided to play hard to get, and stand haughtily unmoved with disdainful expressions and their arms crossed. Perhaps the indifference of the men is a result of a sleep-like trance? (Incidentally, it's clear that Patsy is only using the finger cymbals in her left hand. Her right hand is unnaturally bent back, showing she had little strength in it at the time.)

Eventually, having failed to rouse any response from the pair, Patsy gracefully drifts away. Jack and Joe now decide to ape her movements, arms in the air, then hopping on one leg, then waving their arms, and then as if juggling. (It's worth comparing this with Betty Knox's nautch dance from *On the Air*. The men's gestures are a far closer match to Betty's moves than they are to Patsy's.)

They turn their backs on us and, in time with the percussionist thwacking the rim of the drum, they rhythmically thrust their buttocks from side to side. As the music starts to resemble Grieg's 'Hall of the Mountain King' they circle each other, followed by a few more of Keppel's trademark thrusts close to his partner's rear, before Wilson seats himself on the platform (posing as Patsy did at the start of the scene) while Keppel wheels him offstage. Like most of their routines, what it all means is anyone's guess – but much of the comedy comes from the clear inference that Wilson and Keppel are far more interested in each other than in the seductive charms of their Betty.

Meanwhile, Betty Knox's column continued – with its frequent stark reminders that the war was right on our doorstep. Though, if there was any opportunity to inject a little gentle humour into her report, she would make the most of it:

> Two of America's most distinguished generals, guided by a Scotland Yard detective, went on the usual London sight-seeing tour yesterday. After looking at the bomb damage for some time they politely hinted that they guessed they'd better go home now.
>
> The detective reluctantly admitted that he was lost. He had not been in the City since the blitz and the landmarks he knew were all gone. An American lieutenant-colonel finally guided them to the correct bus stop.

She got a lot of fun out of a booklet called 'A Short Guide to Britain' which was handed out to all American troops as they arrived here. It contained the following couple of gems:

> 'The Upper-Crust speak pretty much alike. You will hear a BBC announcer pronounce all the A's in banana (curious example) like the A in father.
>
> 'Be comforted by the fact that a man from Cornwall would have as much trouble as you in understanding a man from Lancashire.'

There was also the occasional insight into the eccentricities of fellow journalists:

> Fastest talker is British Frank Williams, who nightly telephones the war news to New York at a speed of anything up to 300 words a minute. Williams works for the London bureau of the *New York Herald-Tribune*.

His telephone is at the MoI.

Calls vary from five to 10 minutes. He seldom stops for breath and keeps his voice in a high-pitched monotone, retaining the same volume throughout. Listeners wonder what language he is speaking.

The speech is recorded in the *Herald Tribune* office in New York. When it is slowed down, what sounds remarkably like excited Chinese in London becomes normal English. It reaches the news desk within two or three minutes of being telephoned.

Reasons for the Williams technique are time and money. Williams is 42 and married. He says his wife doesn't think he talks very fast.

One frequently recurring topic was that of food and drink. In particular, the American taste bud – and the culinary revolution it was currently inciting. For instance, NAAFI (Navy, Army and Air Force Institutes) canteens were now serving hot dogs:

> Since 1ˢᵗ November instructions and recipes for American dishes have gone to British NAAFI canteen cooks. Whenever supplies allow, they will have other American foods, such as Shortcake, Johnny-cake, pumpkin and apple pie, doughnuts, muffins, hamburgers.
>
> A recipe for coffee was included in the instructions. Both the Americans and NAAFI are pessimistic about this.

This would not be the last time that Betty cast aspersions on the British nation's inability to serve up a proper cup of coffee. There was one other item of 'hot' stuff also missing from the menu, due to wartime shortages. As Betty solemnly announced, American burlesque dancer Sally Rand had been forced to amend her programme:

> Sally Rand will not do her bubble dance when she comes over to entertain troops, because the firm that makes her bubbles is too busy making rubber lifebelts.

Luckily, or perhaps unluckily, Sally still had her famous ostrich feather fans to cover her modesty. It must have brought back memories of Betty's own considerably less risqué performance in the dance of the seven veils. (Sally Rand was actually two years older than Betty, and continued fan dancing well into her 60s.)

But fan dancing wasn't an exclusively American spectator sport. Britain's own Phyllis Dixey had recently introduced striptease to London's West End – in a clear trend towards more 'adult' content in variety shows. Around this time Wilson, Keppel and Betty appeared on the same bill with her, at the Brixton Empress. This would be the first of many times when their dance of the seven veils (which consisted of very little 'strip' and a whole lot of 'tease') featured alongside a far more explicit version of an identical format.

And so to Deleted Scene number two: The Dance of the Seven Veils according to Wilson, Keppel and Betty. Patsy's immediate predecessor, Eunice Roberts, talked me through the whole routine, so I'll integrate some of Eunice's commentary into my description.

Patsy wafts on to the stage, completely swathed in large flowing veils. Her face is completely covered, other than a small strip around her eyes. (One critic uncharitably nicknamed this routine the Dance of the Seven Army Blankets. She is, admittedly, something of a shapeless mass at the outset.) She waves her arms and spins, forming tantalising shapes under her coverings.

Wilson and Keppel then break the mood by strolling on in their Egyptian headdresses, wheeling on another of their handy gadget assemblages. This one incorporates a large deep basket with a small hand-drum fixed on each side and a gong. They sit behind it, start a rhythmic drumbeat with the back of their hands, then produce two snake charmer's pipes, which they play shrilly and tunelessly as Patsy continues to dance. A large snake emerges phallically from the basket (operated by Jack – yet another nifty contraption from the pair's prop-making workshop) and becomes a third spectator, far more transfixed by the charms of Patsy than of the two pipe players behind him. Patsy casts off the first veil, the one partially covering her face. Keppel displays the veil to the audience, Wilson strikes the gong, and Keppel holds up one finger:

> *Eunice*: Then I had one, two, three, four – four veils down here, pinned onto the dress. I took each veil off and did a comedy bit with them.

Patsy removes the second veil. Another bang on the gong and Keppel (none too subtly) raises two fingers to the audience. The third veil comes off, another gong-bang, and the men beat their chests, drum and clap, chanting something suitably primitive and incomprehensible. Keppel helps Patsy off with the rather long fourth veil, which is appropriately gonged and counted. Wilson gets up and imitates Patsy's hip-wiggling while assisting in the removal of veil number five:

Eunice: I was only young. I had a great figure. My legs were the best part. They used to go mad about my legs.

As Patsy teases Keppel with a glimpse of bare leg, temptation gets the better of him. He leaps up and grabs her leg. Wilson sternly admonishes him. He sheepishly returns to his seat and the pair continues drumming:

Eunice: And then the garment that was covering me up, I just used to pull it and it came off, and I threw that at them.

Patsy discards the sixth veil, which lands on Keppel's head. The gong is struck and six fingers displayed. As Patsy dances ever closer, the snake takes particular interest, extending his long tongue towards her with the rasp of a party blower, making Patsy flee for safety:

Eunice: They had a snake coming up from the basket. They used to go like that (*blowing out the snake's tongue*) and stick it up my bum as I walked past them.

(Jack blew the party-blower tongue himself, by means of a long rubber tube running from the end of his snake-charmer's pipe up into the snake's head – at the same moment as Joe blew into a comedy sound effects device with a rubber bladder to provide the 'razz'.)

Patsy crouches beneath the final voluminous veil. She whispers to Keppel that the glorious moment has arrived. The men drum and chant with increased fervour as the music builds. They advance upon Patsy. Wilson holds up seven fingers while Keppel, with one hand covering his eyes, tugs at the veil:

Eunice: I was turned towards the back and I had my back to the stalls. And they just whipped that one off. On the back of my head I had a mask of one of them, and their outfit on the back of me, like a little shirt thing with a belt.

We are faced with what appears to be either Wilson or Keppel's long-lost brother, with Egyptian headdress and costume, mustachioed and bare-legged. Patsy proceeds to dance as if facing the audience, but actually with her back to them. The dance is extraordinarily comic and grotesque, like a marionette. A lot of hopping, jumping and sliding her legs rapidly together and apart. Sometimes she crosses her arms, apparently across her chest but really behind her back. Finally, after some spectacular star jumps, she turns and reveals how it was done. Wilson and Keppel (who had dashed off the moment the dance started) are happy to leave the final moments of the act entirely to Patsy.

Of course, this surprise ending had been in place ever since Jack, Joe and Betty Knox first devised the routine, but Patsy was able to provide that extra acrobatic zip to its final moments.

Betty Knox's column had news of a different type of entertainment – the 'Show-mobile'. This was a 'theatre-on-wheels' which the American Red Cross was using to provide entertainment for the US forces in Britain:

> These land-borne 'show-boats' are converted Green Line buses, and are self-contained midget theatres, complete with dressing-rooms, loud speakers, lighting equipment, costumes, sleeping bunks, and a company of 18 entertainers. There is a let-down stage for outdoor use when halls are not available.

As if it needed to be said, Betty pointed out that in these shows 'the accent is on girls'. And the producers had located a ready supply:

> They knew the British theatre and the people who make it, but they have found a new theatre. In the back-lines of British choruses they discovered pretty girls who could step out of line and do a specialty. Lots of them are discoveries, and are getting a chance to prove it.

And, if anyone had personal experience of being plucked out of the chorus line, it was Betty. So now the GIs had the girls. But they were still missing a decent cup of coffee:

> Americans are not interested in 'what's cooking' – if it's British coffee – and this column keeps getting requests for American coffee recipes.

There follows detailed instructions for preparing 'Hobo' coffee, drip coffee and percolated coffee, with this final crucial serving suggestion:

> American coffee is never served with hot milk, and must always be at least as hot as the hottest cup of tea.

But Christmas was coming and, in December 1943, Wilson, Keppel and Betty took part in a big show at His Majesty's Theatre, London, for members of the fighting services. *The Stage* revealed an impressive line-up:

Amongst those due to appear are Leslie Henson, Kenway and Young, Will Hay, Flanagan and Allen, Wilson, Keppel and Betty, Eddie Gray, Beatrice Lillie, Hermione Baddeley, Gavin Gordon, Dave Hutchison, Francis Day, Arthur Askey, Anne Shelton, Medlock and Marlowe, Vera Lynn, The Cairoli Brothers, the Ganjou Brothers and Juanita, and the Colleano Brothers.

It's probable that Patsy performed her solo dance on this night. It was a regular part of the act, and a welcome break (and costume change opportunity) for the two men. And it's also our final *Variety Jubilee* deleted scene.

Patsy, her dark shoulder-length hair this time without headdress, wears a bikini top and a long, flowing floor-length skirt, split to allow for some high kicks and acrobatics. Again her movements are Hawaiian in style – arm waving, hip rotating and spinning round. She does a few two-handed cartwheels (though, as in previous routines, her right arm is hardly used at all). She really plays up to the theatre/movie audience with many of her seductive movements. At one point she spreads her arms and leans backwards so the back of her head is virtually waist height. She straightens up and goes straight into a handstand. Then a series of seven or eight one-handed cartwheels, circling round the stage. More of the exotic Hawaiian arm waving and slow high kicks, then three more one-handed cartwheels, this time from one side of the stage to the other. A final few hula-hula moves, then into the big finish – six circular cartwheels, but this time with no hands on the floor at all. It's an astonishing end to a highly proficient acrobatic display.

When you compare it with any of Betty Knox's solo numbers, it emphasises once again the contrasting talents and personalities of mother and daughter – and perhaps the different generations of dancers to which they belong. Both routines conclude with a breathtaking display of spinning round in circles (in Betty's case, while tap-dancing) and both are a reminder that their contribution to the act is far more than good looks and nice legs. (Which, with Wilson and Keppel around, are certainly in short supply.)

But it is December 1943 and, in case we'd forgotten, the war is ever present. Although much of Betty's column came as welcome light relief, there were more sombre items too. At the start of December she interviewed fellow journalist Helen Kirkpatrick of the *Chicago Daily*

News. Helen was the first female war correspondent to have been to the Italian front. Betty let Helen do most of the talking:

> 'The Corsican mountains are no health resort if you are looking for an American detachment in the middle of the night, with guerilla patriots – trigger conscious about Germans – taking pot-shots at you with Sten guns.
>
> 'We abandoned the jeep after 20 miles, when the road narrowed down to a foot-wide ledge hanging over a precipice. That was all German dynamiters had left.
>
> 'Ducking bullets, we walked 10 miles to Bastia.'

Thankfully, for the most part, the Germans had left the area a couple of days previously:

> 'In the morning we found the town square empty – if you don't count about 100 dead Germans.'

15
Zowie
(Britain January–June 1944)

'So on occasions Miss Knox is a very miserable journalist indeed.'
(Marcel Wallenstein, 1944)

BETTY KNOX'S *EVENING STANDARD* COLUMN CONTINUED, three times a week, without a break throughout the first four months of 1944. This was Betty's own view of the war in Betty's own words. We start in January, with a peculiarly English entertainment that she'd witnessed many times, from both sides of the footlights:

> If you see an American soldier at a pantomime, it will probably be the first one he has ever seen. There are no pantomimes in America, and American dictionaries say the word means 'a dumb show of any kind'.
>
> To the GI, it means Charlie Chaplin – before he went in for talkies – or anyone who acts without talking.
>
> The GI doesn't believe in Humpty Dumpty or Cinderella, but when he breaks down and sneaks into a 'kid' show he becomes an ardent fan, and wants to know how long this has been going on.
>
> An American colonel has been here for four years off and on. He had seen all the pantomimes, and was glad to get back from Africa in time to see this year's batch.

She also quoted this poem, written by an unknown American radio-operator-gunner on a Flying Fortress before a raid on Italy:

> Oh, Hedy Lamarr is a beautiful gal, and Madeleine Carroll too.
> But you'll find, if you query, a different theory

Amongst any bomber crew.

For the loveliest thing of which one could sing (this side of the heavenly
    gates)

Is no blonde or brunette of the Hollywood set – but an escort of P38s.

Then there was a story that illustrated future US president General
Eisenhower's zero tolerance policy towards any bickering based on
nationality. (And there must have been plenty of that as British and
American troops attempted to work alongside each other.) He is telling
off an American colonel (Colonel X) for arguing with his opposite
British number (Colonel Y):

> 'You lost your temper; that's understandable. I do it myself. We all do
> under the strains of this job. I'm informed you called Colonel Y a
> blankety-blank. I can understand that too; soldiers use soldier language
> at times. But what I will not stand for is the fact that you called him a
> "British" blankety-blank. For that I'm sending you home.'

For sheer wartime drama, the following account of a Flying Fortress
returning to England after a bombing raid takes some beating.
Bombadier, 1st Lieut. Enver C. Cury pressed the switch to dump their
remaining incendiary bombs in the Channel. However, six of the
incendiaries remained jammed in the bomb bay:

> The bomb veins, which automatically set the bombs off after enough
> revolutions, were spinning merrily in the rush of wind that came
> through the open bomb bay.
>
> Cury aimed frantic kicks at the bombs, hanging precariously over
> nothing but 24,000 ft. of space and a lot of water. Efforts to dislodge
> them by hand were futile.
>
> His walk-around oxygen bottle swung back and forth, threatening to
> break his grip. He finally pulled off the mask in desperation. The ball
> turret gunner, Sergeant John E. Shaffer had come to his aid. The crew
> prepared to bail out.
>
> Cury says: 'I was trying to work out a desperate mathematical
> problem: how many revolutions does it take to set these things off? I
> blacked out before I got around to the answer.'
>
> The pilot grabbed him by the seat of his pants just in time to save
> him from a record high dive. He wasn't wearing a parachute. The
> airplane had settled down to about 16,000 feet when he came to. He
> went back to work.

At that altitude he could not work without mask or gloves. With the aid of Shaffer he managed to dislodge the six bombs.

In February, Betty interviewed a rising star with close family connections to Wilson and Keppel. Colleano's Circus in Australia was where the 'Wilson and Keppel' double-act had originated. Now 19-year-old Bonar (pronounced 'Bonner') Colleano was putting his authentic New York accent to use in West End revue *Sweeter and Lower*:

> GIs in last night's audience have seen a lot of Bonar's relations. Few American kids have not seen Ringling Brothers' Circus – it played everywhere – and where there is a Ringling's there are bound to be some Colleanos. That goes for the theatre, too.
>
> Bonar's father and mother are rehearsing for a new George Black show after closing at the Palladium. It's a big family and they do amazing things.
>
> Uncle Maurice, comedy acrobatic star, now playing in Britain, can accomplish a complete double somersault from floor to floor under his own steam. Uncle Con, wire walker, can and does turn a forward somersault on the wires.
>
> The young Colleano rejects the long line of tradition. His aunts have hung precariously on their heels better than anyone else's aunts ever did. His grandfather, a giant Irishman, took all comers for £5 a try in boxing bouts in his own circus. His grandmother was Australia's greatest equestrian star.
>
> Young Colleano doesn't care, he'd rather be Bob Hope.

At around this time a short movie compilation of variety acts, entitled *Starlight Serenade*, was in the cinemas. Every act featured is named in the opening credits, concluding with the announcement: 'And introducing Bonar Colleano'. He makes an amiable compere, wise-cracking, trading American slang with singer Ike Hatch, doing impressions and even turning to the cinema audience and apologising for an old gag. Wilson, Keppel and Betty are also in the movie – once again doing their 'nudge bells' routine and sand dance. But of especial interest is the fact that Patsy Knox shares a brief scene with Bonar – and, despite being one-third of a famously mute act, she actually gets to speak.

The dapper dinner-jacketed Bonar, with the simple addition of a rudimentary Indian turban, becomes fortune teller 'The Great Colleano'.

He spots Patsy bending to adjust her stocking suspenders, revealing a considerable expanse of bare thigh in the process, and decides to offer his services. 'What's the matter? Hangover?' she says, pointing to his turban. He holds out his hand and (with the aid of a jump cut) a crystal ball materialises. To Patsy's delight he says he can see a lover – dark and romantic, with flashing eyes. He flashes his own eyes and Patsy, realising his intentions, says acidly, 'Isn't his nose rather long?' Slightly hurt, he focuses on a fresh vision in his crystal. Swaying palms, giant pyramids, golden sands stretching away to the blue horizon. He holds the ball ever closer to the camera and the shot dissolves into Patsy in full costume for the 'nudge bells' sequence.

The Wilson, Keppel and Betty routines are well shot, with many close-ups – possibly because the film studio appears to be no larger than the average living room. When the camera angle changes, we are viewing the act almost sideways on. Particularly odd is the sand dance, which appears later in the film. At the start, we see Jack unfold the four-sectioned, hinged wooden sand-board used in place of the earlier rolled carpet. Throughout the routine there are cutaways to Wilson and Keppel's legs and, during the final moments, the camera is firmly glued to their lower appendages. They and the music come to a halt, and there is a slow and laborious pan up their motionless bodies, eventually reaching their faces and raised arms.

When the bells have had their final nudge, we return to the crystal ball. Bonar turns to Patsy, though naturally he doesn't call her by that name. He is still envisaging her future, and plotting to be part of it. 'You know, Betty, I was just thinking …'

'Yes, I know – you beast!'

Patsy slaps his face and flounces off. He is so enamoured with her that it takes a moment for him to remember to say 'Ow!'

Betty Knox's voice was described by Hannen Swaffer as 'a husky contralto'. Patsy is less husky than her mother (perhaps she wasn't such a heavy smoker) but her voice is surprisingly low with a purring lilt to it, and (for someone who had been living here for the past six years) still totally American. Her style of acting and reacting is very assured and a good deal more natural than most other performers in this movie.

Bonar Colleano was at the start of a successful British stage and movie career, often cast as cocky GIs or slick crooks, in films like *The*

Way to the Stars, A Matter of Life and Death, Good-Time Girl and *Sleeping Car to Trieste*. On stage he played Stanley, opposite Vivien Leigh, in *A Streetcar Named Desire*. In 1958 he died in a car crash, aged 34. His son, actor Mark Colleano, was brought up by Bonar's mother, Rubye Colleano, and the two of them met up with Jack Wilson several times in his later years.

In *Starlight Serenade*, singer Ike Hatch and Bonar indulge in what he calls 'a verbal jam session'. ('I'm like the bear, I ain't nowhere.' 'Well, shoot the flipper to me, dipper.') And, at the start of March, similar terminology was peppering Betty Knox's column. Lord Beaverbrook would just have to grit his teeth while Betty reviewed *Hi There! High School*, a book about teen slang, by an American teenage girl whose own name (to contemporary ears) also has slang overtones – Gay Head:

Here are some expressions with definitions:

Drip – 'A wet smack of the human species'
On fire – 'Super-colossal'
Gruesome twosome – 'A couple who go steady'
Jackson – 'Anyone. Most often used in addressing a smooth-looking boy'
Shove in your clutch – 'Get going'
You shredit wheat – 'You figure it out'
Zowie – 'The top current exclamation denoting approval, astonishment or dismay'

When you run across the familiar abbreviation AWOL do not think you are on firm ground, read on and you will find that it has nothing to do with the traditional 'absent without leave'. According to Miss Head, it means 'a wolf on the loose'.

She doesn't bother to define wolf. 'Even the middle-aged understand standard slang,' she says.

A couple of weeks later, on 19th March 1944, Marcel Wallenstein's substantial article on Betty Knox (from which I've previously quoted) appeared in *The Kansas City Star*. Wallenstein is clearly very struck by Betty's feisty attitude. In fact, pretty much every mention she's had (in books, newspapers and magazines) paints an identical picture. She is always herself. And if she isn't happy about something, she won't keep quiet about it. Even if it means openly criticising her employer to a fellow journalist, who is hardly going to omit such strong stuff from his article:

> Lord Beaverbrook frequently uses one of the nine telephones on his desk to blast a paragraph from her column. To date the Beaver has personally killed all her best stories, including the one of the American army private who paid $50 to a stranger in Hyde Park for a barrage balloon and complained the next day to Scotland Yard when it failed to arrive. As Betty Knox wanted to tell the story, the same man had bought Brooklyn Bridge in New York before he left home and wanted the balloon to protect his property.
>
> His lordship would have none of this or any other news or comment which might gnaw at the foundations of Anglo-American friendship, to which he is committed. So on occasions Miss Knox is a very miserable journalist indeed.

It would be highly unlikely for Lord Beaverbrook to find himself casually leafing through a copy of *The Kansas City Star*, so he would have remained blissfully ignorant of such blatant insubordination. It all goes to demonstrate Betty Knox's strength of character. As with the tale of the GIs mistaking the American Embassy for a brothel, if Beaverbrook banned the story she'd simply pass it on to someone else. It wasn't that Betty was any less committed to Anglo-American friendship than her boss. But if two friendly nations are sharing a funny story, does it really matter which one is the butt of the joke?

The photograph accompanying Wallenstein's article is rather surprising. You might have expected a carefully posed portrait, or Betty seated at her desk busily typing. Instead, Betty is onstage with Wilson and Keppel, midway through her dance of the seven veils. In a way, it couldn't be more apt. Betty was brash, extrovert, and had absolutely nothing to hide. Wallenstein's final paragraphs paint a vivid picture of the company she was keeping:

> We were in the Savoy grill, filled at that hour with officers of the Allied forces, members of Parliament fresh from the House; actresses, munitions manufacturers, foreign correspondents, profiteers, chiselers, phonies, men who helped smash Rommel at Mareth and men who have merely made money out of the war. They came and they went and many stopped for a word with the Peden girl of Salina.

London hotels were being used for a variety of purposes during the war. It was certainly not 'business as usual' in even the grandest establishments. The Savoy had become a particularly popular meeting (and working) place for journalists:

> We went up to suite 587, where for 1,000 nights Larry Rue, *Chicago Tribune* correspondent, has held court to his familiars who meet there. The talk ran on, as it always does, late into the night. It was time for me to go, and there were no taxis. There are never taxis in London these nights.
>
> Any minute these sirens would sound an air raid, and it is bad walking in the latter day air raids. Too much hot stuff falls from the sky. The hall porter telephoned to say the taxi situation was hopeless.
>
> Betty Knox picked up the telephone, put it down again and said, 'You'll have a taxi in five minutes.' It was there in three minutes. Apparently the lady has a way with taxi drivers, as well as with theatrical managers, newspaper editors and head waiters.

The day after this article appeared, Betty Knox's own column had further hotel gossip (although, for security reasons, she doesn't divulge its name):

> Reginald of the Ritz is not at the Ritz any more. Instead, he is running one of the biggest restaurants in the world in the former grand ballroom of another hotel.
>
> It is an American officers' mess where 6000 hungry men are fed. Maximum charge is 2s. 6d.
>
> In peacetime Reginald's personal touch and hand-picked staff were famous with café society. Today he has a staff of 400, who dish up a meal every 2½ seconds.

According to Betty, the Americans nickname the place Willow Run (after America's biggest aircraft factory) and Spam Land:

> At first Reginald raised an incredulous Ritz eyebrow at some American tastes. But he admits that he likes most of the strange menus.
>
> Only once have brussels sprouts been served since the mess opened. Americans like them until they run into millions.
>
> On the other hand, things like ham with pineapple rate in the 'not-with-a-barge-pole' class with the British. 'Ham with pineapple! Oh, sir.'

If you imagine the wide-eyed lisping outrage of Eric Blore's stuffy English butler in the Astaire-Rogers movie *Top Hat* (as Betty was surely doing) you get the picture. The American hatred of brussels sprouts was a recurring theme in these columns. From her life so far, it appears that Betty was not the kind of person who could be willingly coerced into eating her greens.

Betty's column had featured many interviews with war correspondents, ever since her piece with John Steinbeck on day one. And it was clear that a journalist covering a war needed almost the same level of fitness as the soldiers they worked alongside:

> An American war correspondent went on one of the hardening up trials designed to prepare correspondents for front line service.
>
> After a ride in a jeep and a night in a hand-made foxhole in the quiet of the English countryside, he wound up with rheumatism. A week later he went on a sterner sortie in a US naval airplane over the Bay of Biscay on submarine patrol.
>
> The correspondent wore the customary electrically heated flying suit. After a dozen or so hours he climbed out of the airplane completely cured of aches and pains.

At the start of April 1944, *Variety* reported:

> Jack Wilson of Wilson, Keppel and Betty, missed his first show in 38 years 4th March when taken to hospital with pneumonia.

Jack was back on stage within days of his illness appearing in print. For anyone doing the maths, the date he is now claiming for his performing debut is 1906. You may care to add it to the list.

Betty, however, was in fine fettle, producing a steady stream of quirky and fascinating tales:

> A sucking-pig went to market in London, and a GI bid for it and won. British bidders applauded, and the soldier made his exit, feeling like a victor, with the pig under his arm.
>
> From there on he became increasingly unpopular. No taxi, bus, or tube would take a GI with a pig anywhere. He finally walked to the station with a mobile audience cheering him on his way and with a decidedly red face. At the station he found a sucking pig is livestock – and must go by freight.
>
> The GI gave up at this point and trudged back to the auction to explain the situation. The auctioneer was sympathetic, but explained that the auction was over and that if he took the pig he'd be in the same fix with no transportation for a pig. Would the GI settle for four rabbits

in a sack? He would and did. Rabbits in a sack can travel any way and he got back to camp brooding over roast pork that might have been.

With one foot in the world of the military and the other still planted firmly in her showbiz past, Betty came up with an amazing range of stories. Sometimes those two worlds collided – as with Sergeant John Sweet, who was about to make his big screen debut in *A Canterbury Tale*:

> Michael Powell, British picture producer, wanted a typical GI who could look and act like he was homesick for Oregon and lonely for his girl. He took one look at Sweet and asked the US army to release him for four months.
>
> They said it was OK, but that Johnny couldn't take any money for it, so Johnny turned the £500 over to the National Association for the Advancement of Coloured People, and made the picture.
>
> Sweet, a teacher before the war, used to spend his civilian evenings with an amateur theatre group. He doesn't know whether he can act or not, and says, 'I'm still a school teacher till proved otherwise.'

His decision to donate his fee to the NAACP is a reminder that racial segregation was still commonplace, both back home in America and in the armed forces serving overseas. But movie-making aside, the Americans were 'over here' for one reason only. Betty's stirring opening words on 21st April 1944 were an indication that the waiting was almost over:

> 'Get set. Get ready. Go!'
>
> It is a phrase familiar to every American schoolboy.
>
> The 'getting set' happened at Pearl Harbour; 'getting ready' has been going on ever since. Today, after 2½ years of planning and building up stores, Service of Supply is ready to put an American army on the continent. And keep it there.
>
> That army will tell you that the toughest part is waiting for the final 'Go'.

And not just the army. American war correspondents were receiving parachute training. The 'paraspondents', as Betty called them, were required to complete five jumps to qualify as parachutists:

> The 'chute school is a hard school. In the morning you spend four hours learning to pack parachutes, and you really care how you do it, because

you jump in your own package.

Lunch is followed by four and a half hours of the most gruelling physical training, where every exercise is done until you literally can't do it again. Parachutists are volunteers. Only tough guys get membership cards.

Into May, and the relentless training continues. Though it has its surreal moments:

Yanks are marching in the dull green uniform and black knee-high boots of the German army somewhere in England.

They are taking orders in German. Not because they like it. The grim fashion show is being presented to show American troops what the well-dressed Nazi will wear when invasion forces move into the Continent.

They will also know what German weapons look like, how to use those weapons, how to break them down, reassemble and fire them.

The weaponry comprised German rifles, machine guns and mines – and set dressing included a red swastika on the wall, and dummy Nazi soldiers guarding the door:

Private Frank Duda, from Chicago, says: 'It's a queer predicament, finding myself a former Polish soldier serving in the US army acting the part of a Nazi heel.'

Meanwhile, at the Savoy Hotel, there was no acting going on. These actors really were soldiers:

Lieut.-colonel David Niven spied Major Jimmie Stewart, authentically shy major now in the USAAF, unsuccessfully trying to hide behind a pillar, and stopped by for a chat. Niven is shy, too, and un-Hollywoodish.

In the grill room Second Lieutenant Robert Preston, who was recently seen in the film *Wake Island*, was earnestly talking to two other United States air officers over coffee.

One officer, who had dined with the movie actor every night since he'd arrived, was asked if Robert Preston was planning to make any more pictures:

'Pictures? I didn't know he's ever been in pictures. He never mentioned it.'

Betty's column of 22nd May 1944 included an interview with Fred S.

Ferguson, President of America's Newspaper Enterprise, who had been a war reporter in World War 1. She asked him how the Americans felt about the coming invasion:

'I believe that lack of personal experience of what a bomb can do, and over-enthusiastic reports in American papers of bomb damage of enemy territory have led too many Americans to believe that Germany is practically wiped off the map, cannot take it much longer, and may even be bombed out of the war before the Second Front gets under way.'

At the bottom of the column is one of Betty's stock-in-trade anecdotes. Yet another example of British pomposity being deflated by a wisecracking Yank:

The doorman of a luxury London hotel looked curiously at the unusual tip an American had pressed into his hand. It was a shilling and a penny. Just before he rode away in his taxi the American explained, 'That's a junior grade guinea, isn't it?'

And that was the last story in the last of Betty's 'Over Here' columns. Without a word of farewell, this thin strip of relaxed, friendly gossip – in a paper otherwise stuffed with grammatically flawless but impersonal journalese – just disappeared. And so did Betty, for a week or two. But she wasn't idle. No one was. Because the waiting was over.

6th June 1944 was D-Day (codenamed Operation Overlord) when Allied troops in their hundreds of thousands landed on the beaches of Normandy.

Betty Knox's 'Over Here' did make one final appearance, in a photographic book with text provided by Betty. *Over Here from Over There* was produced to War Economy standards – a slim volume with card covers and no fancy binding. It almost totally lacked the humour of Betty's column. It was a brief history of British and American co-operation in times of war, told in a style that was relentlessly and flag-wavingly patriotic. Betty wrote what was expected of her, which wasn't so difficult. It was what she believed too. Though one does suspect she'd have liked to 'gag it up' a little. There are odd flashes of wit, as when she describes the first arrival of American troops in 1942:

They were Jewish, Irish, Polish, Scottish, English, Czech, Swedish, German; they were Americans. They were young, eager, brash, but a little smarter than that, for not so many of them this time bragged,

'We're here to win your war for you.' Oh, a few did, maybe; about as few as the British who said, 'It's about time you blokes came.'

In the main, it's information-packed and good stirring stuff. But woe betides anyone who dares to criticise the Anglo-American alliance. You really don't want to get on the wrong side of Betty:

> In Britain, the *Daily Mail* and the *Sunday Dispatch* did their share of the sniping. In the latter newspaper, a writer named Dorothy Crisp berated Americans from time to time with catty vituperation and feminine unreasonableness.

Betty's name didn't appear in the *Standard* for three weeks, and when she returned it was with a new by-line: BETTY KNOX, *Evening Standard* War Reporter. She told how the troops landing in Normandy were being accompanied by a massive freight operation, providing vital equipment and hot meals. She told of American hospital installations operating almost behind the front line. She told of American glider pilot Charles McCann, who had landed in France on D-Day minus one, and fought off Germans single-handed during a six-day siege. But all was not quite as it seemed.

Invasion Journal by Richard Tobin (war correspondent for the *New York Herald Tribune*) was a day-by-day account of his life between April and August 1944, published later the same year. On 27th June, the same month that Betty's Normandy reports had appeared in the *Standard*, Richard was in the Savoy Hotel, London. Unable to sleep, because of the sound of the bombing, he sought out a poker game at two o'clock in the morning. Playing poker with him were writer William Saroyan, and fellow journalists Ken Crawford, Joe Driscoll ... and Betty Knox.

Yes, 'war reporter' Betty was still working from the *Evening Standard* London office, writing articles based on information sent back to her. In the case of pilot Charles McCann, she had interviewed him after his return to England.

But, in just a week or two, Betty would leave London. And go to war.

16

My Tomsky

(Britain and France July–December 1944)

'His eyes glittered as he talked of his leader.' (Betty Knox, 1944)

THE VERY NIGHT THAT BETTY KNOX WAS PLAYING POKER at the Savoy (though several hours earlier) her daughter was onstage at the Grand Theatre, Blackpool for the opening night of *We're Coming Over*. This was something a little different from the standard summer season fare. A completely original show, crafted to showcase the talents of the performers.

The prolific and inventive comedy writer Max Kester scripted this up-to-the-minute tale of an ENSA unit travelling abroad to entertain the troops. Stars of the show were lanky Ethel Revnell and the more compact Gracie West – known collectively as 'The Long and Short of It'. Other talents were the exotically named Afrique (Johannesburg-born impressionist Alexander Witkin) and Medlock and Marlowe, a husband-and-wife dance act, who also did visual impressions of famous celebrities with the aid of caricatured rubber masks.

The plot begins with the company obtaining their passports and inoculations and flying out to Lisbon, where Revnell and West get mixed up in a spot of espionage, but eventually emerge triumphant. *The Stage* takes up the story:

> Thirty-six hours later they are in the desert in North Africa witnessing natives, in the persons of Wilson, Keppel and Betty performing their famous sand and burlesque dances.

This leads into a sequence in which Ethel Revnell dreams she is Cleopatra, Queen of Egypt:

> An argument arises over the way to bring about Cleopatra's death. So they call for the author, and a life-like Bernard Shaw – in the person of Afrique – appears and settles the question.

In the second act the action moves to Cairo, and Afrique obliges with further impressions, including President Roosevelt and Winston Churchill. The whole show sounds quite a romp ('the best revue of its kind seen for years' said *The Stage*) and it must have been a real treat for the performers to have a script made to measure. Even Wilson, Keppel and Betty's tried and trusted old act (which, in the past, had been highly incongruously crowbarred into many a panto) fitted the rest of the show like a glove.

We're Coming Over was far more than the title of a Blackpool summer show – it was the message of the moment. Betty Knox's late-night poker companion, Richard Tobin, departed for France aboard the British battleship *Ramillies*, arriving there on 13th July. Betty must have left at around the same time, as her first genuine report from Normandy appeared in the *Standard* on Saturday 15th July 1944. The previous month, still in London, she had written of hospitals (known as Battalion Aid Stations) being set up only a thousand yards from the front line. Now she is inside one, and there is no mistaking the fact that she is really there:

> Hospitals move fast. Two and a half miles up the road toward St Lo a new battalion Aid Station was being set up. The road had been fought over a few hours before.
>
> In one recent case a casualty was transported from the front line to New York in 40 hours.
>
> In the shock tent at one field hospital were about 40 men being prepared for operations. I asked the tired doctor how many hours a day he was working.
>
> He stopped for a moment and said, 'About 36 hours a day.'

A couple of weeks later Betty reports that 'four-fifths of the US Army's wounded are now being returned to front line service'.

If there was a way to convey the atmosphere of what she was seeing or experiencing, Betty would invariably find it. She wrote that naval gunfire was being directed by army officers on walkie-talkies:

'Walkie-talkie' conversations tell their own history. 'Dog Queen Easy … this is Roger Mike Jig … I have a message for you… target at (blank) enemy pillbox … close supporting fire … commence fire immediately.'

On 2ⁿᵈ August 1944, *Variety*, which never lost interest in the former vaudevillian, reported that Betty was 'just back from flying trip to Normandy'. And *The Newspaper World* gave a generous paragraph to the *Evening Standard's* war correspondents, in which she heavily featured:

Betty Knox has been taking advantage of special facilities with the US Army to visit hospitals in Normandy. She has recently returned from a four-day trip and hopes to be over there again soon.

Within days of that article appearing in print, she was back in France. In early August she told of American locomotives being unloaded directly onto French railway lines from 'sea-trains' – ships that resemble luxury liners, but are specifically designed to transport heavy cargo:

Operating their own cranes – booms that can lift as much as 120 tons – the crews neatly manoeuvre anything up to 100 rolling-stock vehicles over the side, including 65-ton Diesel engine locomotives, steam engines, freight cars, and gondolas within a few hours.

All set to go, complete with crews, oil, coal, and tools, the powerful locomotives are ready to roll within four hours of having been dropped on to the French rails.

A report from Cherbourg heralded the arrival of the first consignment of Allied food supplies. Even amidst the unsettling images, her upbeat style is still evident:

Thin, under-clad children lined the dusty roads. Children's clothes are at a premium. It is not uncommon to see very small boys and girls wearing US army boots. Underwear is something special that goes with having older brothers and sisters.

Few reporters would be able to inject humour into a situation like this, but Betty was never anything other than herself:

There is no coffee, tea or beer in Normandy. Milk is turned into cheese. Under the Germans the cheese was so bad that the Normans described it as 'blotting paper wrapped in glue'. Sugar is short, but it is 12 francs now instead of 200.

The Germans didn't like the local drink, cider. Neither do the Americans.

It remains at five francs a quart – about the only commodity in Normandy that stayed put.

In another article, Betty hitches a ride with an infantry platoon:

On the jeep route to the front traffic was heavy on the hand-made road. Our jeep squeezed past an endless stream of life-saving jeeps bound for the aid station or the collecting station a mile or two back.

It is a rough ride, but it is fast and speed means life.

A few days later she reports from the tent of an American evacuation hospital which is treating three prisoners, two of them German. As is her style, she always brings alive the people she is writing about. They may be the enemy, but they are people too, and Betty wanted to know what made everyone tick.

The first German had a bandaged jaw and couldn't talk, but he'd been writing ever since he'd been brought in:

He was a medical corporal who had been tending an American soldier when the bullet hit his jaw.

In that tent his injury was a relatively minor one.

He would get better in a few weeks.

He scribbled furiously when the interrogation officer appeared.

His note read: 'Here I'll be dead in three days. In a German hospital I'd be helped. So send me back immediately.'

The second German was young, but no younger than many Americans in the same tent.

He was handsome and might well have been the model for the Hitler Youth posters.

He told the Interrogation Officer that he had been a member.

He did not know whether it had been compulsory to join or not. He had wanted to. Hitler was his ideal.

His eyes glittered as he talked of his leader.

On 17th August 1944, three days after Betty's report from the evacuation hospital appeared in the *Standard*, Betty's older brother George was in Elizabeth City, North Carolina, getting married. George Edward Peden, now known as 'Eddie', had worked his way up in the amusement park business, and was on the executive staff of Lewis and Greenspoon, the company that operated the games, rides and attractions at Ocean View Park, Norfolk, Virginia.

Despite a war raging in Europe, the American public – and particularly the American armed forces – flocked to this coastal attraction and Eddie, as manager of the stock department, was kept pretty busy. But not too busy to fall in love. The object of Eddie's affections was Betty Wenzel, who also worked at Ocean View Park. She was a cast member at the park's Republic Theater.

Betty Wenzel was not exactly an actress. The Republic Theater was a 'burly house' – in other words a burlesque theatre. It presented a bill of comedians, strippers and dancing girls. An advertisement for 'Dancers and Showgirls' was placed in *The Billboard* magazine just one week before rehearsals began, and only a fortnight before the show opened. 'No matinees. 5 days a week. Very little rehearsing.'

Clearly the customers were after sexiness rather than slickness. And, with no matinees, the girls would be playing to an adult male audience, including a large military contingent. Betty Wenzel first came to Ocean View Park at the end of March 1944 – and was married to Eddie before the end of the season. A rapid romance indeed. On 17th August, as 42-year-old Eddie tied the knot with his young showgirl bride, at least his parents Charles and Lizzie could comfort themselves with the thought that they weren't losing a son. They were gaining another dancing daughter named Betty.

On 1st September 1944, a fortnight after the wedding, Betty Knox (who, like her sister-in-law, also spent her working hours in the company of American servicemen) was reporting further good news about French food supplies:

> I saw the first cattle convoy of 130 beef cows and six herdsmen leave Le Mans. It was not a motorised convoy. It will walk all of the 125 miles to Paris, running the gauntlet of snipers who still infest the forward areas.

Female war correspondents were mostly expected to provide a 'woman's view' of the war – the human interest stories. Hence the emphasis on hospitals and food in Betty's reports. Women did not have the same freedom of movement as their male colleagues. For instance, female American correspondents were forbidden from riding in army jeeps (something Betty had already done). Betty succeeded in bending the rules more than most. If a good story was out there, she'd take her chances just like the people she was writing about – and, at times, bluff her way into places she really shouldn't be.

The reason there was a significant number of female reporters in France was that many of their male colleagues were currently serving in the armed forces. These women might not have been offered the opportunity of such a high-profile occupation in peace time – and, after the war, many of the most demanding jobs in all walks of life would be handed back to the men. One female war correspondent, Toni Howard (who will be properly introduced later), reckoned that women received roughly half the pay of their male counterparts. Also, being so vastly outnumbered by military males, it wasn't always easy to settle down to a good night's sleep without some unwanted admirer attempting to charm himself into your tent.

When she first came to Normandy, Betty Knox had posed for a publicity shot alongside five other female reporters. The US Army Signal Corps photo is captioned:

> Six women war correspondents are shown as they stopped at a US field hospital to have chow shortly after their arrival in France.

Standing outside the tent where they chewed their chow were Ruth Cowan (Associated Press), Sonia Tomara (*New York Herald Tribune*), Rosette Hargrove (Newspaper Enterprise Association), Betty Knox (*Evening Standard*), Iris Carpenter (*Boston Globe*), and Erika Mann (*Liberty Magazine*). Of these women, it was Erika Mann with whom Betty worked and socialised the most.

Erika Mann was German, born in Munich, the eldest child of novelist Thomas Mann (best known for the novella *Death in Venice*). Like Betty, Erika had an earlier career as a cabaret performer. But whereas Betty had played the Berlin Wintergarten, dancing for Goebbels and Goering, Erika had devised and starred in a political cabaret, entitled *Die Pfeffermühle* (The Peppermill). As she told the *New York Post* (shortly before the show opened in America), for the first two months of 1933 they had played to full houses in Munich:

> 'And then,' recalls Miss Mann, 'we left Germany rather suddenly.'
> A few outsiders, it appeared, had finally got round to seeing 'Peppermill' and its political sketches. They were not amused.

After that, *The Peppermill* toured Europe, but performances in Zurich were disrupted by pro-Nazi demonstrators. When they played America, the show suffered from some patchy English translations of the song lyrics, and the very talented German performers struggled to make themselves understood in an unfamiliar language. Their first night at the Chanin Auditorium, Manhattan in January 1937 got mixed reviews. For John Mason Brown of the *New York Post*, the political background of the show and the considerable courage of its performers counted for nothing:

> Revue – even intimate revue – in our understanding of the term – is scarcely a proper description of the 'Pepper Mill'. It is a frankly unprofessional performance. Only at a church sociable, where friendship reigned supreme and money was being raised for some worthy charity, would such ineptitudes be countenanced by American ticket-buyers as can be encountered in this offering at the Chanin.

He singles Erika out for some faint praise, but says that her fellow performers 'could not seem more like amateurs if they tried', before concluding:

> I would have sat through the 'Pepper Mill', but I honestly did not have the heart to. I felt too sorry for every one concerned. A deadlier, more embarrassing evening I have never seen. The critics should not have been asked to see it. Neither should a New York audience, for that matter.

One reviewer who opted to stay for the whole show was Arthur Pollock of the *Brooklyn Daily Eagle*. Calling it 'by far the wisest revue in town' he took a totally opposite view of that very same performance:

> Erika Mann herself is the mistress of ceremonies, gracious, expressive, simple and wise, and she has written most of the little things, frivolous and serious, that make up the bill. When they are frivolous they are quite child-like; when they are serious they have a wistful poignance, a gentle pugnacity or are simply touching. These are people for whom Germany became too hot a place and, while they are by no means propagandists, they are not silent, having sage and dignified things to say. 'Why are we so cold?' sings Miss Mann at the end of the performance, wondering what it is that makes us worry so little about what goes on in the world so long as it hasn't yet hurt us, what it is that persuades us that the welfare of humanity is not our concern.

Erika was very close to her brother Klaus. They had behaved like twins through much of their life (although he was a year younger) and, as children, even invented a secret vocabulary which only they knew the meaning of. Both had contributed material to *The Peppermill*. Both had written novels (*The Other Germany* was written by them both). And both were currently working as journalists. Klaus was stationed in Rome, where he was on the editorial staff of the American military newspaper *Stars and Stripes*.

On 4th September 1944, Erika wrote to Klaus from Paris, where she and Betty Knox were currently based. In order to get the letters past the military censor more easily, they wrote to each other in English. Her comments on the food situation were much as Betty had reported:

> People look well – not underfed on the whole – and while there are serious shortages only the very poorest have ever been starving.

Erika was of the opinion that the Germans were retreating fast and that there was not much longer to wait. ('The war ought to be over by 10th October.') She had personal news as well:

> … I have had an exciting and exhilarating and tiring and noteworthy time. There is a young female around – an American, working for the London Evening Standard – *gentille comme tout*, if exceedingly crazy and endangered. My Tomsky, as it were. We came over together by chance and accident and have been sharing cots, jeeps and cars ever since.

This needs a little explanation. '*Gentille comme tout*' translates as 'nice as hell', which is fairly complimentary. 'Young female' is interesting. In fact Betty was 38 at the time – so only about six months younger than Erika. On the other hand, Erika was in the middle of a long-term love affair with the conductor Bruno Walter, who was nearly 30 years her senior. There had been other lovers, both male and female, including a serious relationship with fellow *Peppermill* performer Therese Giehse.

But Erika Mann was a married woman. In 1935 she had flown to England and participated in a 'lavender marriage' (a marriage of convenience) to poet W. H. Auden, in order to obtain British citizenship. For the ceremony they wore almost identical jackets and ties. Auden was gay and Erika was bisexual. They never lived together but remained friends, and Auden wrote the English translation of Erika's

Dancing fairies drawn by Alice Peden (the young Betty Knox) aged 16
(Courtesy of Smoky Valley Genealogical Society)

Hobo Flappers to Be Spanked

TOP: Alice Peden, aged 8, with Charles, Lizzie and baby brother Charles Junior (Ken Cuthbertson)
BOTTOM: Runaway teens Alice and Vivian (Courtesy of Louisiana State Museum, Historical Center)

MISS
BETTY
MAE KNOX

TOP LEFT: Keppel and Wilson before Betty, a rare early publicity shot (Newspapers.com)
TOP RIGHT: A typical vaudeville bill at Robbins' Palace, Watertown, NY in 1922 (Fultonhistory.com)
BOTTOM LEFT: Betty Mae Knox of Lincoln, Nebraska – the 'other' Betty Knox (Newspapers.com)
BOTTOM RIGHT: Betty lifts a leg while Wilson pipes, in their pre-Egyptian days (Fultonhistory.com)

TOP: Wilson, Betty and Keppel photographed in Chicago, just months after they became a trio
BOTTOM LEFT: Their names in lights at the Alhambra, Leicester Square in 1932 (Jeanne McKinnon)
BOTTOM RIGHT: Billy Shenton, Joe Keppel's stand-in (Billy Shenton Junior)

TOP: Wilson, Betty (in pith helmet) and Keppel (who penned the autograph)
BOTTOM: Keppel, Betty and Wilson in 1935 on the set of *In Town Tonight*

TOP: Poster for the Berlin Wintergarten, February 1935 (Courtesy of Huis van Alijn, Gent)
BOTTOM: *Soft Lights and Sweet Music* with Wilson, Betty and Keppel in 1936 (Billy Shenton Junior)

Betty's Dance of the Seven Veils, accompanied by Keppel and Wilson and an appreciative snake – notice the rubber tube at the end of Wilson's pipe that operates the snake's tongue

Betty Knox's signed photo from Olivelli's restaurant, Store Street, London (Giovanni Salamone)

Patsy Knox's photo from Olivelli's, taken in 1944 when Patsy was 20 (Giovanni Salamone)

TOP: Normandy, 1944. Left to right: Ruth Cowan, Sonia Tomara, Rosette Hargrove, Betty Knox, Iris Carpenter and Erika Mann (US National Archives and Records Administration)
BOTTOM: Jimmy Smeddle, Joe Young and pianist Jack Wilson in Olivelli's, 1947 (Billy Shenton Junior)

Betty Knox and Erika Mann in California, winter 1944-45 (Courtesy of Monacensia)

TOP: Keppel, Wilson and Patsy doing the Seven Veils in the 1950 movie *A Ray of Sunshine*
BOTTOM: Betty and daughter Patsy photographed by the *Daily Express* in London, 1954

TOP: Wilson attacking Keppel on stage in the Spear Dance, early 1950s (Glen Watt)
BOTTOM: Programme for *London Palladium Varieties* at the Desert Inn, Las Vegas in July 1954

TOP LEFT: Jean Bamberger – Betty in 1933 (Billy Shenton Junior)
TOP CENTRE: Eunice Roberts – Betty in 1941 (Allyson Proudfoot)
TOP RIGHT: Barbara Holt on her wedding day – Betty in 1951 (Barbara Holt Schaller)
BOTTOM LEFT: Irene Scott – Betty in 1951-54 (Giovanni Salamone)
BOTTOM CENTRE: Valerie Cottrell – Betty in 1955-56 (Giovanni Salamone)
BOTTOM RIGHT: Jeanne Curley – Betty in 1956-62 (Jeanne McKinnon)

VALERIE & HENRI MULLENS
PAS DE DEUX CLASSIC

TOP LEFT: Valerie Cottrell's subsequent circus career with husband Henri Mullens
TOP RIGHT: Edwin Hall's 1942 cartoon of Wilson and Keppel in Olivelli's (Giovanni Salamone)
BOTTOM: Jeanne Curley, Joe Keppel and Jack Wilson enjoy a well-earned drink (Jeanne McKinnon)

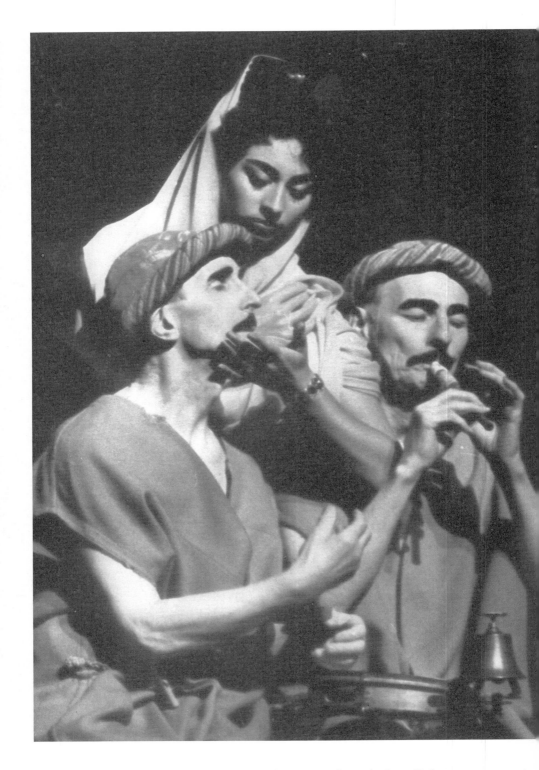

Keppel and Wilson, now in their mid-60s, with Jeanne Curley in the Seven Veils (Jeanne McKinnon)

Peppermill song 'Why are we so cold?' – possibly the best English lyrics in the whole revue.

And finally 'my Tomsky' was a reference to Klaus Mann's own young American boyfriend, Thomas Quinn Curtiss. So, in short, Betty Knox and Erika Mann had become lovers. Betty's zany sense of humour seems to have been the spark that brought the two together – and their relationship would prove to be far more than a casual fling. Erika concludes her letter with one final reference to Betty, comparing her with two mutual friends (one of whom had been recently arrested):

> You would like my room-mate; she is oddly remindful of both Mops and Gert Frank except that I think her rather more attractive than either lost soul.

Another reason for their mutual attraction was the incredible courage of the two women. Erika had a far stronger emotional connection with this war. It was her own countrymen who had turned against her and much of the world. Betty was brave too, but her writing is often so chirpy and gung-ho that it might, on occasions, seem that she regarded the war as one great big thrilling adventure playground.

Although never reporting from the front line, Betty could have had a much safer war. But, offered the opportunity of a good story, good company and good interviewees, she would invariably take it. And the military were more than happy for her to tag along. The same day Erika was writing her letter to brother Klaus, Betty had just set off on her German-hunting escapade with the French Resistance, detailed in Chapter 1.

Erika Mann's prediction of the war ending by 10th October was beginning to look a distinct possibility. But Betty's next report was more sombre. French authorities had arrested five hundred 'war criminals' who were alleged to have collaborated with the Nazis:

> I saw the list of 500 today. By each name is the charge. Some of the charges are trading with the enemy, collaborating and serving with the militia.
>
> Against the name of one woman was: 'Anti-French activities – had her husband shot by the Germans.'
>
> One subject, called in while I was there, was alleged to have denounced 57 Frenchmen to the Gestapo. Her head had been shaved,

but she had obviously received good treatment, and was allowed to wear a turban.

Another woman, a night club singer, admitted that at first she had taken money to denounce members of the resistance movement. Afterwards she thought she was being underpaid, and turned up at the Prefecture to inform on the Gestapo.

On the night of 16th September 1944, a group of war correspondents, including Betty Knox, Erika Mann and Lee Miller of *Vogue*, stayed overnight in an Orléans hotel. Next day they would be taken to Beaugency, to witness the surrender of Major General Erich Elster and nearly 20,000 German troops. Isolated, and under heavy attack from French forces and the American Air Force, Major General Elster had taken the decision to surrender without the permission of his superiors, and a Nazi court later sentenced him to death in his absence. (His face-saving request to stage a mock battle before the surrender was refused by the Americans.)

Betty Knox's bright-and-breezy bravery is frequently on display in her on-the-spot articles for the *Standard*. Erika Mann had considerable reserves of courage too, as demonstrated in this extract from Colonel Barney Oldfield's book *Never a Shot in Anger* about the war correspondents' journey (under the supervision of Colonel E. B. Crabill) to the official surrender:

> The Paris correspondents were briefed the next morning on the complete plans, then Crabill authorised me to take them over. 'Tell them to be careful,' he said. 'We haven't got the Germans in the cage yet, and their guns are loaded.' One of the feminine war correspondents was Erika Mann, daughter of the famous Thomas Mann, who had suffered persecution and endured exile because of Hitler. As we came upon the leading elements of the column and passed alongside it down the road, Erika was emotionally moved, began to talk incoherently, then uttered profanity in the German tongue, and finally as the command car slowed, she got out. When I could get the jeep stopped and get back to her, she was less than a yard from the marching Germans, her hands on her hips, her tongue stuck out, rendering a juicy Bronx cheer right in their faces. That was the end of the ride, because she was bundled up and the retinue went back to the Beaugency Bridge to await the rest of the affair. By then, no Germans would be armed, and it would be a lot safer for her to stick out her tongue.

The following month, Betty is one of a number of journalists mentioned on *The Newspaper World*'s Personalities Page:

> Betty Knox, who recently left the *Evening Standard* and returned to France on a special assignment for the *Daily Mail*, has been ill in Paris.

Betty, who seems to have been dogged by ill health throughout her career, never joined the *Daily Mail* staff. She was now either freelance or working for a news agency. But she kept on good terms with the *Evening Standard*. Her byline would appear on the occasional article – and for years to come she'd supply copy to the paper. But there were no further war reports for the *Standard* bearing Betty's name.

As 1944 drew to a close, Betty's daughter Patsy was again performing in panto. Wilson, Keppel and Betty were one of the speciality turns in *Aladdin* at the Bristol Hippodrome. Dragging up as Widow Twankey was comic Duggie Wakefield. But, as *The Stage* discovered, you don't need to be in a war zone to become a casualty:

> Duggie Wakefield met with an unfortunate mishap in the first scene. A rickshaw in which he was making his entrance overturned and threw him heavily on the stage, badly spraining his right wrist. He carried on with his wrist bandaged.

(Remembering a similar tumble by Joe Keppel on his London Palladium debut in 1932, it seems that an alarmingly high number of stage accidents were rickshaw-based!)

This was one pantomime that Betty Knox never got to see. But not because of the war. Erika Mann had taken her new girlfriend to America. To meet the parents.

17

Hey, Have You Heard?

(America, Britain and Europe 1945–1946)

'… not *precisely* what the doctor ordered.' (Erika Mann, 1945)

THE WAR HADN'T ENDED ON 10TH OCTOBER 1944, as Erika Mann had forecast, but it was certainly in its final months. It might not have been too much of a wrench for Betty and Erika to leave France for America. It was like picking the right time to leave a party and, at this particular party, most of the drama and excitement had now passed and all that remained was the considerable chore of tidying up. For Erika, the trip to America would hardly be a holiday. She was engaged on a lengthy lecture tour, relating her experiences in Europe and looking ahead to how Germany would rebuild and reform itself. Unfortunately, as she wrote to brother Klaus:

> I came back on a troopship, fell sick almost instantly, had to cancel numerous appearances which would have been fine, had I only been able to talk <u>at all</u>. As it went, I spent a week with our dear ones, unable to tell them anything. And there was so much I might have said.

If Erika could say very little, Betty may have talked rather too much. The two saw in the New Year at the Manns' family home in Pacific Palisades, Los Angeles, California. Thomas Mann was a highly revered writer who expected to be treated with due respect and courtesy, even by his own family. Betty Knox was most probably too raucous, too chatty, too zany – and way, way too familiar. One of Betty's great professional assets was that she could talk to anyone and everyone. And she did so by being herself. And, whereas most people present different versions of themselves to different people, there was only ever one Betty. She'd been to plenty of New Year's Eve parties over the years, and this one was by far the grimmest. In her mind, she was just getting everyone to let their hair down.

Thomas Mann first mentions Betty in his diary entry of 29th December:

> *Zum Abendessen E's militärische Freundin und Kollegin, ebenfalls in Uniform.* (For dinner, Erika's military friend and colleague, also in uniform.)

All Allied war correspondents wore what was basically military uniform, without any rank but with a large white letter 'C' on the left arm. In his diary for New Year's Eve, Thomas remarks:

> *Erika's «Eule», etwas verrückt, übernachtet im Wohnzimmer.* (Erika's 'owl', slightly crazy, stayed overnight in the living room.)

'Owl' appears to be a slang term used by the Mann parents when referring to their children's friends – particularly those they disapproved of. 'Slightly crazy' may have been something of an understatement.

Thomas's wife Katia, who quickly realised the nature of Erika and Betty's relationship, was also said to have been unimpressed by Betty's behaviour. In a subsequent letter to her son Klaus, she referred to an occasion when Erika brought her 'owl' to a small select birthday party in honour of Erika's elderly on-off lover, the conductor Bruno Walter. 'Rather inappropriate,' thought Katia.

There is a photo of Betty and Erika in California, sharing a large sun-lounger. Betty wears a two-piece bathing costume and Erika is draped in towels. They are lying back, topping up their tans, and each woman holds a cigarette. How different from just a few months ago in France. They look totally relaxed, totally happy. But something had changed. On 15th January 1945, after all those fraught festive celebrations, Erika wrote another letter to Klaus. When she mentioned Betty (once again referred to as 'my Tomsky') it was with muted enthusiasm:

> My Tomsky has come along – hadn't been here for 6 years – and is now sitting in New York, waiting to meet me in the Middlewest. A strange

acquisition – infinitely uesis, quite endangered, rather worrying and – once again – not <u>precisely</u> what the doctor ordered. People are always getting so frighteningly serious as soon as they are with your sis. But then, one ought to be grateful – and I am after a fashion – for so much wholeheartedness and were it not for the complications – Le monstre and all that – which are bound to arise, I should be happy enough.

The honeymoon would seem to be over. 'Uesis' was one of Klaus and Erika's nonsense code words, meaning an almost child-like (or puppy-like) eagerness to please. '*Le monstre*' (the monster) may be a reference to the jealousy of Bruno Walter. The problem was that fun-loving Betty wanted a serious relationship, while the more serious Erika just wanted a bit of fun. The closeness that sustained them both during the war was destined not to last into peacetime. Erika would return to Bruno Walter intermittently, but she and Betty remained close friends and would continue to work together, and often live together. Since Betty and Donald Knox's teenage romance (and marriage) this is the first serious relationship that has been discovered. There would be others but – for a while, anyway – Erika had been the love of Betty's life.

While Erika, sometimes accompanied by Betty, continued her American lecture tour – and Betty, hopefully, found time to drop in on her parents in Flushing, New York – her daughter, Patsy, was still dashing around Britain with Wilson, Keppel and Betty. The war prepared for its final curtain call, and on 8th May 1945 people took to the streets to celebrate the end of the war in Europe: VE Day. Less than a week later, Wilson, Keppel and Betty were playing the Hackney Empire where the top of the bill was 'Forces Sweetheart' Vera Lynn. For sheer atmosphere it must have been one of the most joyous weeks of their entire touring life – matched possibly, a couple of months later, when Vera and the trio appeared in Coventry (a city that had suffered particularly heavy damage from a prolonged series of German bombing raids).

In July Betty Knox left America and sailed to England. Her destination was, once again, that most improbable hive of journalistic industry: London's Savoy Hotel. By August she was back in Paris. A peacetime Paris, where scores of British and American businessmen were returning to their old jobs, and dealing with the problems caused by inflation and shortages. After her comparatively light-hearted articles twelve months ago on pretty well the same topic, this dispatch to the *Standard* (from 1ˢᵗ September 1945) is more sombre in tone:

> A business man bought an unpretentious country house in 1943 for 100,000 francs (£500). Last week he paid 50,000 francs (£25) to have the walls distempered.
>
> A French secretary lives with her family in a £90 a year four-room flat. Yesterday their landlord offered the family £500 just to move out.

She finishes the piece with one of her typical wry anecdotes, but even this seems tinged with the grim reality of the post-war economic situation:

> Opposite the Café de la Paix is the customary horse-drawn cab rank. I asked the driver of the first fiacre how much it would cost to get to Maxims, about a five-minute walk. He said that he could not do it under 350 francs. He explained quite seriously that his horse was inflation conscious.

A month later, Betty made her first visit (since becoming a journalist) to Germany. Before the war she had danced in Berlin's Wintergarten, but now she was in Nuremberg to report on the war trials for the *London Evening Standard*. This would be far from a fleeting visit.

The idea of prosecuting the losing side of a conflict had begun after the First World War – though the Leipzig trials acquitted most of the defendants. This time there was considerable disagreement amongst the Allied nations about how these trials should be organised. In the event, the 'international' court was largely composed of Americans. Although proceedings opened in October, the trials themselves didn't begin until the middle of November.

Earlier that month (8ᵗʰ November) Wilson, Keppel and Betty were selected, for the second time, to appear at the Royal Variety Performance, this time at the London Coliseum. It was the first Royal Variety show since the war (the previous show had been in 1938). The special Royal supplement of *The Performer* magazine carried an intriguing photo montage of Wilson, Keppel and Betty. The pictures of Wilson and Keppel were taken from an old 1929 photo of the trio, with Betty Knox removed and Jack and Joe pushed closer together. To this was added a photo of Patsy in costume, thus instantly reducing the thirty-year age gap between the 51-year-old men and 21-year-old Patsy to just 14 years.

Anyone who bought the official souvenir programme would have been even more confused, as it contained that same 1929 photo, complete and undoctored, featuring Betty Knox rather than Patsy. The trio spent very little on new publicity photos over the years. They were still using the ones from their old American days whenever possible.

Also on the bill were Will Hay, Sid Field, Tommy Trinder and five members of the Colleano family. Bonar Senior (father of the actor) with Maurice and George did a smart springboard routine – and Joyce and Rubye also participated, the latter being praised for her acrobatic dancing. *The Performer* gave a brief summary of Wilson, Keppel and Betty's act:

> Reversing their familiar routine, Jack Wilson and Joe Keppel began very strongly with their sand dance, which, as always, was productive of great laughter, went into the dance of the Seven Veils (with Betty) and ended with the Spear Dance, each of their grotesque dances, combined with their grotesque appearance, making them immediate favourites.

When it came to providing a potted biography for *The Performer* the trio had a big problem. In their 1933 biography they had maintained (quite falsely) that Betty Knox was not the first Betty, and that they had enjoyed an earlier long career with Betty's mother. Now, by a highly bizarre coincidence, they were performing with Betty Knox's daughter. It was a case of life imitating artifice. They decided to brazen it out:

> An amazing fact is that the two men have had three generations of the Knox family as their girl partners. First there was Betty; then her daughter Betty, who was born at Salina, Texas, and who appeared in the 1933 Royal Performance and recently retired to become a very successful newspaper columnist and journalist (as witness her frequent signed leading articles in the *Evening Standard*); and the present Betty, who is really Patsy Knox, the 21-years-old daughter of the second Betty.

Obviously Salina is in Kansas, not Texas. And obviously Betty Number One is a dirty great fib. The biography concludes with some information (more or less true) about their leisure interests:

> The two men have no special hobbies or outstanding talents apart from those exhibited in the act, except that they are keen on watching boxing, wrestling and other sporting events; but Patsy – sorry, Betty! – Knox is, like her mother, an accomplished dress designer and artist, and she has

some excellent paintings and drawings that give proof of her skill in these directions.

The Nuremberg Trials got properly under way on 20th November 1945. On trial were twenty or so of the most senior Nazi figures. As *The Times* noted, of the many people filling the courtroom, 'members of the international Press are by far the most numerous contingent'. Many books have been written, detailing the events of the trials in painstaking detail. But few, if any, have quoted from an American paperback thriller of 1950, entitled *Shriek with Pleasure*. The blurb on the back cover encapsulates its contents and style:

Nothing Was Taboo. Foreign Correspondent Carla MacMurphy would do anything to scoop a headline – lie, cheat or betray the men who confided in her. A tempestuous and beautiful woman working in postwar Germany she never missed an opportunity to turn a romantic interlude or a political incident to her own advantage.

The author of this steamy romantic escapade was Toni Howard, who had been a foreign correspondent for *Newsweek* and (like Betty) had filed news stories from Normandy and the Nuremberg trials. So when the fictional Carla MacMurphy sits in the press gallery observing proceedings, Toni is writing from first-hand experience:

So here she was, sitting in the press-box of the International Military Tribunal at Nuremberg, her head aching from the weight of these damned earphones and listening to the interminable yak-yak of the handing down of four-power justice ... it was all so hard to follow, it was like a masquerade, everybody dressed up like baccalaureate switchboard officers wearing these silly black headphones and talking into the mouthpieces in too many languages as if they were little boys playing telephone.

Those cumbersome headphones, which needed to be worn fairly continuously if you wanted to know what was going on, were a necessary inconvenience in a trial being conducted in English, German, French and Russian. But, as *The Times* pointed out on the first day of the trial, simultaneous translation would speed up proceedings and reduce the length of the trial by three-quarters:

This system, it will be recalled, was successfully used by the League of Nations at Geneva. Every one in court, judges, counsel, prisoners, and members of the public, is provided with headphones, and simply tunes in to the language he wishes to hear. National teams of interpreters are installed behind glass panels in a corner of the court room a little above the dock and, speaking softly into the microphones, simultaneously translate everything said in court into their own languages.

As Hitler, Goebbels and Himmler had all committed suicide, one of the highest ranking – and most flamboyant – defendants was Hermann Goering, the commander of the Luftwaffe and (before he fell from favour) Hitler's deputy. He was one of very few prisoners who wore uniform (though stripped of insignia and badges). As *The Times* put it: 'Göring in an elegant pale grey *Luftwaffe* uniform, presumably his own creation.' Toni Howard describes how Carla MacMurphy stared across at the defendants, each one sitting stiff and impassive:

> Except Göring, who always sat with his chin on his hand listening to every word and smiling indulgently and switching his earphones from English to French to German and back again, maybe to prove to the court that he really was the Renaissance Man of many tastes and many cultures, maybe so he could hear everything in every language except Russian. Göring, who when the Americans captured him had been a snivelling, dope-sodden spineless wreck, but had now been cleaned up and shaven and trimmed of his flabby fat and somehow made respectable and dignified again ...

Before the war Betty Knox had tap-danced in the Berlin Wintergarten, along with her sand dancing companions, for an audience that included Hermann Goering. Now, in the ultimate example of table-turning, Betty was in the audience and Goering was centre stage. And Betty even got to write the reviews.

None of Betty's Nuremberg reports carry her name, though she wrote the vast majority of those that appeared in the *Evening Standard*. As these are mainly factual accounts and, through necessity, lack the quirky humour and investigative quality of her earlier work, I have generally omitted them – other than a few significant exceptions.

The question has to be asked: is Toni Howard's fictional journalist, Carla MacMurphy, who 'would do anything to scoop a headline' in any way based on Betty Knox? Perhaps disappointingly the answer is no. We know this because we know that Toni Howard met and worked alongside Betty Knox. And (in an audio interview with author and former war correspondent Julia Edwards in the 1980s) Toni portrayed Betty as the polar opposite of Carla:

> Now there is that kind of journalist who was always around in the press clubs – particularly the press club bars – and who, instead of writing his story, talked it. Larry Rue [*Chicago Tribune*] was one of the males that did that. And Betty Knox was the one outstanding female. She'd sit there and tell all the things she'd done that day and what everybody said and did. And the people sitting at the table would, either consciously or unconsciously, steal material from her. Because half the time she didn't write it. And, when she did get around to writing it, it was stale. She talked it. And so, as I said, they'd pick up whatever was interesting or useful – slip it into some story. Not illegally, or not viciously, but just because Betty had told them – instead of going up and writing it first and then getting down to the bar, which everybody else did. Getting it off – then coming down. Betty talked her stories too much. She was a darling. She was a real darling.

In the same interview, Julia Edwards asked Toni whether fellow war correspondent Marguerite Higgins (the first female recipient of a Pulitzer Prize) was the real-life model for Carla MacMurphy:

> I've been asked that before – and I'm required to deny it.

A somewhat diplomatic denial – because Toni wasn't exactly bursting with admiration for the journalist:

> Marguerite was, as far as I was concerned, a complete bitch … the most ambitious and ruthless woman I'd ever known.

But, if Betty wasn't Carla, there's a good chance she was the inspiration for another fleeting character encountered by Carla MacMurphy. Sally Lodge (a name strikingly similar to Betty Knox) briefly becomes the centre of attention in, of course, a press club bar:

> 'Carla!' yelled Sally Lodge, rushing up with the bodice of her dress as usual only half-buttoned, her stringy brown hair hanging lank and dirty on her neck. 'We're taking a poll of all the women correspondents to decide which one of these twenty-one bastards is the most attractive. Then we're going to send a pack of cigarettes and a mash letter [gushingly passionate love letter] to the winner. So here's the question: If you had to go to bed with one of them, which one would you pick?'
> 'Oh, Hess, I think,' said Carla laughing.

'Hess?' screamed Sally, 'you mean because he'd be so unpredictable?' The circle around them was widening, the men listening indulgent and amused. 'Most of the girls say von Shirach, he's the youngest, you know, and the handsomest. He writes poetry too. But you know who I said? Frank! The butcher of Poland. And you know why?' she went on breathlessly. 'Because he's just become Catholic, he spends all his time praying and saying his beads, it'd be so spiritual, like going to bed with a priest!' Laughing, she wandered off, and the circle gradually broke up.

And you wonder why she went down so badly at Thomas Mann's New Year's Eve party! Although this brief vignette perfectly encapsulates Betty Knox's energy and wicked sense of fun – often at the darkest of times – we can only guess that Sally was modelled on Betty. But Toni Howard would have spent many an evening in the press club bar. And these were just the kind of late-night conversations that journalists would have had, as they tried to put all the horrors of the day out of their heads.

But back to Toni Howard's interview. Toni's voice is deep, hoarse and raspy throughout – the characteristic voice of that generation of chain-smoking journos that surely included 'husky contralto' Betty Knox. Just before Julia Edwards steers the conversation on to other matters, Toni shares one final titbit of gossip about Betty:

> She was having a big love affair with Geoff Parsons of the *Herald Trib*. And he threw her over for Drue Tartière.

Betty's relationship with Erika Mann was long over – and now, so it appears, she was head over heels in love again. With all the casual dalliances that doubtless took place, Betty and Geoff's romance must have been quite the 'big love affair' to merit such attention from the journalistic community. Geoffrey Parsons Junior was correspondent for the *New York Herald Tribune*, and Drue Tartière (the woman who eventually supplanted Betty in his affections) was an American actress who married a Frenchman, moved to Paris and worked for the French resistance throughout the war. Drue and Geoffrey subsequently married and he was promoted to Paris editor of the *Herald Tribune*. 'Tis better to have loved and lost,' was starting to become Betty's theme song.

Another writer who knew Betty during her time at Nuremberg was Freda Utley – a controversial author, born in England, who had lived in the United States since 1939. In 1949 Freda would publish a book about American policy towards Germany, during and since the war. It was a highly critical account that could easily be interpreted as anti-American. However, Freda had also lived in Russia and China, and had written similarly damning accounts of their policies.

Although the USA is often thought of as 'touchy' when it comes to criticism, Freda's book *The High Cost of Vengeance* (commissioned by that fairly un-subversive organisation known as Reader's Digest) was considered outspoken, but not an outrage. This extract gives a fair indication of the tone of the book:

> In Berlin, for instance, I found myself in disgrace after having remarked, at a cocktail party in Harnack House, that I thought it was high time we stopped talking about German guilt, since there was no crime the Nazis had committed, which we or our allies had not also committed. I had referred to our obliteration bombing, the mass expropriation and expulsion from their homes of twelve million Germans on account of their race; the starving of the Germans during the first years of the occupation; the use of prisoners as slave laborers; the Russian concentration camps, and the looting perpetrated by Americans as well as Russians.

This is one of several passages from Freda's book to have been appropriated by present-day websites seeking to justify, minimise or deny the Holocaust. But, if Freda Utley trod a tricky path, so too did Betty Knox, who features in the book and was still very much a working journalist when it was published.

Betty Knox was certainly not anti-American, neither was she pro-Nazi. But what did anger her was unfairness, wherever it occurred. If there was to be a war trial, let it be a scrupulously fair one. And, if that meant crossing swords with chief prosecuting counsel Robert Jackson, then (as Freda Utley wrote) that is just what Betty would do:

> Betty Knox, an American newspaperwoman who hails from Kansas, but is now a correspondent of the British Beaverbrook press and has spent three years in Nuremberg, told me that at the International Military Tribunal, although hundreds of copies of the prosecution documents to be presented to the court were available to the foreign press before the proceedings, only two copies in German were provided for the thirty-five defense lawyers, and these only after each day's proceedings. When

165

Betty Knox asked Justice Jackson why more copies were not supplied to the German defense counsel, he said that in the United States there was no exchange of documents. When she insisted that in international law courts it is done, Jackson got furious and exclaimed: 'That would be too good for these bastards!'

When Betty's presence wasn't required at Nuremberg, she was often in the company of Erika Mann. In late November 1945 they both visited Crailsheim, a German city that had been virtually destroyed by Allied bombing. Erika had opted against a repeat of the previous year's festive family gathering, so she spent the Christmas season in the Hotel Urban in Zurich, Switzerland, where she was staying with Betty. Also present were actress Therese Giehse and Erika's brother Klaus. Despite being subject to extreme mood swings, apparently Klaus had a delightful time with his sister and her two ex-lovers.

On 22nd January 1946, Charles Peden (Betty's father and Patsy's grandfather) died, aged 72, in Flushing, New York. His obituary, carried by the *Long Island Star-Journal* on 24th January, described him simply as a 'retired dry goods merchant'. It went on to say:

> Mr Peden was the father of Mrs Alice (Betty) Knox, *London Evening Standard* reporter covering the trial of the Nazi war criminals in Nurenburg, Germany.

Any lingering suspicion that Betty Knox was the disgrace of the family must now be quashed. An obituary that describes the deceased in four words and his daughter in fifteen surely indicates considerable parental pride in her achievements.

Betty Knox continued to divide her time between court reporting at Nuremberg and (whenever the schedule allowed) travelling further afield in search of a good news story. At the start of July (while Erika Mann was in Chicago where her seriously ill father was being treated in hospital) an increasingly rare instance of an article bearing the name 'Betty Knox' appeared in the *Evening Standard*:

> Why are the Russians reluctant to open their zone to Press correspondents? After a 1000-mile tour behind the so-called iron curtain, I find little unfavourable to report.
>
> Once permission for a tour has been granted, Soviet officials do everything to be helpful and co-operative.

No request made by myself and two American correspondents during the past fortnight was refused by Soviet or German municipal authorities in Leipzig, Dresden, Weimar or in smaller cities such as Jena or Plauen.

Requests included unescorted interviews with German officials and ordinary people.

The general tone of the article was that those areas of Germany that were occupied by the Russians were thriving in comparison to those being administered by the British, Americans or French:

From the moment one passes the first Soviet guard on the border, there is an atmosphere of order and sober industry.

Though normally agricultural country, the crops look better than anywhere in Germany and there is a much higher percentage of male labour in the fields.

Without anyone telling you, you feel sure that your car will neither be stolen nor broken into. This is so common in the western zones that losers do not even comment when they become victims.

But one problem all the allies were facing was the stamping out of Nazism. Something that was proving much trickier than had been imagined:

In the American zone, where de-Nazification is taken more seriously than in any zone, polls show that not more than 1 per cent of Germany was actively anti-Nazi.

Frustrated officials admit that exacting de-Nazification laws make it almost impossible to find adequate managerial staff, or any kind of staff, among the guiltless minority.

Few Russian officials said that they believed that the Germans were the victim of anything but Allied defeat.

But you can't sack a nation, and it is more practical to put the German to work, and watch him while he works.

On 1st October 1946, in Nuremberg, the twenty-two accused were sentenced. Three were acquitted, seven were imprisoned, and twelve were sentenced to death (Martin Bormann being sentenced in his absence). Hermann Goering's request that he be shot rather than hanged was refused.

In the early hours of 16th October those executions were carried out. Only eight newsmen were allowed to witness the executions, and their names were picked by lot. The other sixty or so correspondents, Betty amongst them, had to stand (or pace) around and wait – ever conscious of looming deadlines. News agency Reuters was the first to lose patience and dispatch a bulletin saying all eleven prisoners had been hanged. As *Time* magazine reported later that month, it was then that the confusion started. And Betty Knox was at the centre of it:

> All through the night, the truth knocked timidly at the door. In a hallway a GI guard called out to Betty Knox, an American working for Beaverbrook's *London Evening Standard*: 'Hey, have you heard that Göring committed suicide?' She had known the GI since childhood, but she had heard latrine rumors before, so she let it pass.

Another guard told an American radio reporter, who replied: 'A man could ruin himself in five minutes by broadcasting a silly report like that.' So, while the eight reporters who already knew the truth were locked away watching the executions, the others all filed their stories based on assumption rather than rumour. That was their mistake. They should have gone with the rumour. Goering had managed to conceal a cyanide capsule in his possessions, and had taken it (in his cell) only a couple of hours before his appointed execution. The *Daily Mail* stuck by their headline: NÜRNBERG NAZIS HANGED IN PAIRS – GÖRING AND RIBBENTROP DIE FIRST. They maintained that (ignoring the location and method) Goering had, indeed, died first.

So Hermann Goering, who had dominated the headlines throughout the trial, succeeded in grabbing them once more by staging his own death. Could he ever have imagined that the first journalist to hear the news, the woman who had stared at him intently throughout his trial, was the very same girl who had danced before him at the Berlin Wintergarten, sandwiched between those two skinny men with the obscenely bare legs?

We don't know precisely who gave Betty Knox the suicide tip-off. One journalist who she closely associated with during the Nuremberg Trials was Josie Thompson of the United Press news agency. In his 2007 autobiography, former war correspondent Holbrook Bradley mentions that Josie was dating a young Texan captain (nicknamed Tex) who was Herman Goering's jailer, and that Tex had even managed to spirit away Goering's Rolex watch as a souvenir.

The recollections of Marian Podkowiński (a Polish journalist who had worked alongside Betty at Nuremberg) show her lapse of judgement in a far more serious light. Writing in the magazine *Przekrój* in 1970, he remembers Betty as Erika Mann's 'inseparable friend' and goes on to say (in translation):

> Betty Knox, plump correspondent of the *Evening Standard* from London, went down in the annals of Nuremberg journalistic history as the person who learnt from an American guard about Goering's suicide a few minutes before the execution and didn't believe it. She'd been handed a sensational scoop and didn't have the courage to share it with her colleagues. So she ignored the message and lost the chance of a lifetime. Journalists never forgave her. She took to drink out of despair.

This account must have the elements of truth, even if a little embroidered. It's unlikely that her colleagues never forgave her, though they would have made damn sure she never forgot it. At worst, she could be accused of being over-cautious. Had she and her colleagues gone to press, only to discover the Goering rumour was unfounded, the impact on her career would have been far more serious.

She probably became something of a laughing stock. The vaudeville hoofer who let the biggest story of her life slip through her fingers. And there was not a journalist, not an editor, not a potential future employer, who was unaware of the fact.

Nuremberg had changed Betty. Her happy-go-lucky attitude from her performing days had endeared her to many, Erika Mann included. But there were few laughs to be had in Nuremberg and, right now, she was the biggest joke around. Never slim by nature, she no longer had her twice-nightly dance workout to prevent the pounds piling on. At Olivelli's she used to drink the night away to have a good time. Now she drank to forget the bad times. As Marcel Wallenstein had said back in 1944: 'on occasions Miss Knox is a very miserable journalist indeed'.

Compared with the time Betty was having, the ups and downs of Wilson, Keppel and Patsy's career were pretty trivial. In August 1946, Norah Alexander of the *Daily Mail* had some exciting movie news:

> When I ran across them in the Isle of Wight, recently, Wilson, Keppel and Betty were full of plans for a trip to the States in the autumn. (They do that lovely sand-dance, you remember, in long, green nightshirts.)

Wilson was saying that they had a big 'spot' in the new Wesley Ruggles's picture, *London Town*. He was hoping that the picture would be shown in America before they landed, since it would give their act a wonderful boost.

Not for the first time the plot involved a variety theatre – and they would be one of the acts providing breathing space between plot developments. But this was no provincial 'B' movie. This was a Rank Organisation big-budget affair – the first British musical to be shot in Technicolor. Not that it made any difference to Jack and Joe's legs which (at best) were still fifty shades of grey, but their nightshirts would surely gleam in the most verdant hue imaginable. The cast included 13-year-old singer Petula Clark (already a star of stage, screen and radio) and comedian Sid Field – currently a huge sensation on the London stage. The whole production was in the hands of experienced American director Wesley Ruggles. As far as movies went, Wilson, Keppel and Betty had finally hit the big time.

In an early scene, onstage during a rehearsal, we're informed that a couple of speciality acts will be 'coming along later'. They appear in a handful of production stills, including a frontcloth seven veils (with Patsy stripping down to a bikini), and The 'Ampstead Way – where Wilson and Keppel, in 'pearly king' outfits (black caps, sleeveless jackets and shorts, all festooned with mother-of-pearl buttons) treat the crowd to the world's first cockney-Egyptian sand dance!

> Alas, their 'spot' has suffered the fate of a great many other good things.
> It was left on the cutting-room floor.

Thus read Norah Alexander's final paragraph. Cinema audiences were to be denied a full colour glimpse of Wilson, Keppel and (most regrettably) Betty. Possibly as a result of the trio's excision from the final cut, their autumn tour of the States never materialised. But no one involved in *London Town* did particularly well out of it. Director Wesley Ruggles had never tackled a musical before – and the whole movie was a vastly expensive flop. When the American censor saw it, he took great exception to Kay Kendall's daringly low-cut costume and also the camp cavortings of Sid Field and Jerry Desmonde in the photographer sketch. It took several years before a heavily cut version was released in the States. Who's to know whether Wilson, Keppel and Betty's own combination of campery and cleavage wouldn't also have fallen victim to the US censor's scissors?

In November 1946 Patsy's grandmother, Lizzie Peden, took her first trip to England. She was now aged 70, had been widowed at the start of the year, and had undergone an eye operation late the previous year. Her ship docked at Southampton, and her destination was 35 Store Street, London (the address of Olivelli's). It would be a lengthy stay, and she had plenty of opportunity to join theatre audiences and watch Patsy doing routines she had first seen performed by Wilson, Keppel and her daughter Betty in that show in Flushing, way back in 1931.

For Betty, the trial was finally over and the executions had been carried out. But there were darker times ahead. More trials. And many more executions.

18

We Will Teach You Democracy!

(Germany and Britain 1947–1948)

'Neither of them were ever likely to forget their terrible experience.'
(Freda Utley, 1949)

THE NAZI HIGH COMMAND HAD BEEN TRIED and the guilty had been either imprisoned or executed. Except for one – Martin Bormann. He had risen through the ranks to become Hitler's most trusted aide. At the end of April 1945 he was in the bunker with Hitler, who was preparing to take his own life. It is said Hitler ordered Bormann to flee and save himself. Bormann succeeded in escaping and, for years afterwards, his whereabouts remained a mystery. He was tried at Nuremberg and sentenced to be hanged. But, though you can try a man in his absence, it's not so easy to execute him.

And then, on 27th May 1947, an article appeared in the *London Evening Standard*. Sent from Nuremberg, and credited simply to an 'Evening Standard Reporter', it said:

> Elusive Martin Bormann, most powerful man in Nazi Germany after Hitler, is neither in Munich, Liechtenstein, the Austrian Alps, nor dead – according to the testimony of the best-informed Nazis still alive.
>
> These men, who are in a position to have been in possession of the closest Party intelligence secrets, say that Bormann is alive, and has been in Russian hands since the fall of Berlin.

They accuse Hitler's last heir-apparent of having been in close contact with the Kremlin since 1943.

The men could not be named, as they were all awaiting trial, either as witnesses or defendants:

> One of them, describing him as 'indisputably, positively Bolshevik', says: 'Bormann had been working in closest contact with Moscow since 1943.'

This revelation caused quite a stir. One organisation that sat up and took notice was the British intelligence service, otherwise known as MI5. A request was received from Captain R. G. Hodges to contact the *Standard* and obtain the names of the Germans who had made this sensational claim.

All this time Betty Knox was still at Nuremberg, reporting on the various trials (twelve in all) that followed those of the leading Nazi figures. Now on trial were doctors, judges, businessmen, etc. Any idea of an international court had now been dispensed with. All these subsequent, smaller-scale cases were conducted entirely by the Americans.

And when Betty wasn't writing for the papers, she would sometimes appear in them. As often as not she would be the single, solitary individual who was raising her voice, or furiously typing, in protest. In a previous article, she had talked of the difficulties involved in stamping out the Nazi mentality in post-war Germany. Now, in July 1947, a couple of years after the war, *Der Spiegel* magazine reported the formation of a new Nazi party – the SPD. Of all places, they had opted to hold their congress in Nuremberg. But, as this translation makes clear, not everybody was welcome:

> In the company of US journalist Betty Knox is Franz von Papen Junior. He is not allowed to enter. 'We will teach you democracy!' shouts the American angrily, and storms out.

Franz von Papen Junior was a lawyer, and part of the successful defence team that had been responsible for his father's acquittal at Nuremberg. Von Papen Senior had been Hitler's deputy when he first came to power. The comparatively moderate von Papen had hoped to marginalise Hitler but, in practice, it was he who was marginalised. His criticism of Hitler (expressed privately in his earlier career and publicly at his recent trial) was one reason why he and his son were not welcomed by those who still espoused Nazi ideals.

In London, MI5 were still dashing off internal memos in an effort to discover the name of the source who claimed Martin Bormann was in Russian hands. If only their investigative skills could match their neat line in scathing sarcasm, as demonstrated in this typical response:

> The press stories as to the fate and whereabouts of BORMANN offer a variety of sensational turns as the silly season reaches its height. In recent weeks he has been variously, and glibly, reported to be in Switzerland, Bolivia, Argentina, Italy, Norway, Brazil and Egypt.

Presumably the glib report from Egypt claims he was last seen shuffling through the sand, between two skinny old geezers with knobbly knees. On 10th July 1947, the truth was finally revealed by Norman Himsworth, also a master of the deprecating remark:

> The *Standard* story was written by Miss Betty KNOX, who can now be located at Hotel Proubok, Prague. As you can well imagine, it is impossible for us in London to go further than this into the source of the story, with the lady so many miles away. I should tell you, however, that it is the ambition of every newspaper reporter who steps upon German soil to discover the whereabouts of Martin BORMANN, or, should this prove impossible, at least 'discover' some evidence which would justify his writing a story on this subject. No doubt Miss KNOX, if she were interviewed, could enlighten you further as to the source of her information; her answers, I feel sure, would be surprising.

On this occasion it would seem Betty Knox had got her facts wrong. And her punishment was to be death by a thousand sneers. Obviously MI5 would have liked to take the matter further but, apparently, making contact with anyone outside the British Isles (even when supplied with their current address) was a totally insurmountable obstacle.

For a second time, Betty's journalistic instinct had let her down. The previous year she'd dismissed the rumour that Goering had committed suicide, and had been roundly criticised for it. Now she had gone to press with the rumour that Bormann was still alive and, once again, been mocked for her incompetence.

As previously mentioned, Betty Knox worked alongside Josie Thompson of the United Press. It's probable that Betty was working as a 'stringer' – a freelance journalist who is paid for their reports on an individual basis. There were many trials in progress, in different court rooms, often running simultaneously. With so few journalists now remaining in Nuremberg, this was a busy time for them both.

Amongst those on trial were the directors of I. G. Farben, a large chemical conglomerate. Its products included key ingredients in the manufacture of explosives, and the poison gas used in concentration camps. In his book *The Devil's Chemists*, Josiah E. DuBois Junior (who was on the prosecution team) recalled Josie Thompson and Betty Knox in his office, badgering him for newsworthy stories. The big story was that the defence were concealing documents from the prosecution, and Josie's subsequent article in *Stars and Stripes* helped ensure those documents were produced.

In November 1947, Patsy joined Wilson and Keppel for their third Royal Variety Show. This was Patsy Knox's second appearance before George VI, Queen Elizabeth and the young princesses Elizabeth and Margaret. Just like Betty Knox's first Royal performance in 1933, the venue was the London Palladium. In April 1947, the trio had played the Palladium in globetrotting revue *Here, There and Everywhere*, alongside comedian Tommy Trinder and actress Hy Hazell, who were both returning for this Royal show. (The revue had included a scene entitled 'A Date in the Desert', in which Trinder appeared as a tourist, Hy Hazell as Cleopatra, and Wilson, Keppel and Betty as 'The Arabs'.)

The cast for the November Royal Variety show was boosted by the inevitable Crazy Gang and a bevy of female acrobatic and speciality acts. Also onstage (in a sketch entitled 'Buying a Driving Licence') were the great Stan Laurel and Oliver Hardy, in the twilight of their careers but still received with much affection.

The Crazy Gang's Bud Flanagan provided *The Performer* with an exclusive diary of backstage preparations, including a dramatic incident when impresario Val Parnell had to chase a couple of gatecrashers off the premises, one of whom was Al Burnett, current compere of BBC cabaret show *Café Continental.* It was all a misunderstanding, as Bud explained:

> Al told me that Jack Wilson, of Wilson, Keppel and Betty had invited him. Jack said: 'Someone announced from the stage last night that

artistes taking part could invite friends.' We later found out it was Jimmy Nervo.

Yes, yet another Crazy Gang prank. It will come as no great surprise that the review of Wilson, Keppel and Betty's act reads exactly as it did in 1945 – the sand dance, the seven veils, the spear dance. Like every classic comedy routine, the fact that the audience knows exactly what's going to happen next just makes them laugh all the louder. And, as Betty Knox recalled in a 1952 interview for *Stars and Stripes*, the Royal Family were in no way tiring of the trio:

> All told, Betty and her daughter, who is carrying on the Knox stage career under the name Jean Knox, gave six command performances – for King George V, for the Duke of Windsor while he reigned as Edward VIII, and the late King George VI. Betty was an especial favorite of Queen Mother Elizabeth.

The traditional special edition of *The Performer* gives an individual biography of each member of the trio. When read as separate entries, there is far less evidence of Wilson and Keppel's supposed joint career stretching back to childhood. And, although Betty Knox is referred to, there is no mention of the three generations of Bettys as there was in 1945. (The fact that Betty Knox's mother, Lizzie, was currently staying in London with her granddaughter could explain why they suddenly decided to drop this claim.) The Fosters Agency (their representatives since they first set foot in Britain) placed this display advert in *The Stage*:

WILSON, KEPPEL & BETTY
Acknowledge the great honour of being chosen for their
3rd ROYAL VARIETY SHOW.
The only American Act to have this unique distinction.

If there was a record to be bagged, they would happily claim to be an American trio – which, in a way, they once were. They were also shortly heading for Glasgow for the pantomime *Sleeping Beauty*. Being American is not a bad ploy when playing Glasgow. Calling yourselves American and staying mute throughout your act is an even better one.

Wilson, Keppel and Betty spent much of April 1948 at the London Casino (now the Prince Edward Theatre) with a rapidly rising star who shared their talent for physical comedy, though his was of the more frenetic variety: a young man named Norman Wisdom. The Freddie

Carpenter Dancers opened the show, and one of those dancers – Mary Logan – was fascinated by Wilson, Keppel and Betty's meticulous back-stage preparations, as she told *The Stage* in 1999:

> I often stood in the wings to watch their act and it was a revelation to see how self-sufficient they were.
>
> When it was time for their spot, they placed their props carefully in position, which did not seem to differ by so much as a centimetre on any night. Had every light in the theatre fused, they would still have been able to find anything they needed.
>
> Costume changes were kept on hangers and wrapped in dust-sheets. They were hung on the back struts of the scenery, from where the trio made their exits and entrances.
>
> Stagehands were forbidden to come anywhere near or touch anything. In fact the only thing Wilson, Keppel and Betty needed to rely on was the band in the pit.
>
> When they needed any of their props during the act, they incorporated bringing them on into the routine being performed. In the famous sand dance, performed to selections from *Ballet Egyptien*, the mat used was carried on to music, unfolded and sand scattered from a container – all carried out in perfect unison.
>
> Afterwards, they folded the mat and danced off stage without missing a beat. At the end of the week, I doubt whether they had to lay out a single tip for the stage crew.

It was tradition, at the end of the week, for performers to give various theatre staff a small gratuity. Knowing Jack Wilson's generous nature, the fact that the stage hands never so much as touched the props wouldn't have stopped him tipping them. If you have everything where you want it, it is well worth financially rewarding the backstage crew to make sure it stays that way.

In the second half of 1948, the Dachau trials (that had started the previous year) were reaching their conclusion. These were held at Dachau concentration camp, and were American military tribunals dealing with alleged German war criminals. For some of the accused, the result was imprisonment, for others it was execution. Freda Utley's book *The High Cost of Vengeance* expressed the views of many Americans who were deeply concerned about how their countrymen were conducting the trials. Judge Edward Leroy van Roden of Delaware County, Pennsylvania was part of a commission sent to Germany in 1948 to investigate claims that some Germans did not get a fair trial. In one particular case he was in agreement:

> 'There was no jury,' concluded van Roden. 'The court consisted of ten officers sitting as judge and jury, and one law-member, the only person with legal training, whose rulings as to the admissibility of evidence were final.'

He had also heard of statements being taken from prisoners who had been subjected to physical or mental torture:

> 'The tragedy,' said van Roden, 'is that many of us Americans, having fought the war with so much sweat and blood, and having defeated the enemy, now say "All Germans should be hung!" We won the war, but some of us want to go on killing. That's not fighting. That's wicked.'

Freda Utley stated that, in November 1948, fifteen men were being hanged every Friday. Her view was that 'the more victims of the miscarriage of justice who could be done away with, the less evidence of injustice would remain'. Whatever the exact truth was, this would have been one of the darkest times to have been in Nuremberg. In 1946, when the senior Nazi officials had been executed, those journalists who were allowed to witness the hangings were selected by drawing lots. Now, with far fewer journalists around, there was no need to limit the number of spectators. If (as is fairly clear) Betty Knox and Josie Thompson had misgivings as to the validity of the trials, they may have wanted to see for themselves how humanely the guilty were executed. Betty had possibly been fortunate enough to survive her time as war correspondent without witnessing death first hand; but now, three years into peace time, she was watching men being hanged. Freda Utley wrote:

> Betty Knox, whom I have already mentioned, and 'Jose' of the United Press, had attended the previous week's hangings just after I first met them in Nuremberg. Neither of them were ever likely to forget their terrible experience. The Protestant and Catholic chaplains at the Landsberg prison where the executions take place were both convinced of the innocence of several of the men hung. They were in despair at their inability to do anything to stop the crime of killing men, several of whom had convinced the priests or pastors that they were innocent, and all of whom had been condemned by confessions extorted by torture or on the testimony of witnesses proved to have perjured themselves.

One of the men Betty Knox saw had been told on the preceding Wednesday that he was reprieved pending a reinvestigation of his case, and then dragged out of his cell on the Friday to be hung. Another had been promised he should see his wife before dying, after not being allowed to see her for three years. But when she arrived at the prison at the appointed time she was told, 'Sorry, he's already dead; he was hung first instead of last by mistake.'

Before three of the men were executed, Betty Knox had taken down their last words. The first was Cornelius Schwanner, a prison camp commander. One of the charges was that he had killed a Polish prisoner who was too weak to stand, by beating him with his pistol and kicking him in the stomach. Two witnesses testified that he never wore his pistol at roll call. He was also held responsible for an epidemic that killed 250 prisoners. He testified that he did everything in his power to curb the epidemic, even to the extent of purchasing medicine with his own funds. His last words were simple and succinct:

> No, I have nothing to say. Only my relatives I should have liked to see. I am sorry that I could not see my relatives one last time.

The second man was Fritz Girke, who had been the chief of Bensheim Gestapo Office. He was one link in a chain of command that was responsible for executing several American airmen. In one case, his superior (Hans Trimmler) had instructed Girke to shoot a prisoner. Girke then told his assistant to do it, and his assistant passed on the order to two of his subordinates, who carried out the execution. Fritz Girke's last words commenced with a protest that a petition he had filed against his execution had been delayed in the post. He maintained he had done his duty as an officer, and that international law had been violated by his sentence.

Freda Utley explains this violation, claiming that Fritz Girke had previously been subjected to a mock trial in a dimly lit room, where a group of Americans had sentenced him to death, then promised to acquit him provided he signed a confession. He also had a black hood placed over his head and was kicked and beaten. His execution was reported in many papers on 15th October 1948. Because of the similarity between his last words as they appear here, and as they appear in Betty's transcript in Freda Utley's book, it is probable that Betty wrote this article:

Fritz Girke, a former major of Hitler's storm troops and Gestapo chief of Bensheim who was responsible for the deaths of several American fliers who parachuted in his area during the war, screamed 'murderers' repeatedly as he was taken to the gallows.

He shouted from the gallows platform, as the noose was adjusted, that his final petition for clemency had not been acted upon.

'I did my duty as a German soldier when I killed American terror fliers who murdered German women and children,' he cried.

His shouts were cut off as the trap was sprung.

The third man was Willi Rieke, a sports instructor and the commander of a German home guard unit, who was executed for killing an American airman whom he was transporting to a prison camp. His co-accused (Karl Schenk) claimed that Rieke stopped the car at the side of the road, Rieke and the airman got out, and then Rieke shot the man with his pistol. Schenk continued:

When driving back to Friedberg he told me: 'Schenk, when you are asked now in the office, tell them that the flier was shot while escaping or while trying to escape.'

Willi Rieke's son was called to testify, and maintained that his father was, above everything, a sportsman and believed in fair play. Willi Rieke himself insisted that the airman had got out of the car himself, before it had properly come to a halt. He told the man to stop, but:

He continued moving. He didn't stand still, and he turned around, exposing the left side of his body. I grabbed my pistol and fired one, possibly two, but I believe only one shot, in him. Then the flier threw up his arms and fell down.

Willi Rieke's last words, as recorded by Betty, begin: 'I do not want to accuse, nor do I want to pay back what I have received. I want to say that I am innocent.' After sending his final greetings to members of his family, he concludes:

I forgive everybody who was unjust to me and I also forgive those who have rendered false oaths upon which such a sentence could only have been said. May God be a merciful judge for them. My last greetings also go to my beloved sport which is the basis for interior and exterior recovery of our youth. May in the next years the best men of the world meet in a fight, not to win but to be together no matter what nation and what race.

Freda Utley's reaction to the final words of these three men is typically heartfelt:

> How many of the men America has hung, and is hanging now week by week, were innocent, will never be known. Only one thing is certain: they never had a fair trial and their interrogation, condemnation, and execution are a disgrace to democratic justice.

It is almost impossible to write dispassionately about the Nuremberg trials and the trials that followed them. They engender strong feelings, but the precise nature of those feelings will differ from person to person. The sources I have chosen are those with which Betty Knox had a close association. The fact that she not only spoke frankly to Freda Utley, but was prepared to be named, in a book that was published the very next year, demonstrates her serious concerns about how justice had been administered. She saw some horrific sights in October 1948, but it was the human stories behind them that affected her most.

Although the trials were steadily drawing to a close, Betty was in no hurry to leave. Like Wilson and Keppel, she had never stayed still long enough to have a home. Home was wherever she was, and whoever she was with at the time. And once more she had made a whole new circle of contacts and friends. Home, for Betty, was no longer Kansas nor London. It was Germany.

In December 1948, for the third year running, Wilson, Keppel and Betty were in *Sleeping Beauty*, this year at the Theatre Royal, Newcastle-upon-Tyne. As is traditional, each performance ended happily, with the aid of a little pantomime magic. But, as Patsy was soon to discover, fairytale princes aren't the only ones who can work miracles.

19
Hook, Line and Sinker
(Britain and Germany 1949–1950)

'The young man is no menace. He sings quite well.' (Betty Knox, 1944)

PANTOMIME AND SUMMER SEASON are the two times of year when performers can afford to relax just a little. Playing two shows a day to an audience packed with boisterous kids, and coping with elaborate costumes and quick changes, might not be thought of as a rest cure. But at least you have the same digs for a few months. And your day off is just that – a day off. Not a day spent travelling across the country to new digs and a new theatre – knowing you'll have to spend the next morning running through the act with a new pit orchestra and technical team. So, from December 1948 to the end of February 1949, Wilson, Keppel and Betty's whirlwind touring schedule came to a brief halt.

During that winter, playing *Sleeping Beauty* in Newcastle, something quite incredible happened – though it didn't have the most promising of starts. As Billy Shenton Junior (whose father was a close friend of Jack Wilson) recalls – it began with Patsy falling ill:

They were in Newcastle – in pantomime. And Patsy got this cold. And they sent for the theatre doctor – because, you know, in show business you can't just go off with a cold. You just carry on. You get the doctor in and treat it on the spot. And he came in, and he treated her. And he said to her, 'What's the matter with your wrist – with your arm?' And she told him. And he said, 'Let's have a look.' And he looked, and said, 'I think I could do something with that.' And she said, 'Oh, please. I've been told so many times that people could do things with this. But they've all said "no" eventually – it can't be done.'

As previously mentioned, in America as a youngster, Patsy had put her right arm through a glass door, and her severe injuries had been poorly patched up. She was only capable of doing her acrobatics one-handed – and, judging from movie clips, didn't even have the strength and mobility in her right hand to operate the finger cymbals. Fortunately, this doctor in Newcastle was able to offer some hope:

And he said, 'Well, I've been in the services. During the war we had to do a lot of operations on people – mending bones and mending sinews and so forth – that we couldn't do in civilian life, because if it went wrong we'd get sued. But in the services, if it's a matter of life or death, or saving a limb, you can try an experiment. If it goes wrong – tough luck – if it goes right, you've won through and got yourself a new operation. And we perfected this technique – of pulling the sinews down, and joining them on to the other sinews.' And he talked her into it – and she did it. They took time off after the act had finished in Newcastle. And she went in and had this operation.

Of course, it wasn't an instant cure. Afterwards there were weeks and weeks of physiotherapy. Bill remembers her wearing a sling, and doing exercises to flex her wrist muscles and strengthen her grip.

And eventually it came right. Well, fairly right. As right as you could get it.

Just as Betty Knox had been replaced, back in 1933 when she fell ill, Patsy needed another dancer to take her place during her lengthy recuperation – most probably a singer and dancer by the name of Edna May Dibb.

Edna was born Edna May Lark in Bridlington, Yorkshire on 16th October 1904, which actually makes her a year-and-a-half older than Betty Knox. She and her five sisters had already enjoyed success as the Singing Larks, and Edna continued singing and dancing after her sisters left the profession to raise their families.

She was in her mid-forties when she stood in for Patsy. It's said that she didn't particularly get on with Wilson and Keppel. She found them hard taskmasters. However, she managed to stick it out until Patsy was ready to return, which was several months later.

Patsy, during her convalescence, made frequent return trips to Newcastle, to the doctor who had operated on her. But not all those visits were purely medicinal. Billy Shenton Junior explains:

> And she fell hook, line and sinker for the doctor. And this was the big romance, as far as we were concerned.

On 20th May 1949, Erika Mann's brother, Klaus, wrote to his sister from his hotel room in Cannes on the French Riviera, where he was working on a novel. Amongst other matters he suggested that Erika and Betty Knox could join him on a car trip to Prague. Klaus – who was suffering badly from depression, suicidal thoughts and drug abuse at the time – may have been nostalgic for that joyful Christmas he'd spent with them both in 1945. The car trip to Prague never happened. The next day he took an overdose of sleeping pills, and hotel cleaning staff discovered him lying dead in his room.

By late 1949 Patsy was back in the act, appearing in *Aladdin* at Dudley Hippodrome in the West Midlands. The character of Wishee-Washee was played by future *On The Buses* star Reg Varney who, at the time, frequently performed in a double-act with Benny Hill. Benny, meanwhile, was also playing Wishee-Washee in *Aladdin* at Richmond Theatre, near London.

Also in the cast were Billy West's Harmony Boys, whose membership included a teenage Brian Patton – one half of the Patton Brothers, the older brothers of Barry and Paul Elliot, otherwise known as the Chuckle Brothers. Brian recalls Patsy draping the veils over her right arm which (though much improved) would never regain its full strength.

Cine enthusiast Bob Hosier was permitted to film the pantomime in rehearsal, and his few precious colour shots of the trio (almost always photographed in monochrome) reveal how surprisingly multi-coloured the act was. Initially Jack and Joe were attired in long green dragoman shirts, in contrast to the red fezzes and shoes; then pale red mini-togas for the sand dance; and, finally, cream-coloured outfits for the spear dance.

In March 1950, Betty Knox made another appearance in German magazine *Der Spiegel*. It was headlined BETTY KNOX TIPPTE RICHTIG (Betty Knox typed correctly) and was yet another tale of Betty being alerted to an incident of unfairness and campaigning to get it changed.

It concerned the steel-forging industry of the Ruhr, which was being prevented from supplying rail cars to Mao Tse Tung's China, on the grounds that they were 'militaristic'. However, Betty (described in the article as 'pretty and intelligent') discovered that levers on the rail cars were being supplied by British factories, which 'outraged her American sense of justice':

> Betty found it unfair. She tapped many lines on narrow US airmail paper.

Washington senators agreed with her, and the decision was overturned, bringing much needed work to Germany's ailing steel industry.

This was typical Betty. Once more the journalist had become the story. And once more she was making a stand against injustice being meted out to those people she had now chosen to live amongst. The article credited Betty as being special correspondent for *Time* magazine and the United Press agency. Although she was certainly the writer of numerous articles originating from Germany, it has not been possible to attribute any to her.

Friday 14th July 1950 was a busy day for Wilson, Keppel and Betty. First, they attended the Viking Studios in Kensington, to film their act for the movie *A Ray of Sunshine*. Like most of their cinematic appearances, this was a low-budget B-movie showcasing a mix of variety turns, linked together by comedian Ted Ray, star of radio's *Ray's a Laugh*. The plot of the film was negligible, and mainly involved Ted Ray getting progressively drunker so that, by the time Wilson, Keppel and Betty turned up, he could barely stand.

Patsy's previous movies were shot when she was in her very late teens. Now 26, she almost looks like a different woman. The sensuality is still evident, but only occasionally glimpsed behind her cool aloof exterior. The fun-loving flirty teenager has vanished, to be replaced by a 'hard to get but well worth the effort' young lady. Her hair is more styled and she is serenely but effortlessly elegant. The one indication that this woman is still Patsy is her right arm. There is clearly more strength in it since her operation. She is more at ease using that arm and holding the veils in her right hand. But, perhaps out of habit, she still only plays the finger cymbals in her left hand.

Jack and Joe, now well into their mid-fifties, look noticeably older – and not just as a result of their stage makeup. In this six-minute sequence, which must be a sizeable proportion of their stage act, 'Betty' saunters around with a slightly haughty look, suggesting she is quite aware that her companions are putty in her hands. The studio is small and the set dressing minimal. There's a curtain at one side, a painted brick wall behind them, and a large pot plant dominating the background. In the opening shot, a veiled Betty peers through the leaves of the plant. We then have the nudge bells routine, a little expanded from earlier versions. After Betty exits through the curtain, Wilson tries to entice Keppel to dance with him, by jingling his nudge bells. Keppel gives a 'buzz off!' gesture with his own finger cymbals, making it clear that he'd far rather go behind the curtain with Betty. Eventually he succumbs to Wilson's beckoning, making their subsequent dance seem even camper than usual – one of the main reasons why their audiences (Nazis excepted) always found it so funny.

Another peek through the foliage from Betty, and we're into the sand dance. Like the previous routine, this is marred by some cost-cutting. The accompanying music is the best Eastern exotica that the studio's record library could supply, and has obviously been dubbed on afterwards. Wilson and Keppel would have had no difficulty in performing their routine in silence. After all those years, if asked, they could probably have done it blindfolded in separate rooms. But the music is never quite spot-on, and their rhythmic sand shuffling is often just a little ahead of the beat.

Again there are a couple of additions to the routine. As usual, Wilson and Keppel (side by side) do a series of Egyptian hand movements, first facing right, then left, and repeating three or four times. The final time (while Keppel's back is turned) Wilson does a double-handed nose thumbing towards his oblivious partner. Shortly before the end of the sand dance they perform a new gesture – a tossing movement with alternate hands emanating from the navel – possibly to represent scattering handfuls of seeds. Needless to say, it looks vaguely obscene and must have provoked roars of laughter.

Betty re-enters, concealed beneath her many veils. This is, in many ways, the most successful routine, as it relies not on ill-fitting recorded music, but on Wilson's skill on the snake charming pipe (basically a treble recorder). It is a much simpler staging of the seven veils routine than the one filmed around 1943. As the years went on, Wilson and Keppel cut back on their props, so they had less baggage to cart round the country. All they now needed for this routine was Betty's costume, Wilson's pipe, Keppel's drum and a small gong. The voyeuristic snake that used to emerge from the basket and startle Betty with his rasping tongue has been entirely dispensed with.

Other than that, the routine is the same as ever, with each discarded veil accompanied by a stroke on the gong, and Keppel sticking up the appropriate number of fingers. Keppel drums while Wilson pipes – his repertoire including 'Money is the Root of all Evil' and (shortly before the removal of the final veil) the highly appropriate 'Give Me Five Minutes More'. When Wilson and Keppel whip the last veil off Betty, she does the backwards dance as usual, though briefer and less energetic than the earlier filmed version (which could be put down to the limitations of a very small studio, or just that Patsy was cutting back on the acrobatics). The mask that Patsy wears on the back of her head is a more sophisticated affair than the previous version. It is an elaborate *papier-mâché* representation of Wilson or Keppel's face, complete with deadpan expression. Wilson and Keppel join her in the 'star jump' finale, and their act concludes.

The three of them were paid a total of £150 for their time at the studio. However, that was not their total earnings for the day, because their contract stipulated that they 'shall be released in good time for the first performance in which they appear at the Palladium Theatre, London'. Being seasoned and trusted Palladium regulars, Wilson, Keppel and Betty were currently back at the theatre where they had made their British debut, supporting one of the greatest stars of the moment – Frank Sinatra.

The printed programme carries a photo of the fresh-faced, lean, tousle-haired singer and states it is his 'first appearance in England'. Not quite correct. He'd performed in London back in May 1944. And Betty Knox had been in the audience. Her subsequent 'Over Here' column is uncharacteristically cool and dispassionate:

> Frank Sinatra came and went from London without causing more than a ripple of good-natured laughter from curious cinema audiences.

They wondered if it were really true that the 1944 Valentino, nicknamed 'Swoonatra' by US columnists, could produce a feeling of faintness among the weaker sex – or anybody – when he sang. Nobody fainted.

A Sunday night audience watched the serious young man and were politely noisy. Week-day audiences included a few girls who tried lamely to emulate what they had read was Sinatra behaviour among fans reported to be living just for the autograph of America's No. 1 crooner.

The young man is no menace. He sings quite well. People who know him say that he has an active sense of humour and sings with his tongue in his cheek – if that is possible.

Now, in July 1950, when Sinatra stepped on stage to commence his fourteen-song marathon, the packed audience was far more vocal in its appreciation, and (as *The Times* noted) Sinatra was able to handle this idol worship with confidence:

> He is a trim, well spoken, gay young man who laughs when the more excitable of his admirers punctuate his songs with fervent little 'o-ohs' and 'a-ahs,' and who can kiss his hands to an audience without appearing foolish.

By this point in his career Sinatra was as popular (if not more so) in Britain as he was back in the States. He opened with 'When You're Smilin'' and other numbers included 'April in Paris' and the local crowd-pleaser 'A Foggy Day'. The tongue-in-cheek humour hadn't entirely vanished though. Amongst his repertoire was an 'Ol' Man River' parody, retitled 'Ol' Man Crosby'. If Sinatra had any opportunity to glance at his (largely visual) supporting acts from the wings, he would have enjoyed the spectacle of Danish twin girls Krista and Kristel on the trapeze, and been thoroughly mystified by the eccentric walks of Max Wall and the solemn surreal ritual that was 'Cleopatra's Nightmare'.

During rehearsals for his London Palladium appearance (so the story goes) Sinatra sacked one of the musicians. From then on, the whole orchestra hated him – until the end of the season, when he presented each one of them with a gold watch.

Before we leave the Palladium, a few more words on the subject of dressing rooms. Wilson and Keppel were featured performers at the top of their game, and could reasonably be expected to demand the best, both for themselves and for their current Betty. But, as Billy Shenton

Junior recalls, they really weren't that fussy:

> They couldn't care less what dressing room *they* got, as long as Betty had a good dressing room, commensurate with her position on the bill, as Wilson, Keppel and Betty. So she would get a good dressing room. The boys? 'We don't care where we go as long as we're all right,' Joe said. 'As long as the sink is cock-high,' he used to say. 'Got to be able to piss in the sink.'

Billy Shenton Junior once went to visit them at the Palladium. He asked the doorman where they were, and was told to go up … and up … and keep going up:

> He said, 'It's right at the top.' I said, 'Right at the top?' He said, 'Yes. In the flies.' I said, 'You're joking.' He said, 'No.' When we got up there, they literally had four flats roped together, with a door in. A self-made dressing room up there – of flats. Betty had a nice room, but they were up there, in the flies, with the scenery.

On those occasions when their dressing room was something more secure than four pieces of scenery tied together, they would still have the problem of what to do with their valuables while they were on stage. Jack Wilson's money belt has already been mentioned, but Roy Hudd tells of the time when ventriloquist Arthur Worsley shared a bill with them at the Bristol Hippodrome in 1957. The dressing room was full of American wardrobe trunks and suitcases, and mountains of clothes were scattered all over the place. Just before he went onstage, Joe Keppel took off his socks, stuck a roll of white five-pound notes in one of them and lobbed it backwards over his shoulder, explaining, 'If I don't know where the hell it is, what chance have the burglars got?'

Towards the end of 1950, panto season beckoned. This year it was *Aladdin* at the King's Theatre, Hammersmith, London.

But the Betty who danced onstage at Hammersmith wasn't Patsy.

20
Married in Two Weeks
(Britain 1951)

'And that's when the Bettys started to change.' (Billy Shenton Junior, 2012)

SOME PEOPLE ARE UNDER THE IMPRESSION that there was only ever one Betty … or maybe two. Others are convinced that Wilson and Keppel changed their Bettys like they changed their socks – if not more often. But it should be remembered that (apart from a few short-term replacements) since 1928, when the trio was formed, until 1950, there were just two Bettys. Betty Knox stayed with the act for thirteen years and her daughter Patsy for the next eight.

The touring life suited Jack and Joe perfectly. They had no ties. They had no home. But Patsy now had someone in her life. A man she desperately loved. But a man who lived, and worked, in Newcastle. Wilson and Keppel tried to give Patsy time off whenever they could. But, for Patsy, it was becoming an impossible task – travelling constantly around the country, when she really wanted to be in one place with one man. Billy Shenton Junior was aware of the tensions it was causing within the trio:

> The break-up started because she wanted to keep going and seeing the doctor. I don't know all the ins and outs, obviously. I wasn't with them all the time. I tell you what I heard from Jack.

It's possible that Jack and Joe thought they were taking on another short-term replacement when they engaged Barbara Holt for that 1950-

51 pantomime season. Barbara ('an attractive English redhead' says *The Performer*) was born in West Bromwich, Staffordshire in August 1928, and was 22 when she became their next Betty. In a later press interview (with the *Birmingham Evening Argus* in November 1958) Jack and Joe reminisced about their various Bettys, and recalled Barbara with particular fondness:

> 'We had one, she was a beauty,' said Jack. 'She was married in two weeks. That was in Phoenix, Arizona.'

The marriage was actually in London, though Barbara's husband came from Phoenix. And two weeks wasn't that far from the truth. It was certainly only a few weeks into the pantomime, maybe halfway through its run:

> Joe, rather resigned, added, 'We knew we'd never keep her, she was too beautiful for words.'

In October 2012 Barbara Holt Schaller spoke to me on the phone from her home in Arizona. There were several surprises along the way, because that's how her showbiz life mapped out. With no map. No career path. And the most unlikely of beginnings:

> Well, it all started when I was in the army for three years – in Singapore for the last year. And I came home and entered this contest – they called it the 'Carnival Queen of West Bromwich'. That's what I became – Carnival Queen. And from there I went to the Johnny Weissmuller swimming show. And then the Josef Locke show, where I had to very quickly learn how to tapdance.
>
> And then I went to London and got a job as showgirl at the London Casino. And that was when the doorman gave me a message from a Mr Wilson, who wanted to have lunch with me the next day, and that was how it all began.
>
> So I met him next day at a place called Olivelli's. And the day following that, I met him at the theatre where he was working, and met the current Betty. And she put me through the routine – and I became the next Betty.

I asked Barbara what Wilson and Keppel were like to work with:

> Well, I loved Jack. I really loved Jack. Both of them, actually. I mean, they were just sweethearts.

Now in their late 50s, Jack and Joe still paraded the platform-cum-prop-box around the stage with Barbara sitting cross-legged on top. She also had to master the tricky seven veils routine:

> They took that seventh veil off, and I looked exactly like they did. I had the mask on the back of my head – and shoes that were pointing the different way. It was so funny.

Each day Barbara took the bus out of central London to the King's Theatre, Hammersmith – and each evening she would return to Olivelli's, where she'd dine and socialise into the early hours before going upstairs to her room. And it was at Olivelli's that she met her husband-to-be. A whirlwind romance? 'Yes, absolutely!'

On 27th January 1951 (at St Giles Parish Church, Holborn, Central London), Barbara Holt married American trampolinist John Schaller. Jack Wilson was one of a small group of friends and family who attended this fast-tracked wedding. But there was no time for honeymooning. John Schaller and his brother Tony had to leave for an engagement in Paris, while Barbara stayed in London to complete the run of *Aladdin*.

So Barbara's career with Wilson, Keppel and Betty started and finished with the three-month pantomime season at Hammersmith. In later years, Jack and Joe would complain that a whole succession of Bettys had abruptly left to get wed, though few actually did.

But Patsy Knox never did return to the act. And she never quite achieved what she hoped, after leaving to spend more time with the doctor she adored. The story (as Billy Shenton Junior heard it) did not end well:

> What happened after that, I don't know. I understood they were engaged. And I didn't hear about them getting married. But I did hear that there'd been a break up. A big break up. And it broke Patsy's heart. She had a nervous breakdown. And that's when the Bettys started to change. She had to come out of the act. And she eventually went back to the States, and went into a sanatorium.

As Jack Wilson told Billy, Betty Knox travelled back to England, and then took Patsy with her to Texas:

> I think she was the one who took her to the sanatorium. Of course, quite a bit of it was paid for – I think – by Franz von Papen. Because he'd got

money. I mean, Jack had been earning money for years and years and years, but it didn't go everywhere. You know, we're talking about a lot of money, for taking her to America, and into a nursing home or sanatorium. I mean, in America there was no health service, you know. So I think that was paid for by 'his nibs', we think. Because Jack couldn't have afforded it.

Der Spiegel had reported, back in 1947, of Franz von Papen Junior (who had defended his father at the Nuremberg trials) attempting to enter a political meeting in the company of Betty Knox. There was certainly a friendship between the two. Anything more would be speculation. And Jack shared his speculations with Billy Shenton Junior:

> She was sticking to him like glue. We think there was a romance between von Papen and Betty. But all we can say is – we think. Jack sort of hinted at it, but didn't really know himself.

With Patsy now out of the act, Jack and Joe next recruited Irene Scott, a slim blonde from north of the border – Newlands, Glasgow. Irene was born in October 1926 and joined the act aged 25. She was a highly experienced dancer and choreographer who was to become a long-lasting and invaluable asset to the act. Although classically trained, she had little trouble in adapting to their routines – which no longer had such a heavy reliance on 'hoofing'.

She had appeared in a couple of pantomimes at Newcastle – including *Sleeping Beauty*, where Patsy had first met her doctor. Although Jack and Joe weren't looking for a replacement at that time, they'd have had plenty of opportunity to socialise with Irene and watch her at work. After that, she was back in Glasgow for her regular summer job in the chorus line of the *Half-Past Eight Show* at the King's Theatre. But, by July 1950, as the *People's Journal* reported, she had won promotion:

> Now she is ballet mistress of the same show at Glasgow.
> 'Thinking up new dance routines every week is a harder job than dancing in the chorus,' she says.
> Irene often lies awake in bed and works out new dance arrangements for the show.

In October 1951, Wilson, Keppel and Betty were back at the Palladium, this time with Gracie Fields topping the bill. *Variety* noted there was 'a new gal in the show' and *The Performer* described her as the 'invigorating Irene Scott'. But *The Stage* made it clear she was far more than a talented dancer who'd learnt all the moves:

> She is a big success, playing up to the eccentricities of the two clever masters of burlesque in a captivating way.

They finished the year in *Sleeping Beauty* at the Alexandra, Birmingham. Irene had firmly established herself as a skilled and creative member of the team – while over in Bonn, just the previous month, Betty Knox had embarked on her third career.

21

The Title is a Secret

(Britain, Germany and Las Vegas
1952–1956)

'… with a typewriter in one hand and a painting in the other.'
(Omer Anderson, 1952)

MOST JOURNALISTS, IF THEY'RE LAW ABIDING and relatively clean living, manage to keep themselves out of the spotlight. Betty never did. For a start, she would stir up a fuss if she considered it worthy of stirring up. And secondly, if she had a good story to tell, she would share it with anyone – even with fellow reporters. She was never publicity shy herself. Blame it on her showbiz past. And life in her mid-forties continued to be just as eventful.

Omer Anderson, staff writer for the European edition of *Stars and Stripes*, a newspaper serving the US military, had no hesitation in placing Betty centre stage in this article from March 1952:

> Kansas-born Betty Knox, who during more than 20 years abroad made a reputation in the theater and as a war correspondent, is booming along in yet a third career – as a Bonn press club impresario.
>
> Betty's Press Villa Club, since opening last September, has become an indispensable part of the Bonn press scene. It's the only press club in Bonn, and it is operated in the interests of newspapermen, diplomats and officials.

After the war, Bonn had become the capital of West Germany, which continued to have a heavy presence of American and European journalists. Hence the need for an 'international' press club. But there was one unique feature of the Press Villa Club that made it particularly newsworthy:

> It is probably the only press club in the world that prides itself on being 'arty'. Betty has keyed furnishings and décor around a collection of paintings from the Dusseldorf galleries. These include modernists, impressionists, and reproductions of old masters. Shrewdly, Betty has worked out a deal with the galleries whereby club patrons may buy any painting they like and the galleries furnish the press club with replacements.
>
> Betty says half the paintings originally on display in the club have been sold and replaced under this arrangement. Snap-brimmed news-hawks theoretically may be seen departing from Betty's hostelry with a typewriter in one hand and a painting in the other.

When Betty previously complained about unfair treatment given to the German steel industry, it demonstrated her concern that the German economy should rebuild itself. So it's hardly surprising that Betty should ensure this new venture would benefit local businesses. The club was chaired by Jack Raymond of the *New York Times*, and Betty acted as secretary-treasurer:

> Located in La Joachimstrasse, two minutes from the Federal Parliament building, the club has a bar, dining room, conference room and six bedrooms. In a town jammed with the press, Betty's club can't begin to put up all the visiting correspondents. For those she can't she makes reservations for at German hotels.

When Betty had taken part in the Royal Variety Performance of 1933, the act had boasted: 'Despite their world travels, none of the trio speaks any language but English.' Admittedly, at this time, much of their world travel was total fiction – but it was a statement that Wilson and Keppel reiterated in 1945. Quite probably the two men muddled through their foreign tours with a combination of pointing and mime. Betty, however, had now spent eight years living in Germany. When she negotiated on the phone with art galleries and hotels, it would have been with a fair smattering of German. The article concludes with this intriguing sentence:

She is now writing a book on her experiences, although she says the title is a secret.

The photographs that accompany the article show a somewhat stouter Betty Knox than the one pictured in Normandy and snapped sunbathing with Erika Mann in California in the mid-1940s. According to her showbiz successor, Eunice Roberts, she'd started putting on weight even before the end of her dancing career. Then, at Nuremberg, she'd spent hour after hour sitting and listening, with little opportunity for exercise. It was only natural that she'd fill out a little, as Billy Shenton Junior recalled:

> I do know she became very fat. She became very heavy, Jack told me. Which, of course, American matrons do.

Wilson, Keppel and their current Betty (Irene Scott) continued to make Olivelli's their home whenever they worked in and around London. *The Performer* of December 1952 told how the restaurant was organising a number of festive events for its showbiz clientele, with Jack, as usual, at the centre of attention:

> On both Christmas Day and New Year's Eve there is to be a gala dinner and jamboree – with Jack Wilson as chief fun maker and compere – and the charge has been reduced to 8s. 6d. to make it an exceptionally reasonable event.

Just half a year later, in July 1953, Mama and Papa Olivelli reluctantly decided to sell the business. Rita Olivelli proudly showed Noel Whitcomb of the *Daily Mirror* the enormous collection of framed and signed pictures that adorned the restaurant:

> From all over the walls at Olivelli's beam pictures of acts and artists – good acts, acts that are 'resting', acts that are now stars, acts with 'immediate vacancies'.
>
> They are all signed affectionately 'to Mamma and Pappa'.
>
> She looked round the pictures on the wall – 'Such a big family we've got,' she mused. 'Hundreds – thousands of children. All actors. Yet Pappa and me, when we came from Italy – we never even knew an actor.'

With such a priceless collection, it was inevitable that customers would occasionally walk off with a 'souvenir' of their visit. As Billy Shenton

Junior remembered, Jack and Joe (having more than once been victims of theft) devised a novel solution. They had an eight-by-ten-inch caricature drawn, put it in a large three-foot-square wooden frame, surrounded it in heavy anchor chain, and fixed it to the wall with a padlock.

(In 1993, when the current owners of Olivelli's restaurant, Giovanni and Salvatore Salamone, bought the business, the downstairs restaurant was in a very sorry state – packed full of rubbish and debris. It took them a year to clear the place out, during which they discovered a damp and dust-covered box-file, crammed with photos that had formerly filled the walls. A selection of these now has pride of place in the new restaurant – still named 'Olivelli's'. Patrons who glance upwards while dining may spot that very same caricature of Wilson and Keppel, drawn by Edwin Hall in 1942.)

In September 1952, the trio had supported Michael Bentine, just months after he'd left the cast of *The Goon Show*. In April 1953, they appeared with current Goon Peter Sellers (former stage partner of ex-Betty Eunice Roberts) who gave impressions of Groucho Marx and Jimmy Durante. But it wasn't Sellers who topped the bill: it was Wilson, Keppel and Betty.

Tony Hancock, shortly before he became a major radio star, was introduced to Jack Wilson by comedian George Fairweather (a family friend and early mentor). As George told biographer John Fisher (*Tony Hancock: The Definitive Biography*), Jack was hardly a household name at the time, but such was Hancock's admiration for the variety greats he was utterly thrilled to be shaking hands with one of his heroes.

Several times during 1953, Wilson, Keppel and Betty worked with old friend Bonar Colleano, who still managed to slot the odd comedy stage appearance into his busy movie schedule. Jack and Joe continued to provide *The Performer* with quirky little tit-bits about their experiences, including this, which appeared on 5th November:

> Going to the Alhambra, Bradford, the other night, Jack and Joe were stopped by a gang of youngsters with the time honoured and seasonable request to 'please remember the Guy'. They looked at the guys, two of which, with the aid of masks, bore a distinct resemblance to Wilson and Keppel.

Another illuminating article about Betty Knox's current activities appeared in the *Anderson Herald*, Indiana, on 24th November 1953. In the regular column 'Foreign Fax', correspondent John B. Crane brings this report from Dusseldorf:

> The two most famous American woman journalists in Germany since the war are generally considered to be 'Maggie' Higgins and Betty Knox.

Mr Crane hugely overstates his case with this opening remark. Marguerite Higgins, as mentioned earlier, was the likely inspiration for Carla MacMurphy ('would do anything to scoop a headline') in Toni Howard's novel *Shriek with Pleasure* – and, in 1951, was the first female recipient of the Pulitzer Prize for her coverage of the Korean War.

Betty Knox, on the other hand, had always been on the sidelines and, by this time in her career, was a relatively forgotten figure. However, it was Betty and not Marguerite who was the subject of this article, so Mr Crane was just taking the liberty of 'bigging her up'. He went on to relate Betty's current activities:

> Betty Knox, who came to Germany to cover the Nuremberg trials, is still here and is now writing for a string of Canadian newspapers. She never fully recovered from the shock of the trials and the flagrant miscarriages of justice she observed there. She has trunks full of Nuremberg documents and is seriously considering writing a book to reveal for the first time the inside story of the trials.

(This was the book that Omer Anderson mentioned the previous year, the title of which 'is a secret'.) Mr Crane's portrayal of Betty as someone severely shocked and angered by the conduct of the trials is remarkably similar to the picture painted by Freda Utley's 1949 book *The High Cost of Vengeance*. Coincidentally, Freda Utley is the other main focus of John Crane's article:

> I have just come from spending a long and fascinating evening with Betty, during which I sat and acted as unofficial referee between her and Freda Utley, author of the best-seller, 'The China Story', as they argued whether German labor is 'Communistic' or not, and whether private capitalism is on its way out in Western Germany.
>
> Both Betty and Freda are conversational titans in their own right and, when the two get together, it is like watching a world's championship heavyweight prize-fight or the final world series game between New York and the Dodgers.

What follows is a lengthy debate between these two (intellectual) heavyweights about communist influences and corruption in West German industry. Betty had recently interviewed a number of former factory workers who, as a result of post-war 'denazification' measures, had now become industry bosses:

> She reports they are 'living the life of Riley'. One labor director she interviewed formerly made the equivalent of 1,500 dollars a year. Today, as labor director of the plant, he earns 15,000 dollars per year.
>
> As a worker, previously, he could not afford a car. Now he drives a swank Mercedes 300. Formerly he wore a beret. Now he sports a black Homberg hat. He has one son studying in a French university, a second studying engineering and a daughter studying music here in Dusseldorf.

Freda Utley countered that just because the workers are Socialists, it didn't necessarily follow that they were Communists:

> 'Communists and Socialists are all the same,' insisted Betty. 'It all comes to the same thing in the end.'
>
> By this time it was far into the night, both sides were groggy, and I persuaded the ladies to call it a draw. Meanwhile Freda pursues her crusade against Communism and Betty continues her attacks on Socialism.

John Crane surely had his own political axe to grind in this piece, but it's interesting that, once again, Betty had no hesitation in letting her personal and political opinions appear in print. If she'd been working for a news agency, by now she'd be regarded as something of a liability. It would severely limit the stories she could be assigned to cover, and might even have led to her dismissal. So it's a fair bet that Betty's journalistic work was now of a freelance nature and she was operating on the fringes of the profession – which probably suited her fine.

This article also gives no mention of the Press Villa Club in Bonn, where Betty had been working as secretary and treasurer. It appears that this particular club was relatively short lived and that, by now, she probably worked purely as a journalist based in Dusseldorf.

In December 1953, Wilson, Keppel and Betty started their panto run of *Aladdin* at the Globe Theatre, Stockton-on-Tees. A set of photographs (taken during rehearsal or performance) show Jack, Joe and Irene Scott doing the nudge bells, the seven veils and the spear dance –

all performed front-of-curtain. It's the only photographic record of the spear dance in action, and is a vivid reminder of what an orgy of nudity and violence it was – with Wilson lunging at his fleeing partner, in an apparent attempt to make a Keppel kebab.

Soon after the pantomime ended, Irene Scott left the trio, having played the role of Betty for around three years. Like Betty Knox and Patsy before her, her photograph had adorned the walls of Olivelli's restaurant. She later returned to choreography (though with less emphasis on the *pas de deux* and *grand jeté*) for the Boy Scouts' Gang Shows. In later life she rarely mentioned Jack and Joe, but was very proud of her time working with them.

With Betty Knox working in Dusseldorf, and Patsy having left the act in 1950, it would seem the Knox family's involvement with Wilson, Keppel and Betty had long since ended. But, as Eve Perrick wrote in the *Daily Express* in February 1954, the Knoxes had arrived in London to offer Jack and Joe their expertise. Not as dancers – but as talent spotters:

> Right now Betty No. 5 is being sought. And that's the reason Harley-street enters into the picture. To a furnished flat above one of the consulting rooms has come Mrs Betty Knox, who was Betty No. 1, with her daughter Patsy, who was Betty No. 2, to interview would-be Betty No. 5.
>
> I asked Betty No. 1 how come this state of affairs: why, for instance, had she left the act, and her daughter after her?
>
> 'Well, I'd been with the "boys" for 15 years. Then, at the beginning of the war, I felt I ought to be doing something a little more serious than wiggling my hips on the stage. So I became a journalist, and Patsy took over.'
>
> Said Betty No. 2: 'I did the job for ten years, then I wanted some time off to stay with mother, and my friend, Irene Scott from Glasgow, took over. Irene lasted two years, then she got ill and retired.
>
> 'The present Betty, a ballet dancer, is working on a temporary basis. That's why we're auditioning for another Betty.'

As usual, Betty and Patsy's accounts of their careers are far closer to reality than anything Jack and Joe may say. (The 'boys' would happily add any number of years to the length of time Betty Knox performed with them.) But, as Betty Knox told the *Express*, they weren't finding it easy to engage a replacement:

'It's a well-paid job and the act hasn't had to "rest" for a single week since it started. But pretty girls don't seem to want to go permanently on tour. Although the boys are really marvellous to work with.

'They book the rooms, excuse their Betty from Monday morning band-calls – even do her ironing. In my own case they practically brought Patsy up for me.'

Betty's glowing testimonial confirms other accounts that Wilson and Keppel treated all their Bettys well. Their female partner was even allowed a lie-in in her new digs on Monday while Jack and Joe did the band rehearsal themselves. They'd got the act down to such a fine art, they could probably do Betty's moves as accurately (if not as sensuously) as she could herself.

But Betty Knox was a tough act to follow. She'd spent many years with Jack and Joe, touring her own country, then followed them abroad, leaving family and daughter behind. It was generous of her to credit Jack and Joe with bringing up Patsy in England (much as grandmother Lizzie had done in America) but, despite being such a frequent absentee mother, right now she and Patsy were very close. Although Patsy doesn't go into details, if a romantic break-up was the reason for her leaving the act, it seems that Betty had been there for her when she needed her most.

This was one of the last times that Jack, Joe, Betty and Patsy were all gathered together in the same place. And it was an occasion of kind words and fond memories.

Of all the auditionees who danced before the formidable judging panel of Wilson, Keppel and a brace of Bettys, it seems that one made the grade. A couple of weeks later *The Stage*, reviewing a show at London's Finsbury Park Empire, remarked:

Here, too, are Wilson, Keppel and Betty (a new, dark-eyed Betty, incidentally) with that hilarious display of Eastern grotesqueries that never fail to delight.

(One young dancer who unsuccessfully auditioned for the act in the early 1950s was Amanda Barrie. Ironic that the girl who Wilson and Keppel considered inadequate for the role of Cleopatra should, a mere decade or so later, be exercising her comedic seductive charms on Sid James in the title role of *Carry On Cleo*.)

As London Palladium veterans, Wilson, Keppel and Betty were an obvious choice when Palladium boss Val Parnell was assembling a bill to take to America's self-styled 'Entertainment Capital of the World', Las Vegas, Nevada. This single trip would be responsible for some of the best known and often repeated anecdotes about the trio. But, for Wilson, Keppel and Betty, it very nearly didn't happen.

Both Wilson and Keppel had become naturalised Americans in the early 1930s, before coming back to England. Joe Keppel, who regularly returned to his home city of Cork in Southern Ireland throughout his career, had reverted to Irish citizenship. Jack Wilson remained an American citizen, but having made no attempt to return to America since the end of the war, now had an invalid passport. He was, in effect, a stateless person – neither a British nor an American citizen – unable to travel until he could obtain a British passport. Thankfully Val Parnell may have helped speed things through, and the trio set sail on the *Queen Mary* in June 1954.

Wilson and Keppel were among only three people on the ship whose destination was The Desert Inn, Las Vegas. The third person was a dancer by the name of Mary Wemyss – their latest Betty. Mary was aged 35, making her older than Barbara Holt, Irene Scott and Patsy Knox. The notion that Wilson and Keppel picked progressively younger Bettys as the years went on was certainly not the case. They had little interest in a 'glamour girl' if she couldn't dance or get the laughs.

The classic story of their encounter with a New York customs officer was told by Tommy Trinder on the Tyne Tees TV series *Super Troupers* in 1985:

> The customs officer, he picked up this bag of sand, and he said, 'What's this?' And they said, 'Sand.' He said, 'What for?' They said, 'We're sand dancers.' He said, 'Where are you going?' They said, 'Las Vegas.'
>
> Now, I've heard of taking coals to Newcastle, but nobody had ever heard of taking sand to Las Vegas! And they sifted every grain of that sand – the American customs – to make sure they weren't smuggling something into America.

Val Parnell's six-week run of *London Palladium Varieties* was headed by Richard Hearne, a physical comedian whose 'Mr Pastry' character had been a big hit on the Ed Sullivan show. His most famous routine was 'The Lancers', in which he danced with a succession of increasingly energetic (and totally invisible) partners. Supporting acts included singer Pat Kirkwood, the Four Bogdadis (acrobats who genuinely *were* from Egypt), French puppeteer George La Faye and (billed just above a dog act) Wilson, Keppel and Betty. The resident Desert Inn Dancers provided two specially choreographed routines – 'Off the Leash' (to introduce Madame Malta and her Comedy Canines) and 'In Eastern Mood' (for Wilson, Keppel and Betty).

But the true top of the bill in Las Vegas was the gambling – as Val Parnell recounted in the *Daily Express* on his return:

> Nevada State and Las Vegas are built on the rattling of dice and the throw of a coin. The eating, the drinking, the dancing only exist to keep the visitor fit and fine for the casino.

And fitness was vital, if one was to stand the pace:

> ... from 7:30 pm to about 4:00 the next morning, relays of singers or jazz units play without cease. These are by no means poor performers; Artie Shaw was there the week before I arrived.

The *London Palladium Varieties* first-night audience included Bob Hope, who flew in from Tennessee at 6:30 that night and left for Chicago at 3:30 next morning. According to a celebratory two-page ad in *The Performer* he said, 'Well, I just loved it and I have never seen anything greater.' The Maitre d'Hotel added, 'I wish the room was twice as big. We won't have an empty table for the run of the six weeks.'

Val Parnell's bill of twelve acts was contracted to run for one hour and twenty minutes. A seasoned veteran of the Desert Inn bet him it would overrun to more like two hours. But you don't make it in Vegas without being a slick operator. The opening show ran for one hour fifteen minutes and Val pocketed two hundred bucks.

Ralph Pearl of the *Las Vegas Sun* employed a colourful turn of phrase in his assessment of the sand dancing trio:

> As a change of pace, Val Parnell offers Wilson, Keppel and Betty, who engage in a bit of tomfoolery while dressed in enlarged diapers that seem to hang precariously from the emaciated cadavers of Wilson and Keppel, who can never be mistaken for Montgomery Clift and Tony Curtis. Betty, on the other hand, is something else again.

Like those bygone days of midnight cabaret at London's Trocadero, the audience sat at tables, dividing their attention equally between the stage show and their food and drink. A final story comes from the man who later married Pat Kirkwood – songwriter and broadcaster Hubert Gregg (from his autobiography *Maybe It's Because ...?*). After Wilson, Keppel and Betty's first performance they were approached by the manager and told they had to drop the sand dance. When asked why, he said customers at a front-row table had complained 'the sand was getting in their soup'.

The trio returned to Britain at the end of August and saw out 1954 at the Bristol Hippodrome in *Cinderella*. The cast included musical theatre star Adele Dixon (the first singer to broadcast on BBC's high definition television service in November 1936) as Prince Charming, while Buttons was played by Jack Train, the multi-voiced character actor of Tommy Handley's *It's That Man Again*, especially known for his portrayal of the perpetually sozzled Colonel Chinstrap ('I don't mind if I do'). Amongst the six Ladies of the Chorus was Valerie Cottrell, a 16-year-old local girl making her debut on the professional stage. By the end of the run, she'd been recruited by Wilson and Keppel to become their youngest ever Betty.

By now, Wilson and Keppel were both 60 and looking it – not that they'd ever looked exactly youthful. The idea of two old men gazing lustfully at a sensuous teenager might seem distasteful to modern audiences, but the humour (as ever) derived from Jack and Joe's frustrated expectations. Valerie was an accomplished dancer and her age had little bearing on her suitability for the role. As it turned out, Jack and Joe's instincts were right, and Valerie Cottrell became one of the most remarkable Bettys of them all.

Valerie was born in Bristol in 1938. Like Irene Scott, her dance experience was in ballet. Also like Irene, she had been offered the job after Jack and Joe had got to know her and see her at work during the run of a pantomime. And, like Barbara Holt (and, most especially, Betty Knox), the men had succeeded in plucking someone exceptional from a chorus line. In March 1955 *The Performer* wrote:

> Wilson, Keppel and Betty ended their successful pantomime engagement at the Hippodrome, Bristol, last Saturday, and on Monday

opened at Finsbury Park Empire where they introduced the sixth successive 'Betty' to London audiences. The new 'Betty' is 17-year-old Valerie Cottrell, a star pupil of Bettie Vowles, head of the Westbury School of Dancing, Bristol.

Other engagements for 1955 included weeks at the Liverpool Empire, with local lad Ken Dodd ('Britain's New Comedian'), and the East Ham Granada, with Londoner Arthur Haynes. A review of the July London Palladium show confirms that the sand dance, the seven veils and the spear dance were still the principal ingredients of the act, while *The Performer* described Valerie as 'their latest good looking and curvaceous Betty'.

By the mid-1950s, many provincial variety theatres were putting on shows featuring near nudity. This had been available for decades in London and on Broadway, but now there were Windmill-style shows with comedians and daringly bare young ladies almost on your doorstep. Wilson, Keppel and Betty had only rarely appeared on that type of bill. By and large, traditional family variety was still the mainstay of the theatres they played.

The Ipswich Hippodrome, in Suffolk, is an interesting example of a variety theatre progressively changing its programme to cater almost exclusively for an adult audience with sex on the brain. In consecutive weeks in 1954 the shows were: *Girls, Glorious Girls*; *You Mustn't Touch*; *Les Folie de Paris*; *Taking Off Tonight*; *We Couldn't Wear Less*. In 1955 (in addition to *Fanny Get Your Fun*) there was a continuous run of *Yes, We Have No Pyjamas*; *French Tit-Bits*; *How Saucy Can You Get?*; *Call Girl* (with Phyllis Dixey); *Turn the Heat On!*; *A Bit of This and That*.

In August 1955, the Ipswich Hippodrome changed management and immediately closed for refurbishment. When it reopened, new manager Will Hammer told *The Stage* of his plans for its future:

> Mr Hammer says he is very optimistic about his chances of keeping open the town's only variety theatre. 'And there will be no nude shows or vulgarity,' he declares.

Of course, the variety bill on that opening night featured Wilson, Keppel and Betty. But, even with its new clean-cut image, the theatre struggled to attract audiences, and closed its doors to variety less than two years later. A sign of the times for the entertainment industry.

A perfectly reasonable question to pose is whether Wilson, Keppel and Betty's act became any more revealing, as all around cast off their clothes with abandon. The answer is – hardly at all. The sad fact, for all lovers of the female form, was there was far more nudity from Wilson and Keppel than ever there was from Betty.

Despite their appearance in several movies, Wilson and Keppel were extremely wary about performing on TV. As already observed, variety theatres were starting to decline – and the growth in popularity of TV variety shows was being blamed for killing off live theatre. Comedians, who in the past could've told the same jokes for their whole career, knew that one appearance on TV would necessitate them writing a whole new act. Similarly one TV show from Wilson, Keppel and Betty could be seen by a multitude that a lifetime of theatre touring would find it hard to match. Their engagements diary looked healthy enough, but the profession had never felt more precarious – and TV overexposure might spell box office disaster.

They finally took the plunge and made their television debut on 24th September 1955, appearing in episode one of *The Harry Secombe Show* on ITV, just two days after the station had launched. This series, scripted by Eric Sykes, could justifiably claim to be the first sketch show ever to appear on the channel – though it's highly unlikely that Wilson, Keppel and Betty uttered a word of dialogue.

Valerie Cottrell spent around a year as Betty, leaving just months before the trio's BBC television debut. She later married circus performer and horse trainer Henri Mullens, and the couple developed the circus act 'Pas-de-deux', combining ballet with acrobatics on horseback.

Henri enters the circus ring, standing tall, with each foot placed on the back of a liberty pony. Valerie runs to him and he lifts her onto the horses. She does a sequence of ballet poses, supported by Henri, while the two ponies trot round the ring. Finally she is balanced above his head, leaning forward in a Cupid-type pose.

In later years, the two of them switched to training a different type of animal – and Valerie's new dance partner was a chimpanzee. (There must have been many a performance when she gazed into the chimp's eyes, and her thoughts drifted back to earlier days with Wilson and Keppel.)

A brief item on *The Stage*'s TV pages of March 1956 announced

Wilson, Keppel and Betty's BBC debut:

> As guests in 'The Max Wall Show' on April 1, Wilson, Keppel and Betty, one of the longest running variety acts in the country make their first appearance on BBC-TV. Incidentally, Maureen Drew, the present Betty is the fifth in succession.

As that very same journal had previously hailed Valerie Cottrell as the sixth Betty, it seems the Bettys were getting increasingly hard to count.

Despite being pipped to the post by the newly formed ITV, we know the BBC had been after them for some time. And we know they had repeatedly refused. In 1954 a poll of television viewers put Wilson, Keppel and Betty in the top ten of favourite acts, even though (at that time) they had never appeared on TV. BBC producer Michael Mills decided the best course of action was to write to their Betty and hope she could use her powers of persuasion to talk the men round. Unfortunately he was not overly familiar with the act and sent his letter to Betty Knox, assuming her to be a current member of the trio, despite being only two years away from her 50th birthday. Betty, if she ever received the letter, never replied.

Having taken the plunge into TV work, Wilson, Keppel and Betty made three further BBC appearances in the late 1950s. There was *The Norman Evans Show*, *The Jimmy Wheeler Show*, and that roly-poly regular of Saturday night TV – *Billy Cotton and his Band Show*. There is also an unconfirmed story that they appeared on an ITV show with Tommy Cooper. It's said that either Jack or Joe pointed at Tommy's fez and shouted 'Imposter!' – a one-word gag well worth the breaking of around a quarter of a century's self-imposed stage silence.

During this time (when working in London) Joe Keppel often stayed at a family hotel in Vauxhall Road, run by a close friend who was born in the same street in Cork. Joe would scatter sand on the kitchen lino and entertain the kids with a solo sand dance. A family member recalls that, for one of their television appearances, they brought one of the more experienced Bettys out of retirement. After all, it was live TV, and they didn't want to risk an under-rehearsed fluff by a 'new girl' being witnessed by millions.

Remembering Jack Wilson's passport problems before the 1954 Las

Vegas trip, it's fairly evident that travel abroad had played little or no part in Wilson, Keppel and Betty's itinerary since the war. There was plenty of work in Britain to keep them busy, so they didn't feel the need to seek engagements overseas. This was soon to change and all because of the worrying state of British variety. Theatres were steadily closing and it was getting harder to guarantee a full work diary in those lean months between panto and summer season.

Europe would bring new fans, new enthusiasm – and a new Betty.

22
Our Friends are Back

(Europe and Britain 1956–1962)

'... we're going on till Father Time rings down the curtain.'
(Wilson and Keppel, 1957)

JEAN CURLEY WAS BORN IN 1932 in the St Paul's area of Birmingham, West Midlands – a district known as the Jewellery Quarter. She had trained in ballet, tap and modern and, in July 1955, made her debut at London's Windmill Theatre, as a Windmill girl. Amongst the roles she played in this fast-moving, sumptuously costumed revue was a Lady of the Harem in a scene entitled 'Harem Hoo-Hah!' After she left the Windmill, she toured Europe and (as she told Anglia TV's *Bygones* in 1985) it was there she encountered Wilson and Keppel:

> I joined the act when I was with a Spanish Flamenco ballet, when I was in the Chat Noir Theatre in Norway. Walking upstairs after the performance one night, there was this little man, Joe Keppel, saying, 'I would love you to be our next Betty.'

The Flamenco ballet was called Los Flamencos de España – and Jean adopted the suitably exotic stage name of Gina Montes. There is a photo of Jean wearing a traditional Spanish black wide-brimmed hat (*sombrero cordobés*) and strumming a guitar. She joined the company in Brussels and, for the next year, they performed in practically every country in Europe, except Britain. She looked back on those days in an interview with a Birmingham paper:

'We never had much money,' she says with her quick smile, 'but we had an awful lot of fun.'

'I learned a fair amount of Spanish but, at a pinch, it's surprising how far a bit of broad Birmingham will get you.'

In June 1956, *The Performer* mapped Wilson, Keppel and Betty's European progress:

Reappearing in Scandinavia for the first time since the war, Wilson, Keppel and Betty have scored such a solid hit at the Cabarethallen, Liseberg Park, Goteberg, that they have been held over for a further programme. From Goteberg, the irrepressible trio journeys to Oslo, Norway, to appear at the Casino, followed by a month at the Grand Tivoli, Stockholm.

It was while playing the Casino Non-Stop at the Chat Noir (Black Cat) in Oslo at the start of July that they met Jean in Los Flamencos de España and offered her the job – though she didn't join the act until after Jack and Joe had returned to Britain.

This was yet another example of Jack and Joe spotting an exceptional talent onstage, rather than through the audition process. It's easy to see why Joe Keppel was quick to snap Jean up. She had dark hair – as did some (but by no means all) of their Bettys – a great stage presence and the ability to dance 'in character'. All of which won her the job.

Jean brought some much needed stability to Jack and Joe, who had been whipping through a fair number of Bettys in the past months. After Maureen came Denise and (as Jean recalls) her immediate predecessor was a girl called Pippa from a circus family in Manchester.

Over in Germany, Betty Knox had moved house from Bonn to Dusseldorf early in 1955. In September 1956, daughter Patsy took a trip from London to Dusseldorf. This was no flying visit. Patsy had gone to live with her mother in her home in Zietenstrasse.

There was surely a stronger bond between these two women than it would appear. Betty, a young mother through accident rather than design, leaves her daughter behind while she travels round the States, then spends five years in Britain before fetching her over. When Betty stops touring Britain, Patsy starts. And, by the time Patsy has stopped, Betty has set up home in Germany. Betty was now 50 and Patsy was 32. This may have been the longest time they spent in each other's company for the whole of their lives.

Patsy would have had little knowledge of German, so settling in Dusseldorf wasn't the easiest of decisions to make. Her occupation is listed not as actress or dancer, but as a student. If nothing else, a crash course in the German language would seem a priority.

At the end of 1956, in *Aladdin* at the Cardiff New Theatre in Glamorgan, South Wales, Jean Curley made her Wilson, Keppel and Betty panto debut.

Jean Curley, known as Jeanne (pronounced 'Jeannie') to her friends, has rarely given interviews since the 1980s. But, in September 2012, she patiently answered a long list of questions I had for her. Jeanne remembers that she slipped into the role of Betty both quickly and easily: 'It took me no time at all to learn the act. Very little difficult dancing was involved.'

The recent speedy turnover of Bettys had forced Jack and Joe to rethink and simplify the act. In the past, Betty Knox had given bravura displays of fast footwork and Patsy had cartwheeled around the stage. By the time Patsy left, the clog dancing element had been totally dispensed with; the emphasis was now on comedy numbers, rather than the former swift succession of frenetic turns in which the girl's main purpose was to give Jack and Joe time to catch their breath.

Jeanne's *Bygones* interview confirms the picture we've built up of the widely contrasting character and appearance of the two men. After suggesting Joe Keppel was apt to be 'a practical joker,' she describes Jack Wilson:

> Jack was a very loving man. Everybody loved him. Although he sometimes looked like the baggage man when he was walking into the theatre. He had no appearance at all. He was just (*she mimes trudging heavily*) Joe Bloggs, you know, when he was walking in, with the pipe. And he used to like a drop of rum, and Guinness. Joe was dapper. Very, very well dressed. Beautiful shoes.

Joe Keppel never 'held court' as Jack Wilson did – especially at Olivelli's, which is where Jeanne first met them. But Jeanne doesn't agree with the portrayal of Joe as a private man, who preferred his own company: 'Joe was the extrovert – in both clothes and manner.' She also downplayed the idea of Joe having an 'eye for the girls': 'Joe only really joked about the ladies. Nothing more.'

Soon after Jeanne had come on board, Wilson and Keppel did something which, for them, was almost unheard of. They put their hands in their pockets and paid for some new publicity photos. A rare event indeed:

All the previous Bettys used the original Betty's photos with the boys. I insisted on having new ones done.

Photos featuring either Betty or Patsy were still being signed well into the 1950s. Most Bettys never took that trip to the photographer's studio – perhaps because the men wanted to appear as young as they could for as long as they could. But there were at least half-a-dozen new snaps taken – against a shimmery curtain – of Joe, Jack and Jeanne in poses from the sand dance, the nudge bells, the seven veils and the spear dance.

In the spear dance, Jeanne wears a brief two-piece costume – rather briefer than the one Irene Scott had worn for the same routine. In another shot (from the nudge bells routine) Jeanne strikes an elegant pose, arms in the air, while Jack and Joe crouch either side of her. Their arms reach up towards her bejewelled bra – seeming to warm their hands on the heat emanating from those womanly curves. Jeanne maintains an expression of aloof serenity.

Jeanne brought this very bra to a TV interview she gave in 1989 to Roy Hudd. It was highly ornate and deep blue in colour. But, as she told Roy, it was also home-made:

Those were the bras that Joe used to make for me. He designed all my costumes, and sewed the sequins and stones on also.

When they started out, Betty Knox was the costume designer of the team, a fact confirmed by Eunice Roberts. On the other hand, Joe Keppel's skills in this direction did not develop overnight. As a bit of a charmer who enjoyed female company, he probably chose to keep this particular talent to himself. 'I make all my own dresses,' is possibly not the world's greatest chat-up line.

Jeanne told me that Joe added the rhinestone adornments to the bras and belts. He also made the costumes for himself and Jack, while Jack took care of the shoe repairs. Virtually every aspect of the act (props and costumes) had always been under Jack and Joe's total control. The one thing they didn't make was the *papier-mâché* 'Wilson/Keppel' mask that Jeanne wore on the back of her head during the Seven Veils. That was crafted by a group of drama students.

In April 1957, they were back in Europe, playing a season at Paris's L'Olympia Music Hall. The Suez Crisis of the previous year had given their Egyptian lampoon an unanticipated topical twist. President Nasser's decision to nationalise the Suez Canal provoked an intense campaign of bombing and blockades, with Egypt pitted against Britain, France and Israel. The canal had only fully reopened weeks before Wilson, Keppel and Betty's stint at L'Olympia, so (as *Variety* noted) a group of comical Egyptians shuffling onto the stage was guaranteed to provoke waves of laughter from their French audience:

> Present political tensions help this get yocks [belly laughs], and the skilful clowning, invention and actual terp [terpsichorean] qualities make this in for big applause. However, it is thin and timely in essence, and will have to be altered with changing times.

One can be pretty certain that the trio hadn't changed their act one iota to fit in with the times. It just so happened that the times had changed to fit in with their act. And one iffy review wasn't going to cause them to tinker around with routines that would remain fresh in the memory long after some trifling Middle Eastern conflict had been forgotten.

In June they were performing in *Les Montmartre Follies*, back in London's Finsbury Park Empire, alongside Bonar Colleano, who Jeanne remembers as one of the nicest people they worked with. While they were there, the *Salina Journal* in Kansas carried a report about local resident Mrs Elizabeth Peden, who was shortly to leave for Europe to live with her daughter Betty:

> Mrs Peden who is blind ... lives at the Sunny Rest Home, 134 N. 9th.

It's quite a story. A blind lady, aged 81, decides to leave a cosy retirement home in the city she was born and grew up in, to fly to Germany and spend the rest of her days in an unfamiliar place where they speak an unfamiliar language. But, of course, she wouldn't be alone. There would be three generations of the same family living together –

Lizzie, her daughter Betty, and Betty's daughter Patsy. If Wilson, Keppel and Betty's early publicity is to be believed (which it isn't), there in Dusseldorf, living under the same roof, were Bettys numbers One, Two and Three. In reality it was two Bettys (with more than twenty years in the role between them) plus the woman who had shared so many of their triumphs and tragedies.

So Lizzie chose to leave her Salina friends and neighbours, just as Patsy had done with her London friends the previous year, and both were now permanent residents, with Betty, in Germany. One is tempted to ask 'who was looking after whom?' The truth is that all three women needed each other. Betty had not enjoyed the best of health for much of her adult life and was a heavy smoker. Almost every photo from her journalistic career shows her with either a cigarette in her hand, or a packet close by. Patsy, whose emotional state wasn't strong after her relationship broke up, could have settled reasonably happily into the role of homemaker. And Lizzie, an important stabilising element in a frequently turbulent family, would continue to dispense some much needed common sense.

Wilson, Keppel and Jeanne spent the summer season of 1957 on Blackpool's South Pier. Then they were back on tour, with Jeanne Curley loving every minute. As she recalled in 1985, they received a warm welcome wherever they went:

> With the Moss Empire circuit and others, you could play three years and never play the same theatre twice. All that helped to perfect the timing and precision of the act. I can remember Glasgow, for instance. They used to say, 'Our friends are back.' They used to love to see the act again. They're supposed to be the toughest audiences of all, the Glaswegians. They didn't like everybody. And a hell of a lot of comedians fell by the wayside. But they always loved Wilson, Keppel and Betty. I was very proud to be the Betty at that time.

They played the Glasgow Empire again in September 1957, supporting singer Billy Eckstine. While they were there, Macdonald Gillies of Glasgow's *Evening Times* asked the question that anyone who ever saw them on stage was doubtless thinking:

> Just how old are Jack Wilson and Joe Keppel? 'We're both 66,' they chorus. My hunch is they're nearer the 70 mark.

Retiring? I asked. 'Not us,' they say, 'we're going on till Father Time rings down the curtain.'

Good luck, say I.

In fact, they were both 63. Admittedly, they'd never really looked anything approaching youthful. But to be mistaken for septuagenarians when they were in their early 60s, just perpetuates the idea that this pair put the 'Ancient' into Ancient Egypt.

Not that they were in any way starting to slow down. At the end of October 1957 *The Stage* listed their future schedule, again dominated by foreign travel. The piece was headed '55 Not Out' – and repeated the myth that the double act was formed in 1902, when they were 8 years old:

> During this time there have been at least 10 different Bettys, each one leaving after a period, usually to get married. Wilson, Keppel and Betty start their forthcoming continental season with a four weeks' engagement, commencing November 1, at the Moulin Rouge, Paris, after which they will appear at the Ancienne Belgique, Antwerp, and the Ancienne Belgique, Brussels. They then return to England for 'Dick Whittington' at Derby.

A total of ten Bettys is fairly close. But the idea that the brisk Betty turnover was due to them all leaving to get married is certainly not true. The problem with engaging girls in their late teens and early twenties is that, if they don't leave for romantic reasons, they are young enough to want to achieve all they can in a comparatively brief dancing career. The idea of trotting out the 'nudge bells' and the seven veils endlessly – year in, year out – would quickly lose its appeal to many. On the other hand, being plucked from the chorus to become a prominent member of a high-profile threesome could be an excellent way of attracting the attentions of theatre producers, and would look great on any dancer's CV.

There was another tale that did the rounds, explaining why Wilson and Keppel got through so many Bettys. It was a widely circulated piece of gossip, quoted by Tenniel Evans (Leading Seaman Taffy Goldstein in radio's *Navy Lark*) in his autobiography *Don't Walk in the Long Grass*, though he admits he has no idea whether there's any truth behind it. It is said that Wilson and Keppel made demands on their Bettys that were way beyond the call of duty – and that many a Betty had fled her digs late at night, by knotting the bedsheets together and escaping through the window.

Two odd-looking elderly men working with a succession of attractive young dancers were always going to be targets for that kind of rumour. No Betty has ever gone public to confirm this story, and enough of them have spoken warmly of their time with the act to make it seem unlikely. From a purely businesslike perspective, it would make little sense to spend all that time rehearsing a new girl in the role, only to have to start all over again after some unwelcome lusty late-night advances. If Joe Keppel had been tempted, he'd know how perilous it would be to mix pleasure with business. And, after succumbing to temptation, he would never have heard the last of it from Jack. It's obvious from their choice of Bettys over the years that the men never for a moment thought the job could be done by any pretty girl.

While we're in the business of quashing rumours, Jeanne was adamant that there was never any romance between Betty Knox and either Jack or Joe. All those tales of a love triangle, of a long-standing feud, or of Patsy's real father – which all make deliciously spicy gossip – have no basis in fact. Who's to say whether Betty and Jack, or Betty and Joe (or even Jack and Joe, judging from their frequent onstage intimacy) ever spent a night together? If it did happen, it was no more than a fleeting fling. And if it never happened, it wouldn't stop people saying it had.

In December 1957, shortly before they opened in *Dick Whittington*, *The Stage* gave another update on the trio's ever increasing popularity abroad:

> So successful were Wilson, Keppel and Betty in the last programme at the famous Moulin Rouge, that, not only were they held over for the current programme but they are also given top billing in the show. The act has had to turn down several lucrative and immediate Continental offers owing to pantomime commitments in England.

Wilson, Keppel and Betty were now rapidly getting to the stage where they were spending more time in Europe than they were in the UK. In March 1958, *The Stage* again detailed Wilson, Keppel and Betty's forthcoming itinerary:

> Wilson, Keppel and Betty this summer will play another extensive season on the Continent, opening on June 1, for one month, at the Tivoli

Park, Stockholm, followed by the month of July, at the Liseberg Park, Goteborg, with August in Italy, September at the Moulin Rouge, Paris, and the first two weeks of October in Belgium.

Reviewing their July performance at Sweden's Liseberg Cabaret-hallen, the *Götesborgs-Posten* (in translation) said:

> These two gentlemen, whom we have seen many times before, and this lady, who seems to be a new one every time, have merged a grim parody of ballet with Egyptology ... they are, all three of them, extremely funny in a charming and intelligent way.

After Belgium, Jeanne returned home to Birmingham, while Jack and Joe allowed themselves the briefest of holidays, as detailed in a postcard Jack sent to Jeanne:

> Going Dusseldorf to visit Betty & Patsy for 2 days. Will arrive England about Oct. 29 or 30. Will see Delfont & contact you at once with all the dope. We will be O.K. Brush up good we may have to jump in quick.

And 'jump in' they did. Just a couple of weeks later they were back on the British variety circuit, in shows headlined by Chic Murray, Norman Evans and a couple of superb stage drunks – Freddie Frinton and Jimmy James. Variety may have been on the decline, but there were still star-studded line-ups at the larger theatres. *Robinson Crusoe* at Jeanne's local theatre (the Birmingham Hippodrome) took them into 1959, and on subsequent theatrical engagements they met a couple of rising TV stars, Terry Scott and Bernard Bresslaw. So, once again, they were on the road. And this time it really was 'on the road'. As Jeanne told *Bygones*, they needed to move with the times:

> I did make a few changes later. Travelling changes to start with. We had to get rid of beautiful HMV trunks and little picnic hampers that Joe had picked up on the way. But I bought a Volkswagen minibus. And I decided to be the driver – and baggage man – and Betty. Everyone rolled into one.

When Wilson and Keppel had started touring Britain, in the early 1930s, few performers had cars. Everyone travelled between theatres by train, packing their costumes and props into huge trunks. Jack and Joe never had any reason to learn to drive. But they'd steadily slimmed down their props. There was no '5th Avenue Bus', no rickshaw, no staircase, not even a backdrop. The show was far more portable. So a large van could easily accommodate both them and the act.

It's an enormous tribute to Jeanne that she was able to switch on the sexual allure onstage, then afterwards help them load everything into the minibus and drive them off to the next location. In the same interview, she describes the 'nudge bells' routine:

> All three arrive on stage with the bells. We dance around, just using the bells only. Until we arrive in centre stage. Then the girl does a vamp to the boys, showing them what to do with their bodies, and doing lovely vamping movements. And they stop – dismiss the girl – and decide that they are going to do exactly the same.

What this description lacks – something that was definitely a feature of the act in the days of Betty and Patsy Knox – was any mention of carrying the girl around the stage while she sits cross-legged on a platform. When I asked her, Jeanne confirmed that she used to make her own entrance. The two men were now approaching 65, and no longer capable of their former feats of strength. Without the talents and personality of Jeanne – and her willingness to 'muck in' – Jack and Joe might have had to face up to the idea of retirement far earlier than they did.

In June 1959, the *Manchester Guardian* interviewed Jack and Joe, who gave an interesting insight into the Spear Dance, the number that replaced the staircase as their finale:

> They once spent eighteen months rehearsing for four hours a day to polish their clod-hopping sword-fight routine.

As previously mentioned, the spears had a spring mechanism so that Wilson and Keppel could appear to stab each other. Jeanne described it to me in greater detail:

> The Spear Dance was a fight routine which saw Jack spear through Joe's costume. I came on towards the end of the dance as a Major, blowing a whistle to break the boys up. There were bells attached to the spears, which rang as we tap-danced to close the routine.

Jeanne took me through the running order of their act, which was always presented in a single slot on the bill:

1) The Nudge-Bells [finger cymbals]
2) A modern dance solo from Jeanne
3) The Sand Dance
4) The Seven Veils
5) The Spear Dance – with Jeanne joining Jack and Joe for a tap finale.

Jeanne remembered that the running time was always exactly 14½ minutes. After year upon year of touring the same routine, they were one of few acts who could be guaranteed not to overrun by as much as a second. Although Jeanne made no fundamental changes to the act, she did spruce up its visual impact. For a start, she insisted on new costumes and more colourful veils. And (during one of their Paris residencies) she had a hairpiece fringe designed, to make her look more Egyptian.

It's just as well Jeanne was doing something to brighten up the act because, as the *Manchester Guardian* revealed, some of their props were starting to look more than a little shabby:

> The brass tin from which Mr Keppel has been sanding stages for forty years is as old as the dance: his hands have worn through it in several places which are now sealed with plaster.

The reporter then attempts to encapsulate the secret of their success:

> An American writer has said that they have one foot in the grave and another on a banana skin. This is not so. The banana skin implies loss of dignity or at least imminent loss, whereas Messrs Wilson and Keppel are never in danger of losing their dignity because it has never been self-imposed; they were born with it. But what they have lost over the years is Bettys.
>
> Connoisseurs speak boastfully and authoritatively of having seen 'the original Betty' at her best. Others, patently not old enough to have had this experience, tell of the original Betty's daughter. The first Betty, now a journalist, stayed with the partnership from 1919 until 1943. Her daughter Patsy succeeded her for eight or nine years, and since then there have been Irene, Barbara, May, Gloria, Valerie, and the present pretty incumbent, Jean, who has been with them for nearly two years.

The dates, as usual, are way out! (Betty Knox definitely didn't join them at the age of 13 in Australia.) And the number and order of Bettys is a little approximate. The Birmingham *Evening Argus* (November

220

1958) has a more reliable post-Patsy listing, starting with Barbara, then continuing:

'There was Irene, she lasted four years, Gloria, three months, May, a year, Valerie, Maureen, Denise ...'

We'll never know exactly how many Bettys there were. Even to their agent, they were known simply as 'Wilson, Keppel and Betty' – and Jack just split the fee three ways. There were several girls who either replaced Betty or Patsy during sick leave, or briefly 'filled in' between 1950 and 1956. Irene Scott and Valerie Cottrell were the most significant and stayed the longest. Others are remembered by a first name and nothing more. My best attempt at a list of Bettys, in order of appearance, is this:

- Betty Knox
- Jean Bamberger
- Eunice Roberts
- Patsy Knox
- Edna May Dibb
- Barbara Holt
- Irene Scott
- Gloria
- Mary Wemyss
- Valerie Cottrell
- Maureen Drew
- Denise
- Pippa
- Jeanne Curley

In one interview, Jeanne Curley reckoned she was the eleventh Betty. If we include those three unidentified first names, it gives us a total of fourteen. I doubt if even Jack and Joe kept a definitive tally.

In February 1960, *The Stage* said of their Finsbury Park Empire performance that 'it will continue to delight until the sands of the desert turn cold'. In April they made their final BBC television appearance in *The Ken Dodd Show*. A week later they were at the Leeds Empire with Bruce Forsyth, at that time the host of ATV's *Sunday Night at the London Palladium* (one of only a handful of commercial TV shows to feature Jeanne and the boys). After that the British press goes very quiet, and it isn't until almost a year later, in March 1961, that *The Stage* informs us what they've been up to:

> That almost legendary act of show business, Wilson, Keppel and Betty never seem to stop working. They have been in a French revue since last May and are booked up till December, 1961. At present they are in 'Soho Cabaret', at the Etoile, Paris.

And two months later:

> Wilson, Keppel & Betty, now in their eighth month in Paris's 'Crazy Horse Saloon' Night Club, in Avenue George V have had their contract prolonged – twice. The trio have turned down offers from Germany and Scandinavia, but they will play there later this summer.

Paris couldn't get enough of Wilson, Keppel and Betty. They shared bills with such legendary names as Edith Piaf and Maurice Chevalier. And, not for the first time, Jeanne found herself performing alongside girls who wore considerably less. Even so, as she recalls, Joe Keppel saw no reason why they should drop an integral part of their act:

> When we arrived in Paris, we went to a club called the Crazy Horse. Well, as you know, the Crazy Horse is a famous striptease house. And he wanted the veils. He thought it would be very light in between the heavy strip. Eventually we were there two years, probably? Of course, the reason being there was no language barrier. Everybody – internationally – found the boys very, very funny.

One of Jeanne's contracts with the Crazy Horse (running from May to December 1960) reveals she was paid the handsome fee of 150,000 francs. However, this was the year that the inflation-prone franc was finally revalued, and a lesser amount was added in brackets: '(1,500 New Francs)'.

In total (excluding breaks when they were touring Europe or making short trips to Britain) they spent well over a year in Paris. Only Jeanne made any attempt at speaking the language, and all three stayed in different hotels. In June 1961 they succeeded in fitting in a few German dates.

Someone who bumped into Jack and Joe while they were working in Germany was British jazz drummer Ken Harrison. He was touring US bases with trampoline act The Jumpin' Jax. In his colourful autobiography *Jobsworth*, Ken paints a neat picture of Joe Keppel, the ageing roué:

> Keppel wore a tiny pair of silver wings in his lapel. At first glance it looked like a small Air-Force badge, maybe a flying award of some kind, but when I asked what it represented, grinning he turned his lapel over to reveal an erect penis. It was actually the tiny emblem of virility sold as a tourist attraction at Pompeii. Usually owners displayed it on a key-ring, but not Keppel. I laughed, 'Very good, nice touch,' I grinned. Fingering it lovingly, he chuckled, 'Yeah, goes down great with the gals.'

In the autumn they made a brief return visit to England, after an absence of almost a year and a half. One of their first English shows was a week split between the Manchester Southern Sporting Club and the Sale Palace Theatre Club. This may seem a bit of a comedown after their continental stardom. In reality, it was variety itself that was fading fast. In many areas the working men's clubs were the new home of variety, and accepting such an engagement shouldn't be interpreted as 'slumming it'.

The week before Wilson, Keppel and Betty played Manchester, a former Betty was getting married. After her romantic upset of a decade earlier, which precipitated her departure from the act, 37-year-old Patsy Knox attended the Dusseldorf East registry office and tied the knot with 43-year-old divorcee Leo Gilchrist. Leo, born in Texas, was a US Navy WW2 veteran and an offshore oil consultant. ('You've struck oil there,' as the best man might say.) But it was good news that Patsy was settled at last – even if Betty and Lizzie were losing a housekeeper in the process.

By the end of 1961, Wilson, Keppel and Jeanne were back in Paris, which was becoming home for them. Jeanne's happiest memories of working with Jack and Joe were the nine months they spent at the Crazy Horse. During their time in Paris they'd also had two engagements at the Moulin Rouge and three months at the Soho Cabaret.

Wilson, Keppel and Betty could easily have spent far longer than their three months' residency at Paris's Soho Cabaret, were it not for the fact that its perfectionist owner, Alain Bernadin, twice closed down the show and paid off the performers while trying to refine the recipe for his vision of a more sophisticated Parisian nightspot.

Ex-antique dealer Bernadin already owned the Crazy Horse striptease house, but his aim with the Soho Cabaret was a show combining modernistic music, film, lighting and dance, without entirely jettisoning the bare female flesh that had made his fortune. *Variety* chronicled the effort and expense that had gone into this brand new enterprise:

> He spent a pile digging into the foundations of the old Amiral cellar club off the Champs-Elysees and came up with an amphitheatre-type club seating 125, plus fine Japanese décor and a compact stage with treadmills, screen, turntables and all the facilities of a pocket theatre.

Treadmills? In a nightclub? Oh, yes!

> The strip was dispensed with as the girl numbers, with four nudes, had lights playing over well stacked chassis or they trod a treadmill miming trumpet fanfares.

This is a world away from the Windmill's 'starkers but stock-still' policy. Like many a Broadway show of the 1920s, there were pretensions of high art – abstract films and a ballet accompanied by revolving luminous discs – but the solo acts were fairly 'hit and miss':

> Al Carthy does a spirited sketch on the creation of the Frankenstein monster who walks off with the good doctor's head. Martina Cornelius does an okay angular dance and Axo is a sad clown who does not quite hit the needed comic vein to bring it off.

And, in the midst of all this hallucinogenic hokum:

> Wilson, Keppel & Betty do a zany parody on Arab dancing with shapely girl and two spindly men. It is an old house turn that fits into this so-called avant garde show.

And so the trio slotted effortlessly into the newest and most experimental of Parisian cabarets the way they'd slotted into every previous show – by not changing a thing. They never went out of fashion because they never attempted to be fashionable. They'd been vaudeville hoofers, they'd been variety veterans, and now they were continental chic.

They'd become such a fixture of Paris nightlife that young French filmmaker Jean-Daniel Pollet snapped up Jack and Joe for an uncredited cameo role in his atmospheric movie short *Gala* (1961). The sand dance in widescreen; but not so much glorious Technicolor as moody monochrome – a nostalgic nod to the era of 'film noir'. Jack and Joe, now in their mid-60s, had seen their career progress from vaude-house to art-house.

Many of Pollet's movies were set in the world of the dance hall. Several featured the character of 'Leon' played by Claude Melki, a stone-faced young comedian (very reminiscent of Buster Keaton both in style and appearance).

The dialogue-free *Gala* begins with French-Caribbean actor Gésip Légitimus ambling through his deserted nightclub in porkpie hat and overcoat, puffing a cigar, to the accompaniment of a haunting whistled theme. He beckons towards an open doorway, then sits in his chair, positioned just in front of the performance area.

A small band strikes up a cheery theme and Wilson and Keppel shuffle on from the left of the screen. As they go through their time-honoured sand dance, the opening credits for the film appear, often gradually revealed in 'wipes' following the pair across the screen. Leon, the odd-job-man and general dogsbody, hovers in the background, occasionally attempting to imitate Jack and Joe's dance steps. If directly compared with performances earlier in their career, this movie certainly doesn't show the two at their best, though they are still remarkably agile. Jack Wilson, who (as in earlier film appearances) shoots the odd playful glance at his impassive audience, now appears somewhat round-shouldered and stooped. However, the mix of visuals and music (although dubbed on later) contributes a delightfully eccentric start to this, at turns, sombre and quirky movie.

About three-quarters of the way through their act, the manager waves his hands at Jack and Joe, indicating that he's seen enough. They obligingly raise their arms for applause (though none is forthcoming) and proceed to fold up their large and very heavy four-piece wooden sand board and carry it out of the door, leaving just a light sprinkling of sand on the nightclub floor. (As Jeanne recalls, hardly any sand was left on stage, as most of it was already glued to the board.) Hopefully they passed the audition, but their faces give nothing away.

This movie is not Jack and Joe's finest work, but it's a reminder that, even at this stage in their career, they never faded into obscurity. All that had happened was they'd finally become as old as they'd always looked. It may have been their silver screen swansong, but it's a great comic cameo in a stylish movie which – as a rather lovely bonus – went on to win a prize at the 1962 Vienna film festival.

In spring 1962 the trio was back touring the UK – and relieved to find they hadn't been forgotten. The spring tour included another encounter with Bruce Forsyth, together with a glamorous singer poised on the brink of TV and recording success: Kathy Kirby. They also worked with Frankie Vaughan and his top-hat-and-tails mentor, the music hall male impersonator Hetty King who, at 79, was more than a decade older than Wilson and Keppel.

In June 1962, five years after their previous British summer season, Wilson, Keppel and Betty opened at the Wellington Pier, Great Yarmouth, Norfolk in *Secombe Here*. Harry Secombe was top of the bill, supported by comedy songstress Audrey Jeans, ventriloquist Dennis Spicer and young comedian Ronnie Corbett.

A couple of weeks into the run, over in Dusseldorf, Betty Knox's mother died after suffering a stroke. Just nine months earlier Lizzie Peden had been at the wedding of her granddaughter Patsy. She had brought up her daughter and then been largely responsible for bringing up her granddaughter. She had stuck with them through their troubles, shared their triumphs and finally (in her eighties) had left her home city of Salina to spend her remaining years with the two of them. She was 86 when she died. A timely reminder that no one was getting any younger.

In *Secombe Here*, Wilson, Keppel and Betty were honoured with a prestigious spot on the bill. After a Napoleonic sketch ('1812 – and All That') the Pavilion Girls take the stage for an appropriately costumed dance routine: 'The Exotic East'. This sets the scene (and makes maximum use of the scenic backdrop) for: 'Cleopatra's Nightmare with international stars Wilson, Keppel and Betty.' It's a rare thing for variety performers' photos and biographies to appear in theatre programmes – particularly in the case of supporting acts. However, on this occasion, there is both a photo of Jack, Joe and Jeanne in action, plus two sentences, the second one putting the entire secret of their success in a nutshell:

> The apparent simplicity of their act conceals years of toil towards perfection.

They finish their act, Harry Secombe does his top of the bill spot, and then the entire company are onstage for the finale. Their own warm-up act, good billing and an illustrated programme: Great Yarmouth had done them proud. It was a fitting tribute to an act still at the very top of its game. Classic. Legendary. As the *Manchester Guardian* put it, back in 1959:

> Bettys come and Bettys go but Messrs Wilson and Keppel ... show clear signs of immortality.

But no one is immortal. If Wilson and Keppel never seemed to get any older, it wasn't because they stayed eternally youthful. It was because they looked like old men from the start. And now their age had caught up with their appearance. As Jeanne told *Bygones*, she sensed things were coming to an end:

> And it was very sad, a very sad time for me. Because I still wanted to continue. Joe was still very fit. But Jack was tired. He was feeling very tired, and he wasn't feeling very well. Quite poorly towards the end. And he just decided that that was it. And he gave up.

I asked Jeanne what exactly had been the matter with Jack:

> Jack had a bad rupture of the groin before the season at Great Yarmouth and was in a lot of pain – one reason why we decided to call it a day.

Any doctor would have prescribed a long rest as the best way to repair the damage. But Jack and Joe had barely rested since 1920. Jack was in a great deal of discomfort during those last few weeks, and it took courage and stamina for him to continue as long as he did. Uppermost in his mind must have been his determination not to let the other two down. He didn't. And when the decision was made to pull out of the show, it was unanimous.

Reluctantly, they left the show mid-season. There was never any thought of finding someone to deputise for Jack. Ronnie Corbett (who, at that time, had only a handful of TV and film roles plus a spell in the BBC children's series *Crackerjack* to his credit) got the opportunity to do his first ever solo stand-up act. But only for a few days – after which magician Donald B. Stuart was brought in as permanent replacement.

But, for two sand dancers and their veiled temptress, that was it. Somebody once estimated they had performed 'Cleopatra's Nightmare' fifteen thousand times. They would never perform it again. Forty-two years of Wilson and Keppel – and thirty-four years of Wilson, Keppel and Betty – were at an end.

As Jack and Joe predicted, Father Time had finally rung down the curtain. But the old misery-guts should never have been allowed backstage. What the Great Yarmouth theatregoer wanted in the summer of 1962 wasn't a father of time. It was Jack Wilson and Joe Keppel – the fathers of timing.

23

A Distant Tinkle

(Germany and Britain 1963–1977)

'There's the nearest one we'll ever meet to Jesus Christ.' (Rubye Colleano, 1970)

I WOULD LOVE TO END THIS BOOK WITH: 'And they all lived happily ever after.' But, realistically, as our principal characters were all born over a century ago, that was never going to be an option. So this is the chapter when everybody dies. I'll do my best to keep it brief.

Of the original line-up, the first to die was the youngest. Alice Elizabeth 'Betty' Knox died on 25th January 1963, about six months after the trio had disbanded in Great Yarmouth. She died in hospital in Dusseldorf, aged just 56. The causes were 'emphysema, carcinoma and pulmonary trouble' according to the death certificate; all likely to have been brought on by Betty's heavy smoking. Jeanne Curley recalls that Jack Wilson visited Betty in Dusseldorf after the act retired. He would not have seen Betty at her best. Indeed they were both shadows of their former selves. But it was a chance to relive their incredible adventures together – and a chance to properly say goodbye.

Her death notice, placed by daughter Patsy, spoke of prolonged suffering, bravely borne. No one could ever accuse Betty Knox of lacking courage. Unlike Jack and Joe, who'd swapped nationality more than once, Betty remained an American citizen throughout her life. Her occupation, as stated on her death certificate, was 'Manager/Journalist'.

Betty's life had been packed with excitement, thrills, danger, achievement and laughter. If she had the chance, I suspect she'd have done it all over again – provided she could rewrite the ending.

Aged just 30, Jeanne Curley (the final Betty) was too young to retire. As reported by a local newspaper, what she did next was quite amazing:

> When the act parted through ill health, Jean went to Germany after receiving a telegram from a circus. There she set about the task of learning to do a high flying act as a member of a team of four.
>
> In three weeks she was working sixty feet above a safety net and performing before audiences. And, says Jean, make no mistake about that net, it's very easy to break a limb or your neck falling from that height, unless a lot of training is put in.

The trapeze act that Jeanne joined, as a complete novice, was The Flying Croneras; and she performed at the Circus Sarrasani in Berlin, where another ex-Betty (Valerie Cottrell) would appear several years later with her ballet on horseback. Although Jack and Joe started out as a double act in the circus, here were two Bettys whose career paths went in the opposite direction.

Later Jeanne married Andy McKinnon and they became landlords of the Victoria Public House, Birmingham – the theatre bar for the neighbouring Alexandra. After the couple split up, Jeanne took over the Windmill Public House as sole licensee – another theatre bar, five doors from the Hippodrome, where Jack, Joe and Jeanne did panto in 1958. After retiring, Jeanne divided her time between her holiday home in Spain and the city that had always been her true home: Birmingham.

When Wilson, Keppel and Betty disbanded, Jack Wilson needed somewhere to live. He'd stayed in lodgings all his working life and had nowhere he could really call home. Three times (in 1933, 1945 and 1947) Wilson, Keppel and Betty performed before royalty. These Royal Variety performances were charitable occasions, raising money for the Entertainment Artistes' Benevolent Fund – set up specifically to help fellow members of the profession who'd fallen on hard times through ill health or old age. A major focus of the EABF's fundraising has long been Brinsworth House, a retirement home for entertainers, in Twickenham, Middlesex. As Jack Wilson's performing efforts had directly helped maintain it, it was only fitting that he should now reap some of the benefits.

Jack Wilson was first admitted to Brinsworth House in April 1963 and he quickly became the life and soul of the place. At a garden party in 1964, he provided musical entertainment as a member of the Brinsworth Beatles.

Patsy Knox (now Patsy Knox Gilchrist) had kept in contact with Jack Wilson. A series of 'In Memoriam' verses commemorating the anniversary of Betty Knox's death were jointly placèd by Patsy Knox and Jack Wilson in *The Stage* from 1964 to 1967. The last of these also remembered Patsy's 'Dearest Grandma' Lizzie Peden.

Another old friend who sometimes met up with Jack was Rubye Colleano. She'd first encountered Jack at Colleano's Circus in Australia in 1920, where the Wilson and Keppel partnership had been formed. After the death of her son, the actor Bonar Colleano, Rubye had brought up her grandson, Mark. Speaking in 2011, Mark recalled two encounters with Jack, the first in 1967:

> I was about 12 when I met Jack Wilson for the first time. He came down to the little bedsit apartment my grandmother had. And I remember, over tea and biscuits or whatever, they were both talking about their great touring days in England. About the great artists and great comedians and different people that worked on the circuits. And I remember him being very frail, a very skinny man. But he also had this incredible underlying strength. And beautiful humour which I – even though I was very young at the time – responded to and recognised. I immediately liked him. Really took a great liking towards him.
>
> And, of course, then we met him a second time, when my grandmother took me to Brinsworth House. Which was a much more sad occasion, because I could see he was very, very ill at that time. With respiratory problems as well. And, again, very frail. But again there was this humour. He maintained his humour. That's what I remember. I remember him very fondly. Very fondly. And I remember that feeling that I had towards him. He was a very gentle man.

Jack Wilson died on 29th August 1970, from cancer of the throat. *The Stage* published an 'In Memoriam' from Rubye Colleano, recalling nights at Olivelli's restaurant, where she and her late husband Bonar Colleano Senior were frequent patrons:

> Jack used to play piano, and we'd all sing and have fun. My husband Bonar said: 'There's the nearest one we'll ever meet to Jesus Christ.' Well he has joined my two Bonars now and is very sadly missed by my dear

grandson Mark and myself. Mark used to love to sit and listen to Jack and I telling him some of our show business experiences from all over the world. I once made a movie with my dear son Bonar at the age of 4 doing a tap number with our dear Jack and Joe on the roof of the State Lake Theatre, Chicago.

Of the many tributes to Jack in print, there were none from Patsy Knox. By the time of Jack's death she'd moved back to America. Her marriage to Leo Gilchrist lasted only a few years. By 1967 he'd moved away from Dusseldorf, and they had divorced. Leo later married for a third time. Patsy never did remarry. She reverted to her maiden name of Knox and eventually settled in Pearland, Texas. She died on 12th May 1984, aged 60, of liver cancer. On her birth certificate she was Jean Patricia Knox; on her death certificate she was Patricia Jean Knox. The certificate gives no indication of her former dancing career. Her occupation is recorded simply as 'homemaker'. Most of Patsy's friends and neighbours would have had no idea that she was a former acrobatic dancer who'd toured all over Britain, appeared in movies, and twice performed for the King and Queen and the Princesses Elizabeth and Margaret.

In August 1971, a year after Jack Wilson's death, an 'In Memoriam' notice was published in *The Stage*. It was in the very smallest print available, suggesting that the person who placed it was somewhat careful with his money. It is touching nonetheless:

> IN MEMORY of my dear partner Jack Wilson, died August, 1970. Deeply mourned by all his relatives and friends. He was one in a million. R.I.P. Joe.

Before he died, Jack Wilson said he hoped there might be some permanent reminder of him at Brinsworth House. Well, it was a long time coming, but when he finally got his wish it couldn't have been more fitting. In 1984 a bar was installed, where residents could buy drinks, alcoholic or otherwise. The sign above it read: *The Wilson, Keppel and Betty Bar* and Roy Hudd donned a fez for the opening ceremony.

The fact that Wilson and Keppel had little to do with each other in their final years shouldn't be taken as any indication of mutual dislike. They never had socialised together or shared the same digs. Joe Keppel frequently visited his family throughout his life, while Jack did so rarely, if at all. The nearest thing Jack had to family was his fellow professionals, so it was fitting he should finish his days in Brinsworth House; whereas Joe was back where home had always been – Cork, the city of his birth.

Joe moved in with his brother-in-law, Jack Buckley, in Needham Place, Cork. (Jack had married Joe's sister, Mary.) They made an odd couple. Joe, casual and easygoing, always smartly turned out, looking comparatively tall, as a result of good posture and his slim physique. Jack Buckley, on the other hand, was short, bald and walked with a limp. He was an ex-IRA man with a toothbrush moustache and a domineering personality.

Joe was regarded as something of a local celebrity. Jim Hastings, the local grocer, had a floor strewn with sawdust, as was the custom in those days. When Joe entered the shop, he always performed a brief impromptu sand dance, to the amusement of customers. His teetotal lifestyle had relaxed a little. One regular at Dan Turner's pub in Parliament Street remembers that Joe 'liked his Dimple Haig and Bass's barley wine'. He would tell tales of his incredible escapades around the world, and the locals would sit and listen to him for hours.

In 1976 Jack Buckley died. The next year, Joe Keppel was diagnosed with prostate cancer. He died in hospital on 14th June 1977. He was 82. Despite a heart condition, which curtailed his naval service during World War One, he'd outlived both Betty Knox and Jack Wilson. He was interred in St Dominic's Plot (Plot 10) in St Joseph's cemetery, alongside his sister, Nora, and Jack Buckley. The gravestone is in the shape of a book. No inscription was ever added for Joe Keppel – a legendary entertainer in an unmarked grave.

The Times marked the passing of the last original member of Wilson, Keppel and Betty with a brief obituary, remarking that:

> For many years the trio was a top-of-the-bill act in almost every variety theatre and music hall in Britain.

Indeed they were top-of-the-bill; but only rarely. For the rest of the time they were a good, solid, reliable and much-loved supporting act. And, wherever they were placed in the programme, they never failed to give a top-of-the-bill performance.

Both Jack and Joe could tell a good tale. And one of their best comes from beyond the grave. In August 1977, a couple of months after Joe Keppel's funeral, an article appeared in London's *Evening News*, headlined *MISSING FORTUNE*:

> The death at his home in Cork at the age of 82 of Joe Keppel, last surviving member of one of the world's most famous variety acts, Wilson, Keppel and Betty, leaves an intriguing mystery.
>
> He was reputedly a very wealthy man, but nobody knows where he left his money. His family in Eire can find no trace of it.
>
> It is strongly suspected that he buried his money somewhere, but where nobody knows.

The idea of buried treasure – of Keppel's missing millions – is irresistible. And, if Jack had outlived Joe, he'd have embroidered this tale with relish. For some reason they were often perceived as rich men. Ernie Wise, whose screen persona knew a thing or two about keeping a close hand on his wallet, reckoned the pair of them must have left a fortune. Jack Wilson, we know, was generous with his money, treating friends to meals and drinks and, when necessary, helping out a friend who was ill, hard up, or needed a boost with their career. It's less clear what Joe Keppel spent his money on. Certainly on fine clothes, a better class of digs, and having a great time. It's not difficult to squander a fortune. So, whatever the extent of Joe Keppel's riches, he probably spent the lot and had a damn good time in the process.

Of all the kind words that have been written about Wilson, Keppel and Betty, to my mind the best obituary ever to appear in print was actually published in their lifetime: in 1959, when they were still performing. Hopefully they had the opportunity to read it. It was the introduction to their *Manchester Guardian* interview with an unnamed reporter:

> When the last rites are eventually administered to British music-hall, the sound of a distant tinkle, as of altar bells, will reach the ears of the mourners assembled at the funeral feast.
>
> As it gets louder, however, their faces will light up; they will have recognised the exotic click of finger cymbals and the distinctive shuffle of one of the world's best-known sand-dances as Messrs Jack Wilson and Joe Keppel, with the eternally beautiful Betty in veiled attendance, make their last appearance – though from habit they will probably turn up again at 8:40.

24
All the Old Paintings on the Tombs

'People tried to copy them, but they can't, because they just miss that touch of magic …' (Jeanne McKinnon, 1985)

WILSON, KEPPEL AND BETTY HAVE LEFT THE THEATRE. No encores. No autographs. But surrounding each one of them is an unsolved mystery. There's Long John Joseph Keppel and his hidden stash of doubloons. There's the family Jack Wilson never returned to. But the mystery of Betty Knox is the most tantalising of them all. The final sentence of the 1952 *Stars and Stripes* feature on Betty reads:

> She is now writing a book on her experiences, although she says the title is a secret.

And the following year the *Anderson Herald* adds:

> She has trunks full of Nuremberg documents and is seriously considering writing a book to reveal for the first time the inside story of the trials.

It was Betty Knox's eventful life that inspired this book. And the thought that she wrote her own highly critical account of the Nuremberg Trials (which she 'never fully recovered from the shock of', according to the above newspaper) is sensational news. But where is it? We know she could write, and write well – and write fast and well when required. She already had a title, and had started writing in 1952, which gave her more than ten years to complete it. Would she really have bothered with a pseudonym, when her own forthright views on the subject had never particularly been kept under wraps? Is some book with a cleverly devised *nom de plume* at this moment occupying the shelves of second-hand bookshops around the world? Or is the unpublished manuscript lying forgotten in a cupboard somewhere? Or was it thrown away? Or was it never really started? All we know for sure is that it would have been a bloody good read. And it might have helped raise the profile of a woman invariably omitted from accounts of female war correspondents of World War II.

Betty was far smarter than she was ever given credit for. Britain and America were wartime allies, but it didn't stop there being an atmosphere of mutual suspicion and mistrust when hordes of GIs came to our shores. Betty knew America and had got to know the British. Her 'Over Here' column was the perfect vehicle for her talents. She never claimed both nations were the same; she celebrated our differences and (as often as not) laughed at them, without ever taking sides. There was much to be learnt from those columns, but one never felt lectured to. She wrote in her own style – upbeat and totally American – but she was also one of us, having toured the length and breadth of the British Isles over the previous decade.

She wanted to understand the Germans too. Collectively they were the enemy – but that didn't mean they were a whole nation of despicable evildoers. People are people and it was always the personal story that Betty responded to. Nuremberg shook her up badly. And her public outrage over the conduct of the trials probably scuppered her career. But to hell with it! She was also well aware that Nazism wouldn't vanish overnight. Ultimately she chose to make Germany her home, and she made friends the way she always had. By looking below the surface and getting to know people.

If Betty had committed her life story to paper, she might have supplied that vital piece of information about how Wilson, Keppel and Betty dreamt up the Egyptian theme that rapidly led to international stardom. It may not have been her own idea but, almost as soon as she'd joined the act, there was a spirit of close collaboration, of coming up with new ideas, of trying things out, of steadily reshaping the entire act. Without Betty Knox that may never have happened. But, with her, the three of them devised every single routine that comprised their act right through to that very last show.

With Patsy, two new elements were added – acrobatics and eroticism. Betty was sexy, but in the style of a bubbly, cheeky, American flapper. She also played it for comedy, sending up her own role as the alluring female, as well as the attentions of her male admirers. Patsy did it straighter – quite content to let Jack and Joe get the laughs – and also not afraid to play up the sexuality of her performance, whether her attentions were focused on seducing Jack and Joe or whether she was dancing solo for the theatre audience. With Betty's ideas and Patsy's reinterpretation of the role, the act had little need for modification for the rest of Jack and Joe's career.

I hope this book will correct a few popular misconceptions people have about Wilson, Keppel and Betty. But it won't eliminate them. They may be misconceptions, but they are also popular. The gossip, the rumour and the errors will live on. But if I could explode just one myth, it would be this: that Wilson and Keppel were forever changing their Bettys. Betty Knox was with them for thirteen years, Patsy for eight, Irene Scott for three, and Jeanne Curley for the final six. That's thirty years of a thirty-four-year career spread between just four women. The rest either knew they were being taken on as short-term replacements (due to illness or whatever) or did it for a few months and then went on to another job.

Bear in mind the fact that (including matinees) they danced the same routine for perhaps fourteen shows a week. In six months they'd do the same routine more than 350 times. For many girls that would be plenty. Time to move on and do other things. When I spoke to Eunice Roberts and Barbara Holt about the few months they spent with Jack and Joe, they had nothing but affectionate memories. But then other opportunities came along. It had been fun. Great experience. But it was enough.

Fortunately, for Jeanne Curley, not even six years was enough. She would gladly have continued in the role of Betty for many years to come. If Betty Knox proved to be the ideal woman to get the trio started, then Jeanne Curley was a similarly influential figure in their final years. Crucially, she had no problem with making Europe, and particularly Paris, her home for months, even years, on end. As their driver, she made touring less of a chore and upheaval for two ageing non-drivers. And her tireless love and enthusiasm for the act continued to energise Jack and Joe right up until that final performance.

The myth of Wilson and Keppel periodically booting out their Bettys was perpetuated by writer and jazz singer George Melly, who claimed they'd get rid of each one after about ten years. He also wrote in *Punch* magazine that the last Betty's son was 'a brilliant female impersonator'. But Jeanne never had a son. The prodigious pantomime dame and ugly sister is, in fact, James Harman, her second cousin.

So why are Wilson, Keppel and Betty still remembered? Well, for a start, they were performing up until 1962, so there are still plenty of people around who saw them on stage. Jokes are soon forgotten. Songs fade from the memory. But the sand dance, once seen, will stay with you forever.

Then there are the tribute acts, which were around way before Wilson, Keppel and Betty retired. Bert Ross, writing in *The Stage* in 1978, recalled a trio of buskers in London's Leicester Square doing a 'take-off' of Wilson, Keppel and Betty as early as 1933 – just a year after their arrival in Britain. Unfortunately, they were working just outside the Alhambra Theatre, where the genuine article was currently appearing. Jack Wilson stepped outside between performances and was immediately confronted by this troupe of doppelgangers:

> Their 'bottler', the fellow who collects the money, came round the crowd and was doing quite well when he reached the spot where Jack and I stood. Recognising Jack Wilson, he shamefacedly and hurriedly attempted to depart from that particular place, but Jack gripped his arm and held tight. Then, with his free arm, Jack Wilson extracted his wallet from his inside pocket, took out a pound note, and without a word handed it to the 'bottler'.
>
> The relief on the man's face was a sight to see. He just managed to say 'Thanks, Jack' and hurried away.

In later years, one group of buskers dominated Leicester Square with their unauthorised tribute: The Road Stars (brothers Albie and Harry Hollis). Their energy made up for any lack of musicality, precision or talent – and many punters would come away under the delusion (regardless of the all-male line-up) that Wilson, Keppel and Betty had just danced for them. Despite the copycat nature of the act, Harry Hollis's autobiography *Farewell Leicester Square* contains not one single mention of Wilson or Keppel.

Terry Pratchett's Discworld fantasy novel *Jingo* (1997) is crammed with Egyptian references from popular culture, including music hall songs, radio's *It's That Man Again* and Tommy Cooper. After Lord Vetinari, Sergeant Colon and Corporal Nobbs have their clothes stolen, they disguise themselves as Gulli, Gulli and Beti – strolling entertainers specialising in 'exotic tricks and dances'. Vetinari and Colon don long nightshirts and fezzes, while the repulsive Corporal Nobbs is lumbered with the role of Beti – adorned in bangles, veils, harem pants and a pair of strategically placed tin bowls.

The Nazis crop up once more in the shape of Adolf Kilroy, one of many surreal creatures who had supporting roles in Maurice Dodd's long-running *Daily Mirror* comic strip *The Perishers*. Adolf the tortoise had a shell shaped like a German helmet, his evil plans were constantly thwarted, and his favourite curse was 'Vilson, Keppel und Betty!'

Popular music continues to pay homage. Could 'Walk Like an Egyptian' by American girl group The Bangles possibly have been inspired by the trio? Well, writer Liam Sternberg came up with the idea after watching ferry passengers struggling to keep their balance. But the very first line of the lyrics is a clear reference to Wilson, Keppel and Betty:

All the old paintings on the tombs, they do the sand dance, don't you know?

Then there's 'Night Boat to Cairo' with the bent-kneed shuffling of Madness; Steve Martin's 'King Tut'; Michael Jackson's 'Remember the Time'; *Top of the Pops* dance troupe Legs and Co gyrating to 'Egyptian Reggae'; a saucily revamped sand dance from all four Chuckle Brothers; even that chubby curly-moustached GoCompare tenor, sandwiched between a pair of Wilson and Keppel lookalikes and backed by a chorus line of animated wall paintings.

The list could go on and on, but someone would get left out, so best to stop now and leave loads of people out. But not before a visit to a major televisual event.

On New Year's Day 1998, BBC2 devoted much of its schedule to *Day of the Pharaohs* – a lengthy tribute to Wilson, Keppel and Betty's twin inspirations: Tutankhamen and Cleopatra. Centrepiece of the day was a complete screening of Elizabeth Taylor and Richard Burton's interminable blockbuster *Cleopatra*. It's a fair bit longer than Wilson, Keppel and

Betty's version – and in this case it isn't Cleopatra who has the nightmare, it's the film studio executives. It was a production jinxed by massive overspending, bad weather, illness, artistic temperaments and problems galore. It was epic, it was glitzy, it was long and it was dull.

It ran from 3:10 in the afternoon until 7:20 in the evening. Four hours and ten minutes without a single advertisement break. The BBC, not totally insensitive to the physical needs of its viewers, scheduled a five-minute intermission at 5:05 pm. But anyone who chose to absent themselves from their television screens at that moment would have missed one of the true highlights of the day. It was a short compilation, especially made for *Day of the Pharaohs*, entitled *Sand Dance*. The BBC had raided its archives for every sketch, spoof or dance number they could find that owed its existence to Wilson, Keppel and Betty's iconic routine. Apart from footage of the true originals, other programme clips included *Blue Peter*, *The Black and White Minstrel Show*, *Little and Large*, *The Russ Abbot Show*, *Absolutely Fabulous*, *The Fast Show* and, of course, Morecambe and Wise. Enough to make even Jack and Joe crack a smile.

Morecambe and Wise should not be glossed over. When they were starting out, in the late 1940s, they not only saw Wilson, Keppel and Betty perform, they even stayed at the same digs (Mrs Duer's at 13 Clifton Gardens, Chiswick). On TV, a couple of decades later, after they'd sung their closing song and danced off to the back of the stage, they would sometimes be seen in the distance, going back and forth, doing a few Wilson and Keppel moves. But their most direct homage came in 1971, when they teamed up with theatre actress Glenda Jackson in their version of *Antony and Cleopatra*.

Nearly five minutes into this substantial sketch, running at almost a quarter of an hour and scripted by Eddie Braben, Cleopatra (Glenda), having failed to tempt Octavian Caesar (Eric) with food, tries some seductive moves instead. Eric grabs a box labelled 'sand' and swiftly sprinkles the contents on the floor. The band strikes up with Albert Ketèlbey's 'In a Persian Market' and Eric, Glenda and Ernie, in appropriate Egyptian-wall-painting profile, shuffle from right to left, turn sharply and repeat the process a couple of times, finishing with a quick burst of vaudeville hoofing. Another valuable lesson they'd learned from the masters was how to invite applause. Jack and Joe used to thrust their arms high in the air. Eric, Glenda and Ernie conclude with a clap of the hands, before extending one palm towards the audience. To be on the safe side, Eric implores them: 'Be honest, come on!' The trio's efforts are richly rewarded. A routine lasting just eight seconds brings the house down. And, out of a hilarious fifteen minutes, those are the eight seconds that everyone remembers.

(Incidentally, Glenda Jackson showed remarkable courage by playing Cleopatra on stage – in the play what Shakespeare wrote – several years *after* she'd spoofed it with Morecambe and Wise.)

The kindest thing that can be said about all these tributes is that their hearts are very definitely in the right place. But no one has ever taken the trouble to perfect the technique or precisely copy the moves. And Jack Wilson, Joe Keppel and Betty Knox could have taught every one of them a thing or two about comic timing. As could Jeanne McKinnon (formerly Curley) who put her own stamp on the role of Betty in the act's final six years. As she said on *Bygones* in 1985:

> People tried to copy them, but they can't, because they just miss that touch of magic, that style, panache … I don't know how you describe it. It's just there. Perfect timing. Perfect dancing. *(Jeanne looks thoughtfully off to the side for a moment.)* Perfect people?

So, if Jack and Joe were 'perfect people', is it possible to encapsulate the spirit of Betty Knox in just two words? For that you'd need a great writer. Luckily she met one. And, after encountering her, Thomas Mann (recipient of the 1929 Nobel Prize in Literature) did just that.

And I think he was bang on. Two words that explain why she lit up the stage and was such a creative force within Wilson, Keppel and Betty. Two words that explain why every article she wrote for the *London Evening Standard* bristled with energy and excitement. Two words that make Betty Knox the one person in history I would most like to meet. In case you've forgotten them, these are the two words Thomas Mann wrote in his diary. In my opinion, the ultimate epitaph:

Etwas verrückt. (Slightly crazy.)

Acknowledgements

ALTHOUGH THIS BOOK was something of a personal quest, it could never have been completed without the generous help and co-operation of a long list of individuals.

Particular thanks are due to three Bettys – Eunice Roberts, Barbara Holt Schaller and Jeanne McKinnon – who kindly answered countless questions and supplied items from their personal archive. Also to Billy Shenton Junior, whose invaluable recollections helped shape this book and breathe life into the main quartet of Jack, Joe, Betty and Patsy; as did the brief vignettes of personal encounters by interviewees Jean Kent and Mark Colleano.

Thanks to Tiger Aspect Productions Limited for giving their blessing to my idiosyncratic account of their *Psychobitches* sketch.

I'm grateful to Her Majesty Queen Elizabeth II, Baroness Hussey of North Bradley GCVO, Samantha Spiro, Matt Lucas, Glenda Jackson CBE, Peter Nichols FRSL, Victoria Coren Mitchell and Dame Judi Dench for kindly responding to my request for memories and opinions of the trio – and providing this book with such an enthralling Foreword.

Richard A. Baker, Luke McKernan and Anthony Dundon have each written substantial articles about the act, and all three helped me greatly with my research.

Film routines were accessed with the assistance of British Pathé, Richard Jeffs (of Adelphi and Baim Films), Roger Fillary, Tony Hare, Martin Kristenson, Kathleen Dickson and Steve Tollervey of the British Film Institute, Sascha Tauber, Grahame Newnham, Max Tyler, Guy Williams of Wolverhampton City Archives, Dorothy Hosier and MACE (Media Archive for Central England).

The photographs in this book were generously provided courtesy of Smoky Valley Genealogical Society, Ken Cuthbertson, Newspapers.com,

Fultonhistory.com, Louisiana State Museum Historical Center, Jeanne McKinnon, Billy Shenton Junior, Huis van Alijn, Giovanni Salamone, US National Archives, Monacensia, Glen Watt, Allyson Proudfoot and Barbara Holt Schaller. All uncredited photos are from the author's collection. Front cover design was by the Stafford George Quartet.

Genealogical information and archive material came from Kathy McCullough and Nanc Scholl (Smoky Valley Genealogical Society), Marj Spuzello (Iowa Genealogical Society), Janet Buchanan (Phoenix Genealogical Society), Karen Jackson (Greater Omaha Genealogical Society), Renee Lubash (Lincoln-Lancaster County Genealogical Society), Charlene Bonnette (State Library of Louisiana), Sally Jacobs (Wisconsin Historical Society), Kansas Office of Vital Statistics, Texas Vital Statistics Unit, Jackie Cotterill (Birmingham & Midland Society for Genealogy & Heraldry), Tim Glander (Bonn Stadtarchiv), Norbert Perkuhn (Dusseldorf Stadtarchiv), the General Register Office for UK and Wales, the National Archives, the National Archives of Australia, Find My Past, Ancestry, Ensors Chartered Accountants (Ipswich) and Chantry Library (Ipswich).

Newspapers, magazines, books and letters were accessed at the British Newspaper Library, the British Library, Westminster Reference Library, the Goethe Institute (London), Parliamentary Archives, the *Daily Mail*, BBC Written Archives, the Shubert Archive, Kansas Historical Society, Monacensia (Munich) and the Roy Hudd Archive.

Online archive collections include Newspaper Archive, Internet Archive, Newspapers.com, Genealogy Bank, Google News Archive, Google Books, *The Stage*, *Variety* Archives, Illinois Digital Newspaper Collections, Lantern, UK Press Online, Fulton History, Northern New York Library Network, the British Newspaper Archive, Irish Newspaper Archives, BBC Genome Project, National Library of Australia, Papers Past, the *Catholic Herald* Archive, Małopolska Digital Library, the *Guardian* and *Observer*, *The Times* and Gallica.

Special thanks go to: Ken Cuthbertson (Betty Knox's second cousin once removed); Tom Foty (former United Press International correspondent and manager); James Harman (Jeanne McKinnon's second cousin); Giovanni Salamone at Olivelli's Restaurant (for information and archive); Andrea Weiss (for much detailed information about Erika Mann and Betty Knox).

Thanks also to: Anita Abrahams, Rob Aldous, Chris Brady, Bernie

Burgess, Doug Collender, David Drummond, Maxine Fletcher, Manfred Forster, Stephen Garner, Sharon Goddard, Anna Gospodinovich, Sheila Gould, Ike Harrison-Latour, Bertrand Hervy, Georgy Jamieson, John Jeffries, David Kenten, Michael Kilgarriff, Ian Liston, Frank Little, David Lovatt, Anna Ludlow, Peter Noel Murray, Brian Patton, Melody Peters, Maurice Poole, Karen Preston, Hazel Price, Allyson Proudfoot, Colm Reilly, Ellen Ryckx, J. D. Schaller, Frank Schmitter, Jack Seaton, Jonathan Shorney, Don Stacey, Melissa Stein, Una Stubbs, William Taggart, James Thornton, Jeff Walden, Stephen Wallin, Glen Watt, Marjorie Wheaton, Martin Whitehead, Chris Woodward and Armin Ziegler. Apologies for any names inadvertently omitted from this list.

Yet more thanks to Dexter O'Neill, Paul Ballard, Phil Reynolds and everyone at Fantom Publishing for level-headedly rushing in where agents feared to tread.

Finally, I would like to thank family and friends for advice, support and input – in particular Lynda and Jon George and Lyn and Don Smith. Above all, my gratitude to my wife Andrea – who shares my passion for living comedians and indulges my obsession with dead ones.

Bibliography

This book includes quotations from the following:

Over Here from Over There by Betty Knox (Alliance Press Ltd, London 1944)

The High Cost of Vengeance by Freda Utley (Henry Regnery Company, Chicago 1949)

Shriek with Pleasure by Toni Howard (Signet Books, New York 1950)

Never a Shot in Anger by Col. Barney Oldfield (Duell, Sloan and Pearce, New York 1956)

Cronkite's War: His World War II Letters Home by Walter Cronkite IV and Maurice Issermann (National Geographic, Washington DC 2013)

We Opened in One by Rosanna 'Ann Williams' Wheaton (brookswheaton.com)

Jobsworth by Ken Harrison (ken-harrison.com)

And also song lyrics from:

'Picking 'Em Up and Laying 'Em Down' by Gus Kahn and Louis Panico (Leo Feist 1924)

'Ballet Egyptien' by Richard Murdoch (unpublished)

'International Rhythm' by Betty Knox (1939, unpublished)

'I Saw a Robin' by Betty Knox, Charles Irwin and E. Whittam (Cavendish Music Co. 1942)

Betty Knox's 'Over Here' columns and other articles for the *London Evening Standard* are extensively quoted. All were accessed at the former British Newspaper Library, Colindale, London.

Further factual information was drawn from the following autobiographies:

It's Not a Rehearsal (Amanda Barrie, Headline 2002)
High Hopes (Ronnie Corbett, Ebury Press 2000)
Betty (Betty Driver, Andre Deutsch 2000)
Don't Walk in the Long Grass (Tenniel Evans, Bantam Press 1999)
Maybe It's Because (Hubert Gregg, Pen Press 2005)
So Much Love (Beryl Reid, Hutchinson 1984)
The Fool on the Hill (Max Wall, Quartet Books 1975)

And from these:

The Wizard of the Wire (Mark St Leon, Aboriginal Studies Press 1993)
The Devil's Chemists (Josiah DuBois, Beacon Press 1952)
War Correspondent: From D-Day to the Elbe (Holbrook Bradley,
    iUniverse Inc. 2007)
Roy Hudd's Book of Music-Hall, Variety and Showbiz Anecdotes
    (Robson Books 1993)
The Ipswich Hippodrome (Terry Davis and Trevor Morson,
    Terence Davis 2005)
Tony Hancock: the Definitive Biography (John Fisher, HarperCollins
    2008)
Jingo (Terry Pratchett, Gollancz 1997).

I am particularly grateful to two authors whose biographies formed the basis for much of my research and who provided plentiful help and guidance throughout the writing of this book. I would highly recommend the following:

Old Time Variety by Richard Anthony Baker (Remember When 2011)
In the Shadow of the Magic Mountain by Andrea Weiss (University of
    Chicago Press 2008)

Index

NB Mentioned throughout and therefore omitted from this index are:

Wilson and Keppel
Wilson, Keppel and Betty
Wilson, Jack
Keppel, Joe
Knox, Betty (aka Peden, Alice aka Peden, Betty)

Aladdin, 88, 89, 94, 100, 155, 184, 189, 192,
    200, 212
Anderson, Thomas, 9, 19
Antony and Cleopatra, 240
'Arabian Antics', 55, 56, 67, 73
Auden, W. H., 152
Ballet Egyptien, 67, 77, 177
Bamberger, Jean, 71–72, 73, 221
Bangles, The, 55, 239
Barrie, Amanda, 202, 246
BBC (British Broadcasting Corporation),
    72, 89, 117, 126, 175, 205, 207, 208, 221,
    227, 240, 243
Beaverbrook, Lord, 109, 118, 123, 137, 138,
    165, 168
Beggars of Life, 25
Benny, Jack, 39, 41
Berlin Wintergarten, 85, 150, 159, 162, 168
Bernadin, Alain, 223–24
Billy Shenton Trio, The, 73
Blondell & Mack, 50, 55, 69, 88
Bormann, Martin, 167, 172, 173, 174
Braben, Eddie, 240
Brinsworth House, 230, 231, 232, 233
Broadway Vanities, 45
Brooks, Louise, 25, 26
Bryant, Betty, 93–94
Buckley, Jack, 233
Bus Boys, The, 35, 36, 44, 45, 46, 49, 51, 76,
    84
'Cairo Capers', 73

Cardinal, Seb, 1
Carroll, Nita, 94, 100
Chuckle Brothers, The, 184, 239
Cinderella, 89, 133, 205
Cleopatra (Claudette Colbert), 87
Cleopatra (Elizabeth Taylor), 239–40
'Cleopatra's Nightmare', 4, 87, 88, 89, 103,
    104, 105, 125, 188, 226, 227
Cochran, Charles B., 67, 69, 72
Colleano, Bonar Junior, 16, 135–37, 198,
    214, 231, 232
Colleano, Bonar Senior, 16, 135, 160, 231
Colleano, Con, 16, 64, 135
Colleano, Mark, 137, 231–32, 242
Colleano, Rubye, 16, 46, 135, 137, 160, 229,
    231
Colleano's Circus, 15–17, 31, 102, 135, 231
Collegiate Co-Eds, 47, 49, 103
Corbett, Ronnie, 226, 227, 246
Coren Mitchell, Victoria, 4, 242
Coren, Alan, 4
Cottrell, Valerie, 205–6, 207, 208, 220, 221,
    230
Crazy Gang, The, 64–65, 175–76
Crazy Horse Saloon, Paris, 222, 223, 224
Cronkite, Walter, 120–22, 245
Curley, Jean (aka McKinnon, Jeanne), 210–
    11, 212–14, 215, 217, 218, 219–20, 221,
    222, 223, 225, 226, 227, 229, 230, 235,
    237, 238, 241, 242, 243
Dachau Trials, 177

Day of the Pharaohs, 239, 240
Delfont, Bernard, 102, 111, 120, 218
de Mille, Cecil B., 32, 34, 87
de Mille, William, 32
Demri-Burns, Dustin, 1
Derby Winners, The, 34
Desert Inn, Las Vegas, 203, 204
Dibb, Edna May, 183, 221
Dixey, Phyllis, 94, 127, 206
Drew, Maureen, 208, 211, 221
Driver, Betty, 78, 246
EABF (Entertainment Artistes' Benevolent
   Fund), 230
Edwards, Julia, 163, 164
'Egyptian Reggae', 239
ENSA (Entertainments National Service
   Association), 73, 114, 145
Flamencos de España, Los, 210, 211
Flanagan, Bud, 64, 69, 119, 131, 175
Flying Croneras, The, 230
Foot, Michael, 118, 119, 122
Foster Girls, The, 39, 42, 43
Foster, Allan K., 37, 43, 84
Foster, Harry, 57, 63, 68
Front, Rebecca, 1
Gala, 224–26
Gandhi, Mahatma, 66, 76, 82, 83, 84
Ganjou Brothers and Juanita, The, 65, 131
Giehse, Therese, 152, 166
Gilchrist, Leo, 223, 232
Girke, Fritz, 179–80
Glasgow Empire, 64, 215
Goebbels, Joseph, 86, 150, 162
Goering, Hermann, 86, 150, 162, 167–69,
   174
Great Temptations, The, 38–41, 42, 43
Habit, The, 20
Hancock, Tony, 198, 246
Happiness Girls, The, 48
Harman, James, 238, 243
Harrison, Ken, 222, 245
Hello America!, 102
Here, There and Everywhere, 175
Hi-de-Hi, 119, 124
Higgins, Marguerite, 163, 199
High Cost of Vengeance, The, 165, 177, 199,
   245
Hollis, Harry, 238
Holt Schaller, Barbara, 190–92, 203, 205,
   220, 221, 237, 242, 243

Hosier, Bob, 184
Howard, Toni, 150, 161, 162–63, 164, 199,
   245
Hussey, Susan, 3
'I Saw a Robin', 107, 245
'In a Persian Market', 4, 76, 240
In Town Tonight, 75, 79, 85, 117
'International Rhythm', 106–7, 112, 245
Ipswich Hippodrome, 99, 103, 117, 206, 246
ITV (Independent Television), 207, 208
Jackson, Glenda, 3, 78, 240–41, 242
Jingo, 238, 246
Judi Dench, Dame, 4, 242
Kent, Jean, 71, 242
Ketèlbey, Albert, 4, 76, 240
Kiddie, Nor, 103, 111
'King Tut', 239
Knox, Betty Mae, 37–38, 39, 40–41, 43
Knox, Donald Ednell, 27–29, 37, 41–42, 46,
   60, 97, 158
Knox, Edward, 27
Knox, Emily, 41, 42, 46
Knox, Jean Patricia 'Patsy', 29, 37, 42, 54,
   55, 58, 59, 60, 61, 87–88, 91, 92–93, 94,
   97, 99, 100, 107, 109–10, 113, 114, 115–
   17, 119, 120, 124, 125–26, 128–30, 131,
   135–36, 155, 158, 159, 160, 166, 169,
   170, 171, 175, 181, 182–84, 185, 187,
   189, 190, 192, 193, 201, 202, 203, 211–
   12, 213, 215, 217, 218, 219, 220, 221,
   223, 226, 229, 231, 232, 237, 242
Knox, Nellie, 27, 60
København, Kalundborg og -?, 76
Lampe, J. Bodewalt, 78
London Coliseum, 87, 101, 159
London Evening Standard, 5, 107, 108, 109,
   112, 117, 118–19, 122, 123, 124, 133,
   144, 146, 147, 148, 150, 152, 154, 155,
   159, 160, 162, 166, 168, 169, 172, 173,
   174, 241, 245
London Palladium, 62, 64, 66, 67, 69, 99,
   135, 155, 175, 187–89, 193, 203, 206, 221
London Palladium Varieties, 203–5
London Town, 170
Londoner's Diary, 118–19, 122
Lucas, Matt, 3, 242
Luigini, Alexandre, 67, 77
Magness, Celeste, 25–26, 27
Mann, Erika, 150–53, 154, 155, 156, 157–58,
   164, 166, 169, 184, 197, 243

Mann, Katia, 157
Mann, Klaus, 152, 153, 156, 157, 158, 166, 184
Mann, Thomas, 150, 154, 156–57, 164, 241
McKinnon, Andy, 230
Me and My Girl, 110
Melki, Claude, 225
Melly, George, 238
Morecambe and Wise, 4, 78, 240–41
Morecambe, Eric, 240–41
Moulin Rouge, Paris, 216, 217, 218, 223
Mullens, Henri, 207
Murdoch, Richard, 77, 245
Music Hall Artistes' Railway Association, The, 70
Mussolini, Benito, 86–87
NAAFI (Navy, Army and Air Force Institutes), 127
Nichols, Peter, 4, 104, 242
'Night Boat to Cairo', 239
Norton, Frank C., 23
Noye, Harry, 14, 15, 18
Nuremberg Trials, 161, 168, 235
O'Shea, Tessie, 105–7
Oklahoma!, 96
Olivelli's, 95–96, 108, 124, 169, 171, 191, 192, 197–98, 201, 212, 231, 243
On the Air, 75, 81, 126
Once in a Blue Moon, 69–73
'Over Here', 122–24, 143, 187, 236, 245
Over Here from Over There, 143, 245
Owen, Frank, 108–9, 112, 118
Parnell, Val, 69, 175, 203, 204
Parnell, Wallace, 69
Parsons, Geoffrey, 164
Peden, Charles Edward, 8, 10, 11, 23, 29, 42, 54, 149, 166
Peden, Charles Junior, 9, 11, 21, 41
Peden, Elizabeth 'Lizzie', 9, 19, 29, 41, 42, 54, 60, 149, 171, 176, 202, 214–15, 223, 226, 231
Peden, George 'Eddie', 8, 20, 21, 23, 148–49
Peppermill, The, 150–51, 152
Pfeffermühle, Die. See *Peppermill, The*
'Picking 'Em Up and Laying 'Em Down', 33, 35, 245
Podkowiński, Marian, 169
Pollet, Jean-Daniel, 224–25
Pratchett, Terry, 238, 246
Press Villa Club, 195–96, 200

Psychobitches, 1–2, 3, 242
Queen Elizabeth II (Princess Elizabeth), 3, 175, 232, 242
Questel, Mae, 50
RADA (Royal Academy of Dramatic Art), 95, 99
Raleigh Hall, 52, 54, 57
Ray of Sunshine, A, 185
Ray, Ted, 77, 185
Reid, Beryl, 102, 246
Reiman, Bob, 22–23
'Remember the Time', 239
Revels in Rhythm, 67
Rieke, Willi, 180
RKO (Radio-Keith-Orpheum), 50, 53, 55, 68
Road Stars, The, 238
Roberts, Eunice, 103, 110–15, 128–29, 197, 198, 213, 221, 237, 242
Robinson, Bill 'Bojangles', 56
'Romance in Dresden Porcelain', 65
Royal Variety Performance, 3, 65, 68, 69, 76, 159, 175–76, 196, 230
Ruggles, Wesley, 170
Sand Dance, 240
Schaller, John, 192
Schwanner, Cornelius, 179
Scott, Irene, 193–94, 197, 200–201, 203, 205, 213, 220, 221, 237
Secombe, Harry, 207, 226
Sellers, Peter, 115, 198
Seven Veils, Dance of the, 105, 128, 160, 214, 220
Shen Tun Trio, The, 73, 77
Shenton, Billy, 69–70, 72–73
Shenton, Billy Junior, 69, 73, 77, 94, 97, 98, 104, 108, 115, 116, 182, 184, 189, 190, 192, 193, 197, 198, 242, 243
Shriek with Pleasure, 161, 199, 245
Silber, Arthur, 35
Sinatra, Frank, 187–88
Sleeping Beauty, 176, 181, 182, 193, 194
Smith, Herbert, 75
Soft Lights and Sweet Music, 75, 79, 82
Soho Cabaret, Paris, 222, 223–24
Spear Dance, 104, 105, 160, 219, 220
Spiro, Samantha, 1, 3, 242
Starlight Serenade, 135, 137
Steinbeck, John, 123, 140
Sternberg, Liam, 239

Strike Up the Music, 100–101

Swaffer, Hannen, 85, 86, 93, 105, 108, 117, 124, 136

Terry's Juveniles, 94

Thompson, Josie, 168, 174–75, 178

Thoroughly Modern Millie, 42

Three Redheads, The, 73

Tobin, Richard, 144, 146

Trinder, Tommy, 160, 175, 203

Trocadero Restaurant, 67, 69, 81, 104, 205

Tutankhamen, 54, 87, 239

Variety Jubilee, 120, 125, 131

Vinzant, Vivian, 22–26

'Vision of Salome', 78

von Papen, Franz Junior, 173, 192–93

Wakefield, Duggie, 155

'Walk Like an Egyptian', 239

Wall, Max, 96, 188, 208, 246

Wallenstein, Marcel, 19, 28, 109, 110, 118, 122, 133, 137, 138, 169

Walter, Bruno, 152, 157, 158

We're Coming Over, 145–46

Wellington Pier, Great Yarmouth, 226

Wemyss, Mary, 203, 221

Wenzel, Betty, 149

Western Brothers, The, 82

Western, Kenneth, 75, 82

Williams, Ann, 48–49, 245

Windmill Theatre, 39, 71, 206, 210, 224

Wise, Ernie, 234, 240–41

Wizard of the Wooden Shoe, 15

Also available from
fantom
publishing

Andrew Ross

Too Happy A Face

The authorised biography of

Joan Sims

Immortalised through her roles in twenty-four of the iconic *Carry On* films, Joan Sims remains one of Britain's best-known comedy legends. For five decades – through more than seventy film appearances and work on stage, television and radio – she captured the hearts of audiences around the world. Yet behind the laughter was heartache and personal torment as the incredibly private actress battled depression, insecurity, loneliness and alcoholism.

In this authorised biography of Joan, Andrew Ross details her early years on stage and rise to stardom in theatre revue, her failed romances and the intense bond with her parents which ultimately led to the collapse of her one serious love affair.

Revealed is the truth about Joan's relationships with her *Carry On* co-stars (including Kenneth Williams who bizarrely proposed to her), the drink problem which forced her to spend time in a grim Victorian mental institute in the early 1980s and the circumstances behind her reclusive final years and last months in hospital before her death in 2001.

Drawing on first-hand accounts from Joan's closest surviving friends and contemporaries including Barbara Windsor, Fenella Fielding, Dame Judi Dench and Sir Tom Courtenay, as well as exclusive material from her personal archive, what emerges is the story of a determined lady who battled private demons to become one of the finest and best-loved actresses of her generation.

ISBN 978-1-78196-121-6

Available in hardback from
www.fantomfilms.co.uk

Derek Fowlds

My autobiography

A Part Worth Playing

with Michael Sellers

Derek Fowlds is known the world over for his countless appearances in many household favourite television dramas and films.

From apprentice printer to armed forces disc jockey, from the West End to Broadway, from the silver screen to worldwide television fame, Derek's career has seen him work alongside some of the greatest names in showbiz.

He worked in films with Alec Guinness, Kenneth More, Dirk Bogarde and Gina Lollobrigida. He shook Sinatra's hand. He has appeared on screen or stage with Laurence Harvey, Helen Mirren, Daniel Craig and Benedict Cumberbatch. Then there's also been a note or two with Gary Barlow and Simon Le Bon.

On TV, a whole generation embraced "Mr Derek" when he appeared alongside the outspoken Basil Brush, and a nation laughed at the classic BBC comedy *Yes Minister*, in which he starred alongside Paul Eddington and Nigel Hawthorne. He also played Oscar Blaketon in eighteen series of the still hugely popular *Heartbeat* series.

With his heart resting easily on his sleeve Derek talks candidly about his personal life, his adored mother and sister, his two wives, his many lovers and his one true love. It is a story that swings from triumph to bitter disappointment, from glorious unadulterated joy to appalling tragedy.

ISBN 978-1-78196-148-3

Available in hardback from

www.fantomfilms.co.uk